Who's He When He's at Home

Who's He When He's at Home

A James Joyce Directory

Shari Benstock
and
Bernard Benstock

University of Illinois Press
Urbana Chicago London

LIBRARY OF CONGRESS CATALOGING IN PUBLICATION DATA

Benstock, Shari, 1944-
Who's he when he's at home.

Bibliography: p.
1. Joyce, James, 1882-1941—Characters. 2. Joyce, James, 1882-1941—Dictionaries, indexes, etc.
I. Benstock, Bernard, joint author. II. Title.
PR6019.09Z5259 823'.9'12 79-17947
ISBN 0-252-00756-5
ISBN 0-252-00757-3 (pbk.)

To Fritz Senn
(when we first began to assemble the first file cards)
To Fritz Senn
(throughout the agony of the directory in progress)
To Fritz Senn
(in the exaltation and relief when all was done)

THANKS

To Morris Beja, Bradley Goins, Don Gifford, Phillip Herring, Hugh Kenner, Robert Lowery, Pierre Michel, Louis Mink, Victory Pomeranz, John Henry Raleigh, John Van Voorhis, Franklin Walton, Craig Werner, Pamela Wolf, and Stephen Wolf. And multiple thanks to Clive Hart.
And to Carla and Piero Marengo for their eminent domain.

He inquired if it was John Bull the political celebrity of that ilk, as it struck him, the two identical names, as a striking coincidence. *Ulysses,* 662

Contents

Legend xi

Introduction: Name, What's in a . . . ? 1

Directory of Names 45

Anonymous Listings 169

Appendix A: The Joycean Method of Cataloguing 217

Appendix B: Molly's Masculine Pronouns 229

Appendix C: Table of Corresponding Pages 234

Legend (on fold-out page)

Legend

Editions employed:

D *Dubliners* [Viking Press "definitive" edition]

P *A Portrait of the Artist as a Young Man* [Viking Press "definitive" edition]

E *Exiles* [Viking Press]

S *Stephen Hero* [New Directions]

G *Giacomo Joyce* [Viking Press]—named characters only

Ulysses [Random House 1961]

Name in Regular Type : character created by Joyce
Name in FULL CAPITALS : character pre-existing Joyce's fictional use; fictional, historical, legendary, or contemporary
*Name preceded by asterisk : actual resident in Dublin
Name* succeeded by asterisk : not actually a person in this case
"Name" in quotation marks : pseudonym, nickname, alias, nom de plume, conjectured name, misnomer, stage name, mock title, punned name
Name unadorned by either parentheses or brackets : actually present
(Name) in parentheses : mentioned, referred to, alluded to, thought about
[Name] in brackets : appears in hallucination in Circe chapter
! : exclamation mark indicates expletive or ejaculation rather than a person
? : question mark indicates that identity or appearance in doubt

Discrepancies between ACTUAL NAME and Joyce's variant are indicated by inclusion of both, differentiated by appropriate type.

Designation or description of character listed : Well-known historical or fictional persons whose names are obviously unique to indicate themselves alone receive no identification (e.g., Jehovah, Jesus Christ, Moses, Shakespeare, Molière); others are given brief identifications. Joyce's own creations are identified by the roles they play in the works.

Legend

Page and book indicators: *Ulysses* items are offered first, without any preceding letter to specify book; others follow with letters indicating the work as above. If the character never actually appears in the work, his name is in parentheses, and all page numbers therefore are understood to indicate references to him; names without parentheses are characters who appear in person on those pages without parentheses, are referred to on those pages in parentheses, and appear as a hallucination in those pages bracketed.

Animals and inanimate objects: Although this directory is limited to "human" characters, the unusual nature of *Ulysses* dictates that (1) all dogs (like Garryowen) and horses (like Throwaway) must necessarily be included, provided that they have names, and (2) that those inanimate objects that have speaking roles in Circe be included—as hallucinations.

Further references: For fuller information on most of the persons alluded to and on many of the Joycean characters, the following are noted after the entries. Capital letters refer to the specific volume when we feel that the information is essentially accurate; lowercase letters indicate a serious instance of misinformation.

A Weldon Thornton, *Allusions in Ulysses: An Annotated List* (Chapel Hill: University of North Carolina Press, 1968).

N Don Gifford with Robert J. Seidman, *Notes for Joyce: An Annotation of James Joyce's Ulysses* (New York: E. P. Dutton, 1974).

N Don Gifford with the assistance of Robert Seidman, *Notes for Joyce: Dubliners and A Portrait of the Artist as a Young Man* (New York: E. P. Dutton, 1967).

T Clive Hart and Leo Knuth, *A Topographical Guide to James Joyce's Ulysses* (Colchester, England: A Wake Newslitter Press, 1975).

A plus sign (+) also indicates references from the following where especially pertinent; in many other cases the reader can also find additional information in them.

\+ Robert M. Adams, *Surface and Symbol: The Consistency of James Joyce's Ulysses* (New York: Oxford University Press, 1962).

\+ Zack Bowen, *Musical Allusions in the Works of James Joyce: Early Poetry through Ulysses* (Albany: State University of New York Press, 1974).

\+ Louis Hyman, *The Jews of Ireland: From Earliest Times to the Year 1910* (Shannon: Irish University Press, 1972).

\+ Richard M. Kain, *Fabulous Voyager: James Joyce's Ulysses* (Chicago: University of Chicago Press, 1947).

+ Kevin Sullivan, *Joyce among the Jesuits* (New York: Columbia University Press, 1958).
+ *Thom's.* 1904 *Thom's Official Directory of Dublin*

Anonymous listing: For those for whom no name is available (e.g., the boy in "Araby," the Nameless One in 'Cyclops,' the whore with the black straw sailor hat) a separate alphabetized section follows the list of named personages, under designations used in the texts, and cross-referenced where appropriate. This applies to one and two of a kind, but not to unspecified collective groups, unless they are important (Stephen's brood of siblings, for example). In the instances in which those with names appear unnamed, they are cross-referenced, and in the listing of the named, where there is a chance that a page reference does not easily locate the person, an identifying phrase from that page is quoted, obviating the need for line numbers. Noun designations are used for the alphabetized list, except where a vital adjective intrudes (e.g., Croppy Boy under "C"). Where there are many under a particular heading (boy, girl, man, woman), those that stand alone come first; those with succeeding descriptive material next; those with a single descriptive adjective next; those with two adjectives next, etc.

Method of alphabetization: The system used for alphabetical order is that which proceeds through the alphabet until there is a break between words ("Beau Mont" precedes "Beaufort"; "White, Joe" precedes "Whitehouse"). Characters designated by their initials ("A. E.," "H_2O," "H. P. B.") are at the beginning of the alphabet under the first initial. In most cases the surname determines places (for Jesus, see "Christ") except where the prenom is the better known (for Alighieri, see "Dante"). Where confusions might arise, we use the system employed by Thornton (A) and Gifford (N), providing that they are in agreement with each other. For saint names, see the actual name, not under a composite listing of "saints." The deity appears only when he assumes a specific name.

For the convenience of the reader, a condensed version of this legend is available on a fold-out page following the appendices.

Introduction
Name, What's in a . . . ?

Sweet Rosie O'Grady, song heroine who finds herself discussed by Stephen Dedalus and his friend Cranly (P 244), smells as sweet in *Finnegans Wake* (FW 133) as "Roseoogreedy"—or does she? The mutation of names throughout the Joyce canon is a phenomenon that derives directly from Joyce's basic methods of composition: duplication, accretion, modification, comic variation, and ironic juxtaposition. To these can be added a touch of mystification: who, for example, is the O'Grady that Bloom conjectures the dying Dignam might owe three shillings (103)? Even when we realize that this minor debt functions as a balance to the three shillings that Joe Hynes owes Bloom, the identity of this O'Grady remains otherwise in darkness. For the reader of *Ulysses* O'Grady appears and disappears in this evanescent moment, without actually having a present existence. Many others lead such meagre lives in Joyce's works, like the Pennyfeather whose heart Simon Dedalus broke (P 250). Their shadowy substances add to the encrusted surfaces of *Dubliners, A Portrait of the Artist as a Young Man, Ulysses,* and even *Exiles,* present certain problems in the incomplete *Stephen Hero,* and emerge as a major contributory factor to the schematics of *Finnegans Wake.* Wakeans have been fortunate in having Adaline Glasheen as a conscientious census-taker for the past two decades, but no survey similar to hers has been available to the readers of the rest of Joyce's work, which, because of their interlocked systems, function as a single landscape and location.

Who's He When He's at Home has knocked at every door and found almost everyone available for census-taking. Like Adaline Glasheen, whose asterisks have become legend, we have occasionally stood staring at unresponsive doors, but the neighborhood that we have been canvassing is hardly as labyrinthine as that of the *Wake,* so asterisks have proved unnecessary, although an infrequent question mark mars the surface. Some of these do not actually betray our own befuddlement but are intended to anticipate that of the reader: we are confident in our assumption, for example, that Emma Clery makes a solitary appearance in *Ulysses* (215), although we expect that others may not see her in the National Library when Stephen seems to. A conciliatory mark of interrogation is consequently offered.

The following alphabetized directory consists of two parts: a listing of named characters and a listing of unnamed characters, no matter how insignificant. The former group is arranged according to surnames (when such exist), the latter by the key noun that provides the identification in the text itself. Cross-references are included where more than one designation is used in the text, especially for important persons like the central character(s?) in the first three stories of *Dubliners* and the narrator of Cyclops (who appears in Circe as the Nameless One). *Ulysses* of course accounts for an overwhelming proportion of entries, and for most of the quandaries and confusions of identification, but each of the five works catalogued here provides a certain number of interesting cruxes.

Stephen Hero

As a manuscript fragment cannibalized for *A Portrait* and not ostensibly intended by the author for publication, *Stephen Hero* has its obvious lacunae, but like the other books it discusses contemporary people known in their day but obscured in ours. A reader at the turn of the century would have had little difficulty naming the Russian czar who looks like a "besotted Christ." Separated allusions to William Thomas Stead and to the editor of *The Review of Reviews* need only temporarily delay our realization that they are the same person. The footnotes provided by editor Theodore Spencer identify Michael Cusak, Arthur Griffith, Patrick Sarsfield, Hugh O'Neill, Hugh Roe O'Donnell, Terence Bellew MacManus, Paul Cardinal Cullen, but others remain unannotated in the New Directions edition. For example: the Jesuit who was converted to the Baconian theory of Shakespeare authorship; Rousseau's English biographer; the Pope who sent the first Cardinal (belatedly) to Ireland; the Irish archbishop who is also an astronomer; the identity—or for that matter the reality—of the Human Ostrich; the French atheistic writer who died by asphyxiation.

The existence of the published *Stephen Hero* has always been of use to readers of *A Portrait* in its illumination of the finished book. We are in possession of a surname for Emma Clery; a name for the dean of studies, Father D. Butt; a possible prenom for Cranly (if the appellation "Thomas Squaretoes" is understood to retain his actual given name); and something of an identity for the Foxy Campbell of both *A Portrait* and *Ulysses* in "the Very Reverend J. Campbell S. J. in the Jesuit Church, Gardiner St." (S 119). Changes of names from the original to *A Portrait* result in some confusion, the major ones being Madden to Davin and Father Artifoni to Father Ghezzi (while the original professor of Italian lends his name in *Ulysses* to the teacher of music). Even the spelling of certain names has been changed, from Daedalus to Dedalus, and McCann to MacCann—the latter augmentation of the Irish prefix is duplicated in the Lanty McHale who in *Ulysses* becomes MacHale, bringing him into line with the Bishop of Tuam, John MacHale. Stephen's family in the early draft has a far more concise constituency with a brother Maurice (mentioned again in *A Portrait* but shrouded in *Ulysses*) and a sister Isabel (never mentioned again). The Daniels household is not as defined: we know of several sisters (one named Annie) and several brothers, but the exact number remains unknown. Such enigmas are exemplified by Cranly's comment to Stephen, "I heard him speaking of you to someone," and Stephen's reply, " 'Someone' is vague" (S 115). We identify the "someone" as Emma Clery, despite Cranly's purposeful vagueness. Particularly vague is a girl named Lucy whom Stephen contrasts with Emma (S 230–31) and who probably was afforded a greater identity in the missing pages of *Stephen Hero*.

Exiles

Exiles offers few problems. As a self-contained entity and a brief work in dramatic form it has only a handful of characters and a small number of references to people real, historical, or fictional. None of the participants has a role to play in any of the other Joyce works—under the same identity. That young Archie goes for a ride with the milkman reminds us that young Stephen in *A Portrait* does the same, but it is hardly likely that the same milkman services the Rowan household in Merrion and the Dedalus household in Blackrock. Jonathan Swift is mentioned in *Exiles*, as in the other works, but the most pointed redeployment of a historical character is that of Archibald Hamilton Rowan, the patriot who seems to have supplied young Archie with his given name despite Richard Rowan's disclaimers; his associations with Stephen's Clongowes are of dramatic importance in *A Portrait*.

Dubliners

Readers of *Dubliners* have on occasion noted that Joyce practiced a tight economy in awarding names to his characters. His own given name he attached to Father Flynn, young Doyle, and Mr. Duffy, each of whom has a five-letter surname (containing a y) like the author's. Two main characters are named Thomas (Kernan and Chandler), while two sons of main characters (Farrington and Conroy) are also named Tom. Jack is used for four characters of varying importance: the boy's uncle in "The Sisters," Polly's brother in "The Boarding House," the caretaker in "Ivy Day," and Mr. Power in "Grace." Certain surnames serve dual purposes as well: the Mooneys of "The Boarding House" are echoed by Ginger Mooney in "Clay"; old Leonard, the Catholic wine merchant, has his shadow in Paddy Leonard drinking at Davy Byrne's; Jack Power is complemented by Miss Power in "The Dead." *Dubliners* is a small world where a girl who loses a brother named Ernest can find a lover named Frank, and where a Cotter is an intrusive element in one boy's life and a Mercer is in another's. Given the commonness of names like James and Tom and Jack and Joe (Hynes, Donnelly), the coincidences seem intentional, and the economy practiced mirrors the narrowness of perspectives and possibilities in Dublin.

Having to share a name is hardly as much a deprivation as having none at all, and anonymity plagues several important persons in *Dubliners.* Most noticeable is the boy who is central to the first three stories, whose namelessness contributes to the important conjecture that he is the same boy throughout. His nameless aunt and uncle (the latter called Jack in "The Sisters)—and his implied parentlessness as well—add to the negative evidence of his continuity as a character. The one surname that we can be sure is not his own is Smith, the alias used in "An Encounter" (no one would actually use his own name for an alias), but that hardly narrows the range of possibilities. It is incidental that Mahony's sister has no given name ("An Encounter"), but pointedly significant that Mangan's sister ("Araby") lacks one. Also worth noting is that Farrington has no given name (and almost becomes totally nameless when repeatedly referred to as "the man"—which, as Coilin Owens indicates, derives from the Irish word for man that is incorporated in the first syllable of his surname). Farrington's loss of a given name is balanced by Maria's loss of a surname. If the latter were known, it would blur the ambiguity of her relationship to Joe and Alphy since as a spinster her name would be the same as theirs if she were an older sister (a relationship that parallels Eveline's to her young siblings). It is important to note how a character is referred to in *Dubliners,* although far from easy to understand why: some primarily by first name (Eveline), some only by last name (Lenehan), some preceded by Mister (Cunningham), some quasi-anonymously (Farrington as "the man"), some fluctuating between first and last names (Gabriel Conroy). Often, the tone of a story depends upon such references to name forms.

A Portrait of the Artist as a Young Man

Verisimilitude has often been credited as the rationale for nomenclature in *A Portrait,* as in *Dubliners.* The notable exception of course is Stephen's own surname, modified from the totally mythic form in *Stephen Hero* to the only slightly more "acceptable" form of Dedalus. "You have a queer name, Dedalus," Athy comments (P 25) with the candor of schoolboys (calling attention to his own as well), in which he anticipates the more pointed remark by Davin: "What with your name and your ideas. . . . Are you Irish at all?" (P 202). To call attention to the anomaly of the Dedalus name would have been disastrous for a lesser writer, but Joyce manages to weigh the mythic significance with evidence that the name is intended as appropriate within the national context as well. Stephen's retort to Davin makes this quite specific: "Come with me now to the office of arms and I will show you the tree of my family" (P 202). And Temple augments its Irishness by claiming to have found the Dedaluses in Giraldus Cambrensis ("*Pernoblis et pervetusta familia*"—P 230).

Three important clusters of names in *A Portrait* derive from Stephen's panoply of classmates and mentors at Clongowes, Belvedere, and the University. The middle group is the smallest, and each member plays a significant role in relation to him—particularly Mr. Tate, the teacher who announces heresy in Stephen's essay. Even so peripheral a figure as Bertie Tallon has his importance, dressed as he is in girl's clothes for the theatrical performance. His name echoes that of Tusker Boyle of Clongowes fame, whose effeminacy is circumscribed by his care of his nails. "Tallon" is one of the rare aspects of the use of charactonyms in Joyce's process of naming, combining in its echo of "talons" the tusks and nails of Master Boyle and corroborating the tagname of another Belvedere boy, Vincent Heron. Here Joyce calls elaborate attention to the birdlike features and name of Stephen's adversary, but surrounds him with two boys whose names fail to resonate on their own, Boland and Nash. Yet as a triumvirate of tormentors Boland and Heron and Nash become names to reckon with. When Stephen outgrows Belvedere and such companions, he finds himself at the University, where he remains aloof from his real associates and immerses himself in a mystic company of writers and musicians. Hauptmann, Newman, Cavalcanti, Ibsen, and Ben Jonson have been commented on often, but less ostentatious is Stephen's trio of Elizabethan madrigalists and lyricists, "Dowland and Byrd and Nash"

(P 233), presumably chosen to replace (through pun and generic classification and echo) the discarded triumvirate.

The Clongowes cluster, where the largest cast of incidental characters is amassed, has often drawn attention from those readers who found the names purposely peculiar, yet, as Kevin Sullivan has carefully documented, names like Thunder, Kickham, and Lawton, despite their unusual resonance, actually belonged to Joyce's own compeers at Clongowes. In surrounding Stephen with a horde of fellow Clongownians, Joyce primarily employed those who were actually at school with him, although distancing the death of Little to precede Stephen's tenure at the school. Of the boys and masters a significant group are fictional. Beside Athy, whose punned name is paired against Stephen's own, the common characteristic of the fictitious is their basic unwholesomeness, from the pandybat-wielding Father Dolan to the ones involved in the smugging, Simon Moonan, Tusker Boyle, and Corrigan, as well as such punishing mentors as M'Glade and Barrett. (The names seem to have been changed to protect the guilty, although Gleeson and Wells have actual correspondences in the real Clongowes of Joyce's day.) The sycophantic Moonan may, however, have an afterlife in *A Portrait,* if it is indeed he who is a colleague of Stephen at the University. The dean of studies praises Moonan obliquely by asserting, "Take Mr. Moonan. He was a long time before he got to the top" (P 190), but this seems to refer to someone of attainment higher than just a new graduate. Yet when Donovan is ticking off the failures and successes at the examinations he notes, "Moonan got fifth place in the Indian" (P 210). Either as a direct development or as a coincidental namesake, the new Moonan (or Moonans) reminds the reader of the calibre of Stephen's "competition."

The roster of National University students is as prodigious and varied as that of the Clongownians and ranges from Stephen's associates (Cranly, Lynch, MacCann, Davin) to casual references far and wide. The attempt at autobiographical accuracy in assigning names is not repeated in this later instance: instead, all the participants serve under fictional designations. The importance of these classmates to Joyce makes their roles in *A Portrait* worth noticing, especially as they relate to the later situation in *Ulysses.* Dixon, for example, with Cranly in the library while the latter is ostensibly reading *Diseases of the Ox,* is in all likelihood a medical student, and in *Ulysses* the young doctor who attends to Bloom's beebite. More important, the early indications of Buck Mulligan have been noted by Hans Walter Gabler in the presence of a Goggins in the last chapter of *A Portrait* and the mention of a Doherty, both based on Oliver St. John Gogarty.

Ulysses

Despite the usual demands for the literal naming of characters and the logical references to known personages, *Ulysses* provides an unusual catalogue of proper names and enigmas in nomenclature. It is a delight to correspondence hunters, a quagmire for the unwary, and a deluge of whodunits for the literary detective. The first page of the book presents a mysterious name that is not fully identified until hundreds of pages later. When Stephen looks at the gold points of Mulligan's teeth, the name Chrysostomos comes easily to his mind, punning on the literal meaning of "goldenmouth" and recalling at least one of two great orators so designated. Determining which Chrysostomos was intended may be relatively insignificant (a secular orator is as apt in context as a religious one, except that Mulligan is performing the mock functions of a priest in a chapter characterized by religion). The name game had already begun with Mulligan's appellation of Kinch for Stephen Dedalus, a nickname he augments, qualifies, and even declines unto the previous generation—Mr. Simon Dedalus he refers to as "Pa Kinch" (425). By calling attention to the absurd Greek name of Dedalus and the "Hellenic ring" of his own rhythmic name, Malachi Mulligan opens the Pandora's box of name association, but it is not until his own full designation, Malachi Roland St John Mulligan (417), that the box bears fruit. "St John" suggests the prototype, Oliver St. John Gogarty, but also St. John Chrysostomos, the ecclesiastical orator, while Roland pairs off with Gogarty's actual Oliver and mocks the fraternal friendship of Childe Roland and his loyal friend.

Cases of mistaken identity abound in *Ulysses,* both by face and by name, as when Kernan thinks he sees Ned Lambert's brother Sam (240). Bloom actually does see John Howard Parnell, brother of Charles Stewart Parnell, earlier in the day (165), but he is mistaken when he thinks he sees his own name in the Elijah throwaway (Blood of the Lamb) and Hugh Boylan's in the *Telegraph* (H. de Boyes), which proves to "tell a graphic lie" (647). The close coincidences of naming distinguish the technique of *Ulysses,* a work of parody and parallel, substance and shadow, illusion and reality.

Joyce's use of *Thom's Directory* highlights the duality, and it is not insignificant that Bloom once worked for Alexander Thom: the tome classifies reality by listing the residents of Dublin and multiples mysteries by containing a full complement of mistakes. We need no Hermes Trismegistus to tell us that the line above is often reflected in the line below in any alphabetized listing, and the margin for error (the reader's as well as the compositor's) is great. Individuality is a shared phenomenon, and incorrect association its natural concomitant. Leopold Bloom is not Mr. Bloom the dentist, nor is he related to him, but those "facts" need not prevent Jack Power from wondering if they are cousins (337) nor Poldy from passing himself off to the Watch as the dental surgeon, as well as cousin to von Bloom Pasha (455), nor the dentist chasing him with tweezers in Nighttown (586). The mystic association of the fictional Bloom with his "real" namesake proves to be far from casual, and there is good reason to think that had they been the same person an accidental clash among the wandering rocks might have been avoided. When Bloom first calls Mrs. Breen's attention to Cashel Boyle O'Connor Fitzmaurice Tisdall Farrell (a name to conjure with!), it is to prevent him from colliding with her as he makes his circuitous way outside lampposts (Bloom touches her arm and guides her out of his way). Later, Bloom takes the blind stripling's arm and guides him across the street, but without Bloom's guiding hand to save him, the blind boy walks into Farrell—in front of the dentist's window.

The economy in naming practiced in *Dubliners* has its comic counterpart in *Ulysses,* as many commentators have noticed. In Wandering Rocks, where such conflations are rampant, Hart and Knuth's *Topographical Guide* notes the presence of three Dudleys: the viceroy (whose humble name is Humble) is the Earl of Dudley; Conmee's counterpart is the Rev. Nicholas Dudley; and the barrister Dudley White fails to salute his viceregal namesake, although he stands outside the premises of a partial namesake, Mrs. M. E. White, and her initials in turn are those of the vice-council for the Austro-Hungarian Empire, a justice of the peace named Solomons. (That naming and renaming is a constant process in which Joyce played a part as neither first nor last in a series becomes apparent when the *Guide* duplicates the order of M. E. for both, while current editions of *Ulysses* reverse them for Solomons; *Thom's* for 1904 [p. 2015] and the first editions of *Ulysses* are in agreement, however, and the authors of the *Topographical Guide* have wisely made their "silent emendation.")

Duplications and triplications of disparate persons at times provide ironic couplings, at others merely odd coincidences. The revivalist Charles Alexander is distinct from the William Alexander who was primate of the Church of Ireland, while F. Alexander was the owner of Throwaway; Mary Anderson was an actress, Micky Anderson a watchmaker; Andrews provides a name for an Italian grocery firm in Dublin and a noted juror; the Aristotle of the *Poetics* did not produce the *Masterpieces;* John Barrington manufactured soap, Jonah Barrington, Irish bulls; Judge Barton investigated Shakespeare, while

James Barton drives a hack; Nancy, Phil, and William Blake pursued divergent paths; and so on through the alphabet in twos and threes and even fours. When lookalikes are clustered close together, as in Wandering Rocks, the intentional confusion makes itself apparent, but when distributed widely across the terrain of the book they are often overlooked. Even so, many can be accepted at face value, as the likely repetition of names found within a community, while others should call attention to themselves by implication and inference. At its most pointed, the process also involves new packaging of separate entities, particularly in Circe where simple confusion becomes multiple hallucination, and such English Celtophiles (folklore and history respectively) as Haines and the Rev. Hugh C. Love are wedded together as "The Reverend Mr Hugh C. Haines Love M.A." (599), comparable elements in one sense but opposites in another (*haine,* French for hate). And what's sauce for Haines is saucier for Mulligan who combines with the fictional Father O'Flynn to produce Father Malachi O'Flynn (599), the revered priest of the song and mock priest of the Black Mass, the self-styled "Fertiliser and Incubator," and the cleric who "makes hares of them all."

The various nominal cruxes of *Ulysses* are compounded as the work progresses, and what begins as a relatively straightforward play on names in the early chapters magnifies considerably thereafter. As one reads the novel chapter by chapter various parallels emerge, cohere, and develop, as do new problems in identity, relationship, correspondence, and symbolic significance.

Telemachus

Mulligan's spotlight on the resonance of names brings several "teasers" into the open: the genuine Christine, for example, or Algy or Kinch. It is quickly apparent that identification of literary allusions plays its part in solving several instances of casually inserted names, but Kinch has continued to puzzle commentators of *Ulysses.* William York Tindall has offered "kinchin" for child, but the cumulative effect (Buck sounds the motif over a dozen times in the first chapter alone), especially "toothless Kinch" and "Kinch, the knifeblade," makes it seem stronger than that, perhaps the Irish slang for twinge or crimp, which would reinforce Stephen's "agenbite of inwit." Of peculiar interest are several acquaintances of Mulligan's mentioned here but never referred to again, including revelers in Clive Kempthorpe's rooms in Oxford that Stephen recalls probably from Buck's recounting. Seymour in particular is memorable, since once invoked by Mulligan he is reported back in Dublin and spooning with "that red Carlisle girl, Lily" (22). It is assumed that Carlisle is her surname, rather than her place of origin.

Nestor

This chapter is distinguished by several lists of names. Stephen's students at Mr. Deasey's school generally sound English or even Scottish (Cochrane, Armstrong, Comyn, Talbot, Halliday, and Cyril Sargent) befitting the "better" families that dominate the social class of the locale, and Stephen mentally fabricates hypothetical names for their girl friends, "Edith, Ethyl, Gerty, Lily" (25). The last echoes the Lily Carlisle whose "father is rotto with money" (22), while Gerty anticipates the Gerty MacDowell of Sandymount Strand. To complement the names of the pupils, there are those of the titled personages whose horses are pictured on Mr. Deasey's wall. But Stephen's private list is the most interesting of all, his mental tabulation of creditors, from Mulligan to his former landlady, including the unaltered names of several of James Joyce's Dublin friends, the two editors George Russell and Fred Ryan, and two names from University days in *A Portrait* and *Stephen Hero* (Temple and McCann—in the original spelling). It is a compilation that embodies in miniature the range of the fictional work (names from the present novel combined with those from both real life and the past novelistic attempts at depicting reality). To add spice to the reality of identification, there is Deasy's reversal of historical personages in recounting the elopement of the wife of O'Rourke with the king of Leinster, Art MacMurrough.

Proteus

The flotsam and jetsam of Stephen's intellectually cluttered mind toss up a plethora of names in this episode devoted almost exclusively to the interior of that mind. Poets and mystics, philosophers and journalists, missionaries and politicians, all easily identified in the standard reference sources, attest to the eclectic jumble. Arius returns to remind us of the catalogue of heretics in Telemachus, but a parallel list here consists of royal pretenders to political power. Other similarities with the first chapter, suggesting that the Telemachiad operates in sonata allegro form, include a counterpart to the Oxford scene of the ragging, this time a Paris recollection that is Stephen's own and involves another mysterious person mentioned only once, Esther Osvalt. Memories of his stay in Paris also offer members of the Egan family and references to French writers and political figures, as well as a hypothetical vignette of early morning in Paris which pictures a ladies' man,

Belluomo (anticipating the masculinized Bella Cohen of Circe) and a pair of Parisiennes in a *patisserie.* A more consistently developed vignette is Stephen's projected visit to the Goulding family and its household members slated to reappear afterward in other contexts. The tantalizing quartet (or trio) of "Temple, Buck Mulligan, Foxy Campbell. Lantern jaws" (39) is the best example in the chapter of purposeful association disguised to look like random listing: their common denominator is their facial resemblance to the horse (Stephen will later unsheathe his "dagger definition": "Horseness is the whatness of allhorse"—186). Triggered by an image of Swift as a mad Houyhnhnm pursued by Yahoos, the "oval equine faces" ironically come into focus. The first two are mockers of Stephen's acquaintance, but the third is a Jesuit, possibly the one whose full name is given only in *Stephen Hero,* while the fourth is not actually a separate person but an aspect of the third: "Was it not a mental spectre of the face of one of the jesuits whom some of the boys called Lantern Jaws and others Foxy Campbell?" (P 161).

Calypso

With Bloom's mind now replacing that of Stephen Dedalus, the names of heretics and Jesuits give way to those of shopkeepers and purveyors of foodstuffs. Taken as a whole, the catalogue is immense and justifies Hugh Kenner's comment that *Ulysses* is a survival kit for those who suddenly find themselves marooned in the city. Local merchants mentioned or met are Buckley, Dlugacz, Hanlon, Larry O'Rourke, M'Auley, Cassidy (essentially butchers and publicans); "merchant princes" of far-ranging importance include Andrews, Findlater, Tallon, and realtors Towers, Battersby, North, MacArthur (for all of these check the *Topographical Guide*); brand names offered are Plasto, Boland, Denny, Drago, for hats, bread, sausage, and hairdressing. This confraternity is only the first contingent of a parade of mercantiles in Bloom's repository, but his mind contains more personal names as well. Those of wife, daughter, dead son, father-in-law, neighbor, family midwife, friends, and acquaintances from past and present join with political notables (also past and present) and an occasional author and composer. Notes on Molly's desultory conversation while dressing produce two names of note, Roberts and Gretta Conroy. The latter establishes at least a casual relationship between the Blooms of *Ulysses* and the Conroys of *Dubliners* that will be of importance later, while the first presents a delectable mystery. Neither *Allusions* nor *Notes* glosses him, and the *Topographical Guide* does not include him as a business address, yet it is tempting to think in terms of Joyce's *bête noire,* George Roberts of Maunsel and Co. Not only is he listed as a "Robber" in *Finnegans Wake* (FW 185), but he is given his full name when mentioned by George Russell in Scylla and Charybdis. The context of Molly's remark indicates that this particular Roberts owes (or owed) Bloom money, apparently having advertised through the canvasser's auspices. It is highly likely that a publisher would advertise his wares in a newspaper, but Russell's remark is even more appropriate: "George Roberts is doing the commercial part" (192).

The Lotus Eaters

Local color continues to dominate as Bloom walks through the city and ticks off businesses he passes (Leask's, Nichols's, Meade's, Conway's) or that pass him (Prescott's car) or are frequented by him (Sweny's). He thinks of several others (O'Neill's, Clery's, Hamilton Long's) and of various named products (Pears's soap), but mostly of drink, from Cantrell and Cochrane's ginger ale to Wheatley's bitters to Guinness's porter (the Guinness brewers themselves are referred to by their titled appellations, Lord Iveagh and Lord Ardilaun). A reference to Ponchielli in the previous chapter now multiplies into a congregation of composers, Rossini, Mercandante, Mozart, Palestrina, but mostly the chapter expands the circle of Bloom's fellow citizens, many of them having had previous existences in *Dubliners,* like the Gretta and M'Coy mentioned in Calypso (there is even a good possibility that the Kearney who was Bloom's guarantor at the Capel Street library is Kathleen Kearney's father—Molly knows the musical daughter—since his business is on Ormond Quay in the immediate vicinity). M'Coy and Bantam Lyons accost Bloom; the former mentions the latter, as well as Hoppy Holohan and Bob Doran, while Bloom thinks of Tom Kernan and Martin Cunningham. Since opiates permeate Lotus Eaters, the paralytic world of *Dubliners* logically casts up its cast-offs, even to the extent of reviving the simoniac Jesuit, Father Purdon, in his real person as Father Bernard Vaughan.

Marx's assertion that religion is the opiate of the people must have seemed obvious to the author of *Dubliners.* Bloom's temporary respite in All Hallows augments the references to clerics that include Vaughan as well as Father Conmee of Stephen's childhood, a Father Farley, Dr. Walsh, the priest officiating, and a mysterious one who has eluded tenacious researchers, "the priest in the Fermanagh will case" (83)—the last's tenure in a "witness box" follows Bloom's speculations on the confessional. An analogue to Stephen's nicknamed Jesuit is found in Bloom's less prestigious Brother Buzz, while a pair of saints (Peter

Claver and the local particular, Patrick) join archangel Michael, deities Christ and Buddha, prophet Mohammed, nemeses Pilate and Satan, and biblical figures Martha and Mary, Peter and Paul, Saint Joseph and the Blessed Virgin.

Lotus Eaters can also be viewed as the first full indicator of anonymity in *Ulysses,* as the Odysseyan Noman wanders ghostlike through Dublin. Bloom's trick of mind in the previous chapter, designating people whose names he cannot remember as "whatdoyoucallhim" and "Chap you know" (61) is compounded here and will resound in Cyclops, Circe, and Eumaeus. M'Coy perpetuates the habit ("what do you call him Bantam Lyons"—74), but the chapter contains a large number of unnamed characters seen and remembered and discussed, particularly the drowned man, plus the pseudonymous persons of Henry Flower and possibly Martha Clifford. (The climax of the chapter hinges on the name of Throwaway, yet, as Fritz Senn reminds us, the name never appears: "I was just going to throw it away," says Bloom [85], and "I was going to throw it away"—86). Misnomers figure prominently as well: Bloom's mind is playing tricks on him as he tries to recall the circumstances and performances of Mosenthal's drama, *Deborah,* shown in Dublin as *Leah, the Forsaken,* and the series of actresses conjured up offers Rachel in lieu of Leah, an error occasioned by the biblical pairing of sisters Leah and Rachel. More important is the misnamed Invincible, Denis Carey, whom Bloom originally conceived of as Peter Carey. His correction from Peter Carey is based on his realization that his mind had been clouded by having seen the notice about Saint Peter Claver, but his "correction" posits an even greater mistake. The terrorist in question was actually *James* Carey, but Peter was not a bad guess since there was a member of that name also indicted. *Denis* is a gratuitous intrusion, and the weight of that given name will be in the balance in Bloom's later musings.

Hades

By now the Bloomian tendency to note the names along the way and remember a host of others by associative processes has become well established, and the route to Glasnevin affords numerous opportunities. Of particular interest are the statues along O'Connell Street and the list of businesses on the west ("dead") side of the street. Several nameless figures appear in this chapter on death: the "dullgarbed old man" selling bootlaces (93), a bargeman on the Royal Canal (99), and the mysterious mourner in the macintosh (109). Each incidental and anonymous, they nonetheless reverberate later on: the bootlace vendor appears among the "mute inhuman faces" leering at Bloom in Circe when he is being accused by "The Sins of the Past" (538); the bargeman bobs up in Wandering Rocks "moored under the trees of Charleville Mall" (221) and quoted in Oxen of the Sun on the state of the drought in Ireland (396); and the man in the macintosh accidentally acquires a surname derived from his garb and becomes ubiquitous thereafter. Determining whether the bargeman is necessarily the same person in all three instances involves the same sort of ratiocinative process applied to the boy in the opening three stories of *Dubliners*. Geographically and chronologically the first two cohere: seen at Crossguns Bridge about 11:30 P.M., he could have lazily made his way down past two more locks to Newcomen Bridge in two and a half hours. In all three cases the barge contains turf, and in the first and third the speculation centers on the drought-ridden land through which he had traveled. On a decidedly smaller scale the bargeman, like M'Intosh (or the Rosevean or the Elijah throwaway), is a mysterious emanation appearing and reappearing in various places, a wandering rock.

Several more refugees from *Dubliners* make their initial appearance in Hades, and in particular the main characters of "Grace" are recalled: Cunningham, Power, and Kernan are at the funeral, M'Coy's name is offered as present in spirit, and Fogarty is asked about. To these can be added Ignatius Gallaher, Paddy Leonard, Crofton, little Peake of Crosbie and Alleyne's, Mrs. Sinico (mentioned), and Joe Hynes (present), while from *A Portrait* there are Mrs. Riordan (mentioned) and Simon Dedalus (present).

Various name games are played throughout the chapter, including the namesake one: Bloom thinks of the "crown solicitor for Waterford" (93) with the same name as his father-in-law; Daniel O'Connell is buried in Glasnevin, while John O'Connell is the caretaker of the graveyard. Near namesakes are represented by the grave of Robert Emery that Bloom sees, which makes him think of Robert Emmet; punned names, by Father Coffey and Reuben J. Dodd (the first appreciated by Bloom, the second saved for "Odd Miss Doddpebble"—dead stone, German *Tod*—in *Finnegans Wake*). The name not matching the face occurs in the anecdote on Terence Mulcahy impersonated by the statue of Christ, while the intrusive name appears in the initial sounding of the "Goulding, Collis and Ward" joke that re-echoes unto staleness, while the alphabetized obituary will provide a later ploy for polytropic Bloom. Two cases of missing names are suggestive, that of the "nice young student" who dressed Bloom's bee sting (97) and will appear under his own name in Oxen of the Sun, and Mrs. Dignam's brother, present but unnamed at the funeral. The latter will undergo interesting name play before the book is over, but here he suffers an identity crisis in the mind of Leopold Bloom. Musing on the widow remarrying, Bloom tries to match her with a present but impossible man. ("She would marry another. Him? No"—102), and after a reverie on Victoria and Albert returns to reality to see Ned Lambert greeting Dedalus. Later he focuses his thoughts on Lambert ("His wife I forgot he's not married"—110), but earlier he had looked at the bereaved family and wondered "Who is that beside them? Ah, the brother-in-law" (101). Bloom's matchmaking mind had almost lined up brother and sister, but he quickly realized his error and changed to the next nearest male, one that he was at least subliminally aware was a bachelor.

Aeolus

A radical influx of new characters and new references characterizes the seventh chapter, including from *Dubliners* such stalwarts as Lenehan and O'Madden Burke, with an honorable mention for Gabriel Conroy. O'Madden Burke is a candidate for the namesake game since jockey O. Madden is alluded to here (as well as the famous Edmund Burke and a pub named Burke's), but the three-Madden situation will have to wait several more chapters. Paddy Hooper has his analogue in the alderman Hooper (in real life his father) referred to in the previous chapters, while the Seymour Bushe there recurs in confusion with his brother Kendal Bushe; and Dick Adams, "the besthearted bloody Corkman the Lord ever put the breath of life in" (137), echoes fellow Corkonian Dick Tivy. John Gray's statue is reprised but Gregor Grey is a new addition.

Initial and title replace anonymity as the basic disguise in Aeolus. A. E. and "Tay Pay" (137) are sufficiently well known as George Russell and Thomas Power O'Conner, but allusions to "His grace" and "the archbishop's letter" (118, 121) stir odd recollections of the sanctimoniously revered counterpart of Bismarck and Gladstone (S 74) and the derided "Billy with the lip" (P 33). The letter in question appears in the *Evening Telegraph* and is seen by Bloom and Stephen in Eumaeus, but this epistolary counterpart of Garrett Deasy remains unnamed in that chapter as well. (His full name, however, is contained casually in Lotus Eaters, "Dr. William J. Walsh D. D."—80.)

Somewhat more mysterious are "Long John," "Number One," "Messenger," and the "yankee interviewer" (119, 138, 140). The first will appear on his own as John Fanning the subsheriff in Wandering Rocks; the second refers to the leader of the Invincibles in this context, but confusion persists, both in Bloom's mind and in the comments of O'Molloy and Crawford: "Tim Kelly, or Kavanagh, I mean" (136). The yankee interviewer, mentioned again in the same context in Scylla and

Charybdis, has been identified by Richard M. Kain as an American professor named Cornelius Weygandt; but the "Messenger" is baffling. His act of lighting a cigar is superfluous to the action in the newspaper office and can only be explained as a digressive "literary" thought by Stephen and not indicative of anyone present or actually alluded to. Stephen takes advantage of O'Molloy's self-interruption in lighting a cigarette before resuming his quotation to create a short piece of literature which sounds unaccountably like Beaufoy's piece on Matcham. (And according to the syntax, Messenger is a surname rather than a common noun, yet what identity does he actually have in the vignette?)

The main complement of characters in Aeolus are constituted from the pressgang, publisher, editor, typesetter, dayfather, foreman, and newsboys, with an army of orators and journalists and politicians and classical figures supplementing those in attendance. This chapter comes close to duplicating the nostalgic cataloguing that was evident in "The Dead," particularly in the movement backward toward the remote past that was apparent in the glorification of operatic singers. Yet for all the news hounds and goldenmouths evoked here, one tantalizing ghost goes unidentified, even though he is treated to a major caption, "WHAT WETHERUP SAID" (126). Wetherup's distinction is to be quoted for his pithy sayings, here by Bloom and again in Eumaeus, but he has no other function or characteristics. Robert M. Adams is disdainful of Stuart Gilbert's identification of Wetherup with M'Intosh (paralleling one unknown with another helps very little) and runs him down as a W. Wetherup who was a friend of Joyce's father, but Adams obviously considers this dirty pool. One can sympathize with Nannetti in the press room, searching for the dayfather and asking, "Where's what's his name?" (121).

Lestrygonians

Recalling names is a difficulty that Bloom acknowledges, and here he excuses his limitation by remembering Nannetti's lapse ("Well, if he couldn't remember the dayfather's name that he sees every day"—156). His particular gap is someone he remembers as "Pen something" and he hesitantly lights upon "Pendennis" (156). He is not particularly satisfied with the guess and it will be a while before he recalls it more accurately. His "choice" of Pendennis mystifies—it hardly seems likely that Thackeray's Arthur Pendennis has any grip on Bloom's imagination. But the intrusion of Mrs. Breen in his thoughts might present the answer (he could have seen her long before acknowledging her presence on Westmoreland Street in his conscious mind), and signifi-

cantly her complaint is about her demented spouse, Denis Breen. It will eventually be admitted that Bloom fears the possibility of lunacy, and that his premarital interest in Josie Powell, the future Mrs. Breen, puts him into a strange relationship with her actual husband. That the name Denis persists in his mind as a bugaboo of sorts can be evidenced both from the substitution of Pendennis for Penrose, and earlier Denis Carey for James Carey. Only a few hundred yards later Bloom rethinks the older enigma ("Like that Peter or Denis or James Carey"—163), having broken through both the deceptive visual evidence of the church announcement and the mental block that he carried with him to arrive at the real name. A half hour later Penrose will eclipse Pendennis (181).

If Penrose's name had been an item of food it might have jogged Bloom's memory a bit earlier. With food on his mind he makes obvious inadvertent allusions as he wanders toward lunch, and the punned names become obsessive. Graham Lemon leads off, a candy vendor no less, followed by circus man Pepper, a friend called Hancock, the biblical Cain, a publican named Rowe, the provost of Trinity, Dr. Salmon (a pun Bloom makes purposely), an impresario named Whitbred, composer Meyerbeer, the bailiff Rock, the biblical Ham, butcher Coffey, Pygmalion, and even a plumber named Miller (not to mention a horse named Zinfandel). And if a few more liberties were taken with other names that are somewhat suggestive, the list could be expanded.

Hunger may have sharpened Bloom's ability to recall missing names since he does clear up the Penrose dilemma, specifies Dixon as the bee-bite doctor, and seems to have correctly arrived at a royal Otto after being temporarily derailed by a namesake Leopold. But others still elude him. It is understandable that he cannot be exact as to which Dedalus daughter he sees; he trips over the name of the "nice nun" at Tranquilla Convent (she is later identified as Sister Agatha—552); and he makes his first blunder over Mina Purefoy, conflating her with Philip Beaufoy. Yet he is undoubtedly skillful in making it through Farrell's six-part handle a few moments later.

The same associative process that derails him over Purefoy/Beaufoy works in his favor when he reads the handbill on "Dr. John Alexander Dowie" (151) and remembers last year's evangelists from America, Torry and Alexander (Gifford and Seidman spot Reuben Archer Torrey and Charles McCallom Alexander). Coincidental names continue as a pattern: Bloom has no sooner hummed his way through lines from "Father O'Flynn" than he enters Davy Byrne's and finds Nosey Flynn seated there. But the person he fails to find during the lunch hour provides a significant mystery in Lestrygonians. His name is given only once and he plays no further role in *Ulysses,* yet he points to Bloom's lonely search for a sympathetic companion, a young man with whom he can establish a friendship. "Or will I drop into old Harris's and have a chat with young Sinclair?" he muses; "Wellmannered fellow. Probably at his lunch" (166). The search for Sinclair leads to the Burton where Bloom's disgust would have naturally led him away sooner had he not been looking for him: "Not here. Don't see him" (170). There have been interpretations of this incident which identify *him* as Blazes Boylan, but Bloom is obviously looking *for* someone and delays leaving the doorway while doing so. Young Sinclair is never found on 16 June 1904, and Bloom finds young Stephen instead.

Scylla and Charybdis

The shift back to Stephen's world returns us to tougher nuts to crack. More obscure than the wealth of intellectual lore that pervades the chapter—most of which easily surfaces when the necessary research is done—is the Dedalian habit of thinking in specifics without bothering to name the referent antecedent. A short passage at the beginning smacks of Molly's soliloquy with its profusion of masculine pronouns: "Cranly's eleven true Wicklowmen to free their sireland. Gaptoothed Kathleen, her four beautiful green fields, the stranger in her house. And one more to hail him: *ave, rabbi.* The Tinahely twelve. In the shadow of the glen he cooees for them. My soul's youth I gave him, night by night. Godspeed. Good hunting" (184–85). Discarded friend Cranly exists as the frame for the thought since it is to *him* that Stephen had confided in their nocturnal peregrinations. His Wicklow origins (which includes Tinahely) locate him quite specifically, but also point to John Millington Synge (the title of *In the Shadow of the Glen* is unavoidable). That Yeats may be involved as well stems from the echoes of *Cathleen ni Houlihan,* although annotators are quick to add that allusions to Kathleen and the four fields of Ireland and the English strangers pre-exist Yeats's reworking. If we accept the assumption that it is Cranly who is "cooeeing" for his fellow Wicklowmen, drumming up his insurgent dozen (are they *his* disciples or is *he* the twelfth disciple?), we are still confronted by a Christ figure being hailed. Has Cranly changed roles from the precursor to Christ in the course of the transfer from *A Portrait* to *Ulysses,* and is he being hailed by the final adherent? That would give him his twelve, but he only asked for eleven. Or are Synge and Yeats included here in addition to allusions to their works? Stephen has his reasons to resent Yeats's sponsorship of Synge, and snubs by Russell and Moore corroborate his isolation from the Dublin literati.

The literati are very much in evidence in Scylla and Charybdis, and many more are talked about in the library. The chapter contains more "real" names than any other, although many are noted only once or twice. The three librarians plus the visiting A. E. lend an air of literal reality unspoiled by the presence of fictional Stephen and Mulligan and the intrusion of Bloom. George Moore, the shadowy Piper (see *Notes to Joyce*), Padraic Colum, James Starkey, George Roberts, Ernest Longworth, W. B. Yeats, Susan Mitchell, Edward Martyn, George Sigerson, Stephen MacKenna, Lady Gregory, James Stephens, and J. M. Synge are clustered together in several contiguous paragraphs as the dramatis personae of the Celtic Twilight invoked in the National Library. A second grouping of the alive-and-well consists of the theosophists and mystics, from A. E. through Blavatsky and Daniel Dunlop, William Judge, Isabel Cooper-Oakley, plus such mere glimmers as Louis H. Victory and T. Caulfield Irwin. (The A. E. pseudonym allows Joyce an opportunity to toy with other sets of initials: H. P. B. for Blavatsky, K. H. for "Koot Hoomi," and O. P.—ordinary person.) A third category consists of Shakespeare biographers, commentators, and theoreticians, from Ben Jonson and Robert Greene through G. B. Shaw, Frank Harris, Georg Brandes, Oscar Wilde, Sidney Lee, and Judges Barton and Madden. The initials W. H. add conjectures of "Willie Hughes . . . Hughie Wills, Mr. William Himself. W. H.: who am I?" (198). In this chapter, as Fritz Senn notes, names tend to lose their solidity.

A cast of hundreds populates the chapter, from the Dublin walks of life to the Elizabethan: Shakespeare's family and relations (unto the third generation), rivals and contemporaries, dramatic personages and incidental characters. Philosophers and poets from antiquity down to Joyce's contemporaries rub shoulders with various kinds of writers and their literary offspring, along with another group of heretics and mockers (rarely absent from any chapter in which Stephen dominates). That Ann Hathaway plays so important a part in Stephen's theory probably accounts for the numerous wives who populate the chapter: King Henry VIII of course has the lion's share, but those for whom the monogamous limit is honored are Odysseus and Menelaus, Aristotle and Socrates, Pericles and Adam, and gratuitously the Quaker librarian Lyster, plus the Ann shared by the murdered Edward and the murderer Richard.

The gathered intellectuals are rather casual with their references to the great and the known, so that Yeats is referred to by his initials, Jonson as "old Ben," and most of the contemporaries by their last names alone, resulting in our difficulties over the wandering Piper. By contrast, Algernon Charles Swinburne attains his surname at last, after being familiarly glossed over as merely "Algy" in Telemachus and Proteus. Many names suffer from rough handling by the narrative voice, especially those of Eglinton and Best. Francis Bacon's name results in the obvious gastronomic pun—a throwback to Lestrygonians—and Stephen gives voice to the "Lawn Tennyson" appellation that he had harbored since his solitude along Sandymount Strand. Queen Elizabeth is reduced to a homey "Eliza Tudor," yet fares distinctly better than the Blessed Margaret Mary Alacoque ("Anycock"—202). Scant reverence is afforded Gautama Buddha, pluralized as "buddhi" on one occasion and truncated to "Buddh" on another (185, 192). And a handful of pseudo-Shakespeares are felicitously run together as a cumulative "Rutlandbaconsouthamptonshakespeare or another poet of the same name" (208).

Two pseudonyms in particular are of interest, Christfox and Ikey Moses. The first exists apparently in Stephen's imagination rather than in conversation, and it follows from the reappearance of Quaker Lyster. Collated are Jesus Christ and George Fox with William Shakespeare in a strange amalgam involving their attraction/repulsion of women. Stephen's own ambivalance toward women (remaining aloof yet lusting after them) is contained in the passage, and his identity as the fox persists from the schoolroom riddle, although in Scylla and Charybdis he retains his totem as "Bous Stephanoumenos" (210).

"Ikey Moses" (201) is Mulligan's anti-Semitic tag (adopted from a comic strip) for Leopold Bloom. Buck plays fast and loose with the naming of characters, particularly his own in the list for his piece of parodic drama, and his attempt to label Bloom with a characteristically Jewish name backfires in its resonance, the biblical Moses here vouchsafed only a glimpse of the promised land of the intelligentsia (Bloom plays Moses in this instance to Stephen's Christ). An earlier sobriquet for Bloom, stemming from adolescence and remembered by the hungry Bloom in Lestrygonians as "Mackerel" (162), will backfire later when the Cyclops narrator labels him a "cod" (315).

As always some characters are blessed with a surfeit of names, while others are deprived of any. That William Magee the librarian had as his pen name John Eglinton gives rise to a play back and forth between the two, but Shakespeare biographer Sidney Lee is burdened with the suggestion that his name was actually Simon Lazarus. The relative position of the mistress to her dying protector blends together the name of Aristotle's mistress with that of Charles II into "Nell Gwynn Herpyllis" (204), and Stephen also enjoys the homophonics of Mananaan MacLir and King Lear: "Lir's loneliest daughter" (192). However, two people once very close to Stephen go unnamed. If it is Emma Clery that he sees ("Is that? . . . Blueribboned hat . . . Idly writing . . . What? Looked?"—215) (and no alternative possibility for this intrusion is offered in the text), her face registers on his mind without allowing him to register the name. Even more pointed is his recollection of the brother who had served as his first audience, "Where is your brother? Apothecaries' hall. My whetstone. Him, then Cranly, Mulligan: now these" (211). The Maurice who figured prominently in *Stephen Hero* and resurfaced in *A Portrait* is here reduced to anonymity.

Near-anonymity shrouds a shadowy figure in the halls of the library, one of the two patrons who draw Lyster away from Stephen's lecture (the other is Ikey Moses Bloom). Known only as "Father Dineen" (211) he has been recognized by many as *the* Father Dinneen hard at work on his Gaelic-English dictionary. The discrepancy in spelling has caused many a quick hand to reach for a pencil, but Joyce often deletes a single letter from real names, usually an unnecessary duplication or a silent vowel (as in Torrey or Nashe or Bandmann-Palmer). The accident of time and place is too tempting here, and the irony that a Gaelicist would interfere with Stephen's discussion of the prince of English writers (Haines after all has gone off to buy Douglas Hyde's translations) also proves too great a temptation. To reinforce the identification Joyce later has Lyster in conversation with a "priesteen" (U 215): his name and his vocation are interpunned, and the English word "priest" takes on a Gaelic diminutive ending.

Wandering Rocks

Once back out on the streets we find that the offices of commercial Dublin augment the shops of mercantile Dublin in providing the basic array: the names that line the thoroughfares compete with those bandied about by the Dubliners in conversation with each other, and those in the thoughts of Father Conmee, Tom Kernan, young Patsy Dignam, and Boylan's secretary, Miss Dunne, as well as Bloom and Stephen, plus the occupants of the first two carriages of the viceregal procession and those their path intersects. Needless to say, this is the chapter that the *Topographical Guide* devotes the most space to and has the most interesting conjectures about. Attempting to identify the "stout lady" (225) with either Mrs. M'Guinness or Lady Maxwell proves irresistible.

The two named ladies between them bracket the attentions of Father Conmee: the titled one has taken up part of his afternoon and represents an attention to the higher social order, particularly the jaded aristocracy of the eighteenth century, that preoccupies his thoughts as he wanders. The pawnbroker characterizes the world of sordid reality that forces itself upon him, like the necessity of having to accommodate one of the Dignam orphans at Brother Swan's. Ironically, the three cherubic youngsters he encounters and employs to mail his letter derive from backgrounds as seedy as that of Mrs. M'Guinness, but only by tracing them back to their parents by way of *Thom's Directory* (an investigation undertaken by Robert M. Adams) is the irony made manifest. Adams starts out strong but finishes rather inconclusively, offering as parents to two of the boys a pawnbroker (again) and a bookmaker, actual denizens of Dublin, and a coincidental namesake in the fictional Ignatius Gallaher for the third. The text itself corroborates one of the references when Lenehan ducks into Lynam's to check the odds on Sceptre.

Conmee's associates from the earlier reference to him recur in his thoughts: he muses over his talk on Saint Peter Claver and recalls the same sermon by Father Bernard Vaughan that Bloom had heard (Conmee's attitude toward his fellow Jesuit is condescending, but Bloom's comment on the Christ-or-Pilate sermon is cleverer). Much of what transpired for Bloom in All Hallows is recapitulated in Conmee's walk, including aspects of the interexistence of Catholic and Protestant clergy in Dublin; Conmee sees an announcement for "The reverend T. R. Green B. A." (220) just as Bloom had seen the announcement for Conmee, but apparently does not see "the reverend Nicholas Dudley C. C." (222) whom he intersects at Newcomen Bridge. His most auspicious contact and most gratuitous blessings, however, are reserved for the "flushed young man" and the "young woman with wild nodding daisies in her hand" (224) emerging from a hedge. These lovemakers will later be identified as Lynch and his Kitty.

Several minor mysteries surface in Wandering Rocks. An early one concerns the conversation between Corny Kelleher and constable 57C in which the latter reports ("with bated breath"), "I seen that particular party" (225). We suspect that Kelleher is a police informer—his pull with the night watch will get Stephen out of trouble in Nighttown—and many have conjectured that this reference to a "particular party" should be read in that light. Police informing is probably the best solution to the enigma, although for a while there was a temptation to interpret the policeman's secretiveness as more salacious. Discussion of amorous constables begins with Bloom's conjectures about the next-door maid ("a constable off duty cuddled her in Eccles Lane"—60), which turn out to be specific rather than just general. The constable in question re-emerges in the chase scene in Nighttown as "the constable off Eccles Street corner" (586–87), and when Bloom mimics the maid

("O please, Mr Policeman, I'm lost in the wood"—60), he is punning merrily on the name of her employer ("Woods his name is"—59). But constable 57C is not likely to be the maid's cuddler since he is "on his beat" (221) here in North Strand Road, quite a distance from Eccles Street corner. On the other hand, one of the archetypal lovers paraded through Cyclops is "Constable 14A" who "loves Mary Kelly" (333).

Somewhat more mysterious is Miss Dunne, Boylan's secretary, who appears only in this chapter and is permitted a bit of interior monologue. Her role is perfunctory enough, except that several annotators have credited her with being Martha Clifford (if Bloom can operate under a *nom d'amour* and a post office address, perhaps his paramour, with post office address of her own, has a real name of her own). This sort of neat juxtaposition can be tempting, except that Martha began her correspondence in all innocence by answering an advertisement for a typist and could hardly have expected to be employed under a pseudonym. What Miss Dunne is reading is of greater importance. Molly in her soliloquy engages in some literary criticism, dismissing *Moll Flanders* categorically because "I dont like books with a Molly in them" (756). Her own name is actually Marion, and Miss Dunne is reading *The Woman in White,* where the heroine is named Marian (given in *Ulysses* as Marion), and rejects it as well. The Molly-Marion-Mary construct has numerous reverberations in Wandering Rocks: Miss Dunne does like books by Mary Cecil Haye; she admires a poster of Marie Kendall; Conmee broods on Mary Rochfort, daughter of Lord Molesworth; the pea soup in the Dedalus household was donated by Sister Mary Patrick; Bloom surveys the pages of *The Awful Disclosures of Maria Monk;* and Conmee recalls that Mrs. M'Guinness had a fine carriage like Mary, Queen of Scots.

The same complex of names-without-identities and identities-without-names carries on in Wandering Rocks: who is the Crotty that Ned Lambert expects when O'Molloy enters? An unnamed stout lady gives the sailor a coin (Molly, considered stout by some of her detractors, does the same), while an elderly female haunts law firms; Boylan makes his purchases at Thornton's from an unnamed shopgirl, claiming that they are for an "invalid" (227), while they are actually for Molly, who will fulfill his prophecy by spending the evening hours in bed with him, although she belies it in this chapter when she tosses the coin from her window. In Stephen's literarily creative mind a pair of characters take shape, inspired by his view of jewels in the lapidary's window (this Russell is no effete A. E.; his stones conjure up belly dancers and crusty seamen in Stephen's imagination). But Stephen's presumed midwives, to one of whom he had given a name on first sight and both of whom he names in fabricating his parable, now reappear in their "actual" guise as "two old women" (242) remaining anonymous. And Dignam's brother-in-law, deprived of a name at the funeral, begins to come into focus: Patsy Dignam knows him as "uncle Barney" (250).

Wandering Rocks also presents a double dollop of bicyclists, nine quartermilers, and four halfmilers. The latter group had once tantalized symbol hunters, because the forerunner was J. A. Jackson (237) whose name reads like a multiple play on Joyce's own and puts him out front. But the literary detectives defused the High Symbolism of the bicycle race by finding the names just where Joyce found them, in the Dublin newspapers of 17 June 1904. Not as easily uncovered is the jumble of names in Kernan's thoughts about his coat: "Stylish coat, beyond a doubt. Scott of Dawson street. Well worth the half sovereign I gave Neary for it. Never built under three guineas. Fits me down to the ground. Some Kildare street club toff had it probably" (240). Kernan does not know the original owner but assumes it was a "toff" (another such Bloom remembers fired a gun carelessly); Kernan knows the tailor to have been Neary, but Scott remains a puzzle, as Hart and Knuth indicate (see *Topographical Guide,* pp. 67–68). Even if Joyce made the mistake they suppose, misreading *Thom's,* where Robinson the tailor appears before a Scott, why are there *two* tailors implicated? Possibly Neary sold secondhand coats and was the middleman between Robinson (alias Scott), the toff, and Kernan.

Sirens

The musical structures that inform this chapter have their effects on the play on names (Bloom's "Naminedamine" provides a name for the game—257), but much of the sense of theme and variation had been anticipated throughout *Ulysses.* New techniques center on the running together of names like notes of music ("Big Benaben," "Lionelleopold," "Simonlionel," "Bensoulbenjamin," "Siopold"), while the tones of the scale are sounded in the truncated names of the singers at the Ormond bar: "First Lid, De, Cow, Ker, Doll, a fifth: Lidwell, Si Dedalus, Bob Cowley, Kernan and Big Ben Dollard" (290). The coincidental sound-alike of names is also exploited (the previous chapter had juxtaposed Mrs. M'Guinness with Denis J. Maginni)—Lydia Douce and George Lidwell ("Lidlydiawell"—278), Mrs. de Massey and Joe Maas, Cantwell's offices and Cantrell and Cochrane, Messrs Pick and Pocket—while Hugh MacHugh provides his own echo. And even demented Farrell's walk outside lampposts suggests a series of musical notes as Bloom parodies it: "Like Cashel Boylo Connoro Coylo Tisdall

Maurice Tisntdall Farrell, Waaaaaaalk" (286)—the seven vowels in the last word parallel the seven tones of the scale.

In comparison with other chapters Sirens has very few new names, and the ones that accumulate here are sounded over and over again. Yet the commonplace name given the deaf waiter, Pat, conceals its resonance, until the persistent "tap" of the blind piano tuner's cane sets up its mirror image. Bloom himself plays upon one unusual name when he passes the jeweler's shop: "Bloowhose [his own name has picked up the echo of a conversation outside his hearing] dark eye read Aaron Figatner's name. Why do I always think Figather? Gathering figs I think. And Prosper Loré's huguenot name" (259). Bloom's memory may have contained a name like Aaron Figatner's that had concerned him in Calypso and duplicated the initials: Adam Findlater (58; see *Thom's,* p. 1869). Adam "gathering figs," Clive Hart notes, corresponds to Adam Findlater's profession as a wholesale food merchant.

The "Bloowhose" mentioned here is *not* the object of the barmaids' derision, despite the persistent misreading of the passage that occurs, an error which is occasioned by a failure to take into account the musical elision taking place in Sirens. Lydia and Mina are laughing themselves silly over "that old fogey in Boyd's," the local chemist's, with a "goggle eye" (259) and a "bit of beard" (260). None of this description fits Bloom, but the laughter over "greasy eyes" creates a counterpoint with Bloom out on the quay, which the narrative voice then dubs "Greaseabloom" (260) in melodic echo of Lydia and Mina. Bloom remains as unaware of their laughter as they are of his proximity, and even after he has had his dinner in the Ormond dining room, the two barmaids apparently are never conscious of Bloom's existence. The Boyd in question, by context and by reference to *Thom's* a chemist, may not be the same Boyd that was the subject of the Power-Cunningham conversation in Wandering Rocks, where these two Dubliners demonstrated an uncanny ability to guess the referent even when no name is given: "You could try our friend," suggests Power; "Boyd?" responds Cunningham, "Touch me not" (246). Adams opens his essay in detection by lining up the Boyds of *Ulysses* with those of *Thom's* and finds himself fingering his way through flypaper, but he asserts that the Boyd being solicited is a Y.M.C.A. man, not the chemist.

Several names attach themselves to Blazes Boylan in this chapter, especially when he is anonymously seen as "a young gentleman" in a hackney car—on his way to Molly. His outfitting includes a hat by John Plasto and a suit by George Robert Mesias, by coincidence the suppliers of Bloom's hat and suit as well. The Jewish tailor, by no means a singular figure in Dublin, may also be alluded to by Dollard when teased about his ill-fitting trousers: "Bad luck to the jewman that made them" (244). And the driver of Boylan's cab offers an odd instance of name reversal (from the reading of his license presumably), "Barton James of number one Harmony avenue" (279), but this reversal will be straightened out when he reappears in Circe.

An easily overlooked character of unusual recurrence is the "frowsy whore with black straw sailor hat" that Bloom successfully bypasses after he leaves the Ormond. Although she remains nameless in all of her manifestations, she acquires mythic proportions, not only in her significance to Bloom but also to Stephen. The hat is her emblem (hats are often symbolic euphemisms in Joyce's books for female genitalia—see *Finnegans Wake,* page 229—and in Penelope the dozen hat references are symbolic of one of the four cardinal points), and it is by her black straw hat that we locate and recognize her. Bloom uncomfortably recognizes her here as a prostitute that once accosted him and who has seen him with Molly (note that she refers to Molly as a "Stout lady"—290). Bloom carefully avoids prostitutes, and he lets this particular siren sail by, but she is rerouted past him again at the cabman's shelter: "The face of a streetwalker, glazed and haggard under her black straw hat" (632). If Bloom had been dismayed by her looks in daylight, he is no more pleased by her face at night, and he assumes that she is rotten with disease. Stephen in the shelter had failed to see her, yet if he had he might have remembered her since she once accosted him by the Grand Canal just after he left Emma ("A black straw hat was set rakishly above her *glazed* face"—S 189). She becomes the recipient of Stephen's financial generosity and the source of his bemused speculations ("the woman in the black straw hat gave something before she sold her body to the State," he tells Lynch; "Emma will sell herself to the State but give nothing"—S 203). Eventually in *Ulysses* the emblem subsumes the person, and we learn in Ithaca that Molly Bloom also owns a black straw hat (730), although Molly's soliloquy, festooned with an array of hats, fails to include the black straw now resting on the commode—instead she innocently recalls the "white ricestraw hat" she wore when tantalizing Mulvey (760).

Cyclops

The epic catalogues alone make Cyclops a census-taker's nightmare, the lesser problem being the listing of the cast of hundreds in alphabetical order. Each grouping presents certain difficulties of its own, and the basic concept of giganticism and name manipulation calls into question other ordinarily accepted names. For example, the curate at

Barney Kiernan's is obviously called Terry, and it is logical that his Christian name is Terence, but is his surname O'Ryan? "Terence O'Ryan" (299) is the only indication of his full name, but the practice of adding "O' " to certain names as a super-Irish comic touch occurs in several instances in the chapter (O'Bergan for Alf Bergan, O'Dignam for Paddy Dignam, and even O'Bloom—297). Sandwiched in among these and in a paragraph of mockheroics Terence Ryan may have been over-Irished in jest, but there seems to be no way of knowing from the text. (The only Terence O'Ryan in *Thom's* is the other kind of curate.)

"O'Bloom, the son of Rory" ushers in a host of tamperings with known names in Cyclops. Lord Iveagh and Lord Ardilaun, the Guinnesses famous for their bung-holed barrels of stout, are "the noble twin brothers Bungiveagh and Bungardilaun," (299); scientific Bloom is rechristened "Herr Professor Luitpold Blumenduft" (304); Bob Doran has been calling himself "Joseph Manuo" (314); Bernard Kiernan has been Gaelicized into "Brian O'Ciarnain" (316); John Wyse Nolan presides over a forest wedding as "Jean Wyse de Neaulan" (327), where the organist is "Senhor Enrique Flor" (327), a Portugese version of our own Henry Flower; Orangeman Crofton from *Dubliners* reappears as a confused Crofton-Crofter-Crawford (336); Bloom's father, as "old Methusalem Bloom" (366); and Bloom under various aliases from those already cited to "Mister Knowall" (315), "Old lardyface" (333), "old sloppy eyes" (336), "Junius" (337), "Ahasuerus" (338), and "Elijah" (345).

Principles that govern alteration of names or creation of pseudonyms vary from catalogue to catalogue. On the most straightforward level there is the procession of Dublin clergy from "the very rev. William Delany S.J., L.L.D." to "the rev. J. Flanagan, C. C." (317-18), culled from *Thom's* and probably never assembled in such profusion before, two dozen strong. Equally coherent and homogeneous are the dozen Irish "jurors," listed as "the high sinhedrim of the twelve tribes of Iar" (323). But the other religious procession, the hordes of the annointed and the blessed, has its anomalous factors. Although the progression begins logically enough with monks and friars of the various orders, followed by a vast body of the saintly, one begins to suspect even before the saints lose their names and become "S. Anonymous and S. Eponymous" (339), et cetera, that some of the names verifiably belonging to the canonized are also of characters closer to home: "S. Martin of Tours and S. Alfred and S. Joseph and S. Denis and S. Cornelius and S. Leopold and S. Bernard and S. Terence and S. Edward" (339). Surnames fall easily into place for these nine: Cunningham, Bergan, O'Molloy or Hynes, Breen, Kelleher, Bloom, Kiernan, O'Ryan, and Lambert (those in or near the pub on Little Britain Street), especially since the saint between the last of these and the anonymous faction is "S. Owen Caniculus," a canine named Garryowen. Each of these makes an appearance in the pub except Breen and Kelleher, both of whom are subjects of conversation there, while two unnamed characters, the Citizen and the narrator, and the named characters Bob Doran and John Wyse Nolan are missing, although earlier we find "S. Simon Stylites and S. Stephen Protomartyr and S. John of God," strangely familiar as well. An unusual pair consists of an acknowledged "Brother Aloysius Pacificus" coupled with a fictive "Brother Louis Bellicosus," anticipating a brotherly battle. The procession culminates with Father O'Flynn, and although Robert M. Adams insists that there is no reason to assume that "Father Malachi O'Flynn" in Circe has any connection with St. Malachi but only with Mulligan, here is O'Flynn "attended by Malachi and Patrick" (340).

Other cohesive clusters include the English-sounding names read from the births and deaths columns of the *Irish Independent* (where a purposeful mispronunciation of "Cockburn" provides for grim venereal humor—298); the lower-class English names of the murdered and the hanged in Rumbold's letter (303); humans punned into arboreal figures in the wedding in the woods (327); the scurrilous names of the parliamentarians (315–16); and the multilingual names and titles of the seventeen delegates of the "Friends of the Emerald Isle" (307), from which "real" Hi Hung Chang has been ferreted out by Hugh Staples as having been a Chinese envoy to the Court of St. James. The announced schedule of "Irish heroes and heroines of antiquity" produces the greatest surprises and the least homogeneity: it starts out with legitimate heroes but soon incorporates traitors as well, and once it reaches Goliath, wide and wild disparity runs rampant. The principle of coupling is soon limited to similar sounds (Thomas Conneff, Peg Woffington), nationalities (Dante Alighieri, Christopher Columbus), vocations (Marshall MacMahon, Charlemagne); names are replaced by captions, surnames clash with given names to produce hybrid compounds, and people are replaced by places (Dolly Mount, Sidney Parade, Ben Howth). See Appendix A.

Far more muted in tone is the coupling of lovers, ten logically matched sets covering an enormous range, with some of the specific pairs proving particularly interesting. The amorous bobby, earlier identified as the 14A who once almost arrested Bob Doran as drunk and disorderly in a bawdy house, now is seen as "Constable 14A [who] loves Mary Kelly" (333). Gerty MacDowell, viewed in Wandering Rocks, is credited with loving a bicyclist, who will later be identified as the brother of the W. E. Wylie who cycles through Wandering Rocks (237). That the man in the macintosh "loves a lady who is dead" has resulted in speculation by John O. Lyons and others that M'Intosh is actually the James Duffy of "A Painful Case," and the lady, Mrs. Sinico (whose funeral Bloom attended last year—114). And a further enigma is posited by the news that "M. B. loves a fair gentleman": the initials fit Molly Bloom and the description fits Boylan, but there is also the possibility that they are *Milly* Bloom and Alec Bannon, for whom there is no description.

Cyclops, a chapter in which jumbled and disguised naming is a structural principle, proves to be a maze of blurred identities. "L-n-h-n and M-ll-g-n" (307) are easily recognizable although they have lost their vowels, and a reversed "Owen Garry" (311) can soon be righted, but the single letter "P." signing an article of satiric lampoon goes unexplained. Nolan had expected the pseudonym "Shanganagh" for Arthur Griffith, but the single initial points to someone else ("a very good initial too," notes Hynes, the loyal Parnellite—334). No name at all can be even more mystifying, especially when two friends talk of a third without needing to identify him:

> —What about paying our respects to our friend? says Joe.
> —Who? says I. Sure, he's in John of God's off his head, poor man.
> —Drinking his own stuff? says Joe.
> —Ay, says I. Whisky and water on the brain. (293)

We only know that "our friend" in his case is not the Citizen, since he is the next topic of conversation, but if the drunkard in question is Bob Doran (the fact that in *Dubliners* he worked for a wine merchant might account for his drinking his own stuff), then Joe Hynes registers no surprise at finding him in Barney Kiernan's. Doran's drunken insistence on calling Paddy Dignam "Willy" follows logically from the pairing of Willy Murray and Paddy by Alf Bergan, but the identity of Willy Murray remains Joyce's personal aside since he has already based the character of Richie Goulding on his maternal uncle of that name. "Our friend" may well be, as Clive Hart suggests, a euphemism for drink itself—or Kiernan himself.

As enigmatic as "our friend" is the narrator's conjecture that Bloom has a "friend in court" (313) who helped him out of difficulties over the Royal Hungarian lottery tickets. Bloom is unlikely to be closely associated with any Dublin jurists, but he had already indicated that there was trouble about the tickets at a "lodge meeting" (156). That Bloom had once been a Mason but no longer is (he wonders if Kernan is) may be explained by the role Sir Frederick Falkiner might have played in both keeping the scandal out of the courts and having Bloom booted out of the Masonic Order.

Nausicaa

After the congestion of Cyclops the next chapter is relatively free of crowds, although like every chapter of *Ulysses* it introduces its share of new characters. Gerty MacDowell has already had a partial introduction, and her grandfather Giltrap been mentioned as the owner of Garryowen, but other members of her family, and her friends Cissy Caffrey and Edy Boardman materialize for the first time. The narrative tone of Gerty's half of the chapter, the euphemistic and coy nicknaming of God's creatures, colors not only vocabulary but specific names as well. Spoiled beauties are "the Flora MacFlimsy sort" (346); a rosebud mouth is a "cupid's bow" (348); the determiner of taste in clothes is "Dame Fashion" (350); a lavatory is "Miss White" (353); and sleep is personified by "the sandman" and "Billy Winks" (363). Gushy Gerty is not the only practitioner of such verbal abuse. The males in the novel are no less capable of such personifications: Bloom thinks of the ideal husband as "Mr Right" (369), the returning soldier as "Johnny" marching home (378), and the ocean as "Davy Jones' locker" (379), and, like Gerty, he resorts to the cute diminutive "wifey" (352, 373).

Several names are skilfully inserted in Nausicaa for immediate or delayed effect. The quarreling twins are aptly named Tommy and Jacky, since they represent warring soldiers and sailors (Tommy Atkins and Jack Tar respectively). Gerty has an acquaintance named Winny Rippingham, a name that Molly would have enjoyed making fun of. Cissy renames Bloom "uncle Peter" (361), and Bloom hypnotically plays upon the name "Grace Darling" (376, 382), at first in the accurate context of the heroine who rescued the shipwrecked, but later, as he dozes, in a romantic-erotic context because of the oddity of her surname.

The most significant name play in Nausicaa centers on Father Conroy, one of the three clerics conducting a benediction at Mary, Star of the Sea Church in Sandymount, within earshot of Bloom and company. Nowhere in the chapter is his Christian name given—or anywhere else in *Ulysses* for that matter—but neither is Canon O'Hanlon's, although Father John Hughes, S. J. is fully accounted for. Conroy's missing prenom causes Robert Adams some difficulties: having found that Father Bernard Conroy was actually a priest at the Sandymount church, he claims that "Dignam went to confession to Father Bernard Conroy, supposed to be the brother of Gabriel" (p. 60) and that "Joyce, finding a Conroy at the Star of the Sea, altered the name he had already given, and rebaptized Gabriel's brother as Bernard" (p. 61, *n* 6). By avoiding the use of Father Conroy's first name Joyce avoids rebaptism assiduously; by having Bloom, a scant acquaintance of the Conroys at best, assume that this Conroy is Gabriel's brother Joyce compounds the joke; and by having Father Hughes quote "the great saint Bernard" (356) Joyce doubles the compound, while having Father Conroy in hearing Gerty's confession refer to "the archangel Gabriel" triples it. Would a "senior curate in Balbriggan" (D 186)—if the events of "The Dead" can be proven to have occurred prior to 16 June 1904—now find himself assisting at the Star of the Sea?

The mysterious figure in Nausicaa is the man seen by both Gerty and Bloom strolling along the Strand, actually a quite ordinary personage until he becomes tangled in Bloom's imaginative conjectures. Gerty barely notices him but has developed an antipathy for him nonetheless. His evening walks are apparently habitual, and she thinks of him as "the gentleman off Sandymount green," while Cissy more colorfully refers to him as "the man that was so like himself" (354). Bloom notices him returning and classifies him as "this nobleman" (357), and he builds a minor portrait of a postprandial stroller with money in the bank. His oblique self-identification is soon followed by another urge to write a marketable tidbit, and his title comes quickly to mind, reflecting his own image: *"The Mystery Man on the Beach"* (376).

Oxen of the Sun

The scores of names usually associated with this chapter are not contained in its pages since they are the writers whose prose styles Joyce parodied and embellished here. Secondary allusions, many of them to the Latins (Virgil, Ovid, Tully) nonetheless abound, but it is on the actual denizens of the Lying-In Hospital that most attention needs to be focused. The hospital director, Sir Andrew Horne, is not actually in residence, and Doctor O'Hare (as Bloom learns) is dead, but the two nurses, Callan and Quigley, are at work, as is Doctor Dixon. The common room boasts a party of revelers, mostly the medical students Lynch, William Madden, Francis (Punch) Costello, and the Scottish student J. Crotthers. Oxen of the Sun is rather generous in supplying given names where none had hitherto been available: Lynch for the first time is identified as Vincent, Mulligan proves four-named, and Lenehan is enhanced with the initial T. Mock doctors are more plentiful than real ones—witness Doctor Rinderpest (399), Doctor O'Gargle (406), Doctor Diet, and Doctor Quiet (423)—unless one includes the legendary medicinemen of Ireland, "the O'Shiels, the O'Hickeys, the O'Lees" (384). The Irishness of these names echoes Stephen's prejudices about low-Irish names: Father Dolan ("It was like the name of a woman that washed clothes"—P 55); Father Moran ("whose name and voice and features offended his baffled pride: a priested peasant"—P 221), and especially the Christian Brothers on the bridge, where the one name spoken ("—Brother Hickey") summons up three others in his mind ("Brother Quaid./Brother MacArdle./Brother Keogh./Their piety would be like their names, like their faces, like their clothes"—P 166).

Surrogate names are often applied to those present as the literary styles change, most particularly when the group takes on Bunyanesque denominations. Stephen's touches of self-glorification here, including the lie that he had been paid for something he had written, labels him "Boasthard" and "Young Boasthard" (395–96), while Bloom's basic characteristic earns him the title of "Calmer" and "Mr Cautious Calmer." One name is self-descriptive ("Mr Dainty Dixon"); another is explained by a reference back ("Mr False Franklin" re-echoes "a franklin that hight Lenehan"—387); but the other three, "Mr Cavil and Mr Sometimes Godly, Mr Ape Swillale," are best applied to Lynch, Madden, and Costello respectively. A licentious anecdote on John Fletcher and Francis Beaumont results in their being renamed, "Beau Mont and Lecher" (393); Nicholas Breakspear (Pope Adrian IV) and Pope Nicholas II become "Father Nicholas," while Kings Henry II, VII, and VIII share the role of "Lord Harry" (399–401); Theodore Purefoy appears as "Glory Allelujerum" (408); M'Intosh is both "Dusty Rhodes" and "Bartle the Bread" (317); and St. Peter reverts to a "Peter Piscator" (391).

Pope Peter and the now-familiar Joseph the Joiner are included with other members of the Holy Family in a game of "This is the house that Jack built" being played by the carousing medicals. Stephen seems to be the instigator as he conjectures about the virginal conception, and when Costello calls for a song from Stephen (*Etienne chanson*), the following is forthcoming:

Behold the mansion reared of dedal Jack,
See the malt stored in many a refluent sack,
In the proud cirque of Jackjohn's bivouac. (394)

The house in question is either the world God created, or the Church created on the rock that is Peter, or the distillery of John Jameson and Son, or Daedalus's labyrinth, or even the shaky household of the Dedaluses. Stephen's name is attached (*"Etienne . . . dedal"*), but so is Joyce's own father's. That J. J. and S. constitute the Holy Trinity is well worked over in *Finnegans Wake* ("Jhon Jhamieson and Song . . . of the twelve apostrophes"—FW 126) and the storage of the malt here in "the crystal palace of the Creator" (394) carries the same allusion. It is tempting therefore to return to the cryptic colloquy of the nameless one and Joe Hynes early in Cyclops regarding "our friend . . . in John of God's . . . Drinking his own stuff . . . Whisky and water" (293).

During the course of the chapter Lynch's paramour of the afternoon is identified as a girl named Kitty (apparently not the Kitty Ricketts who will occupy him later at Bella Cohen's), and Bloom's first love, Bridie Kelly, occupies his thoughts in the hospital common room. The birth at long last of the ninth Purefoy child occasions a catalogue of all their children (some with nicknames, some with christened names, some with both), paralleling Bloom's cataloguing of Mat Dillon's six daughters in Nausicaa. The identity of the Yeats sisters, long delayed after the references to the "weird sisters" in the first chapter (13), now comes closer, at least about their number: "To be printed and bound at the Druiddrum press by two designing females" (424).

Three other identifications of note occur late in Oxen of the Sun, as the hospital revelers end up at Burke's pub. An anti-vegetarian diatribe centers on an old married couple, Darby Dullman and his Joan ("A canting jay and a rheumeyed curdog is all their progeny. Pshaw, I tell thee!"—423). The names are obviously intended to be basically typical, but there is the supposition that this is an offhanded comment on the companionate marriage of the Shaws and G. B.'s avowed vegetarianism. "Pshaw" parallels the same pun in *Finnegans Wake,* where "this is Pshaw" (FW 303) locates him among seven Anglo-Irish writers and "Jeebies, ugh, kek, ptah" (FW 590) locates G. B. U. K. Shaw as an Englishman. The final note is the appearance of Bantam Lyons among the celebrants in Burke's ("I shee you, shir. Bantam"—426), a late entry into the festivities.

Circe

No two readers of this phantasmagoria make the same decisions as to what constitutes reality and what is hallucination, and Hugh Kenner is probably accurate in reading the entire sequence as something different from either literal reality or distorted fantasy. For the purpose of tabluation, however, it is necessary to make certain distinctions about what actually transpires in the events of the plot. That the Cissy Caffrey of Nausicaa is on Mabbot Street with Private Carr may seem incontrovertible, but the presence of Edy Boardman is unlikely and that of the twins totally unacceptable. Dictates of logic govern any such selection, and although it is feasible that slum children of the neighborhood are still in the streets at this hour it is not conceivable that the toddlers of the suburban middle class are there. Separating the young from the old surrounding Rabaiotti's cart is not easy in the strange dim night light, but the stunted gnomes of hallucination can finally be detected as real children as moments of clarity intervene. Thus the "pigmy woman" (429) is a child on a swing, but the gnome among the rubbish is a rag-and-bone man.

The conditions imposed by the opening tableau govern the rest of the chapter, and the suspicion persists that if these conditions can be satisfied all else will fall into place. However, the opening is devoid of a hallucinator since neither Stephen nor Bloom is yet on stage, although Stephen soon appears and passes through. Edy and the twins are known to Bloom from the evening exposure on Sandymount Strand, but there is no reason to assume that Stephen knows them. Nor does Bloom know Bertha Supple, although Gerty *thinks* about her while Bloom is looking at Gerty. Edy's bickering places her legitimately in the squalid surroundings of Nighttown; her grammar is of the streets and her vocabulary of the gutter, a far cry from "A penny for your thoughts" (360), one of the few lines of recorded speech that she has in Nausicaa. Even if we accept the fact that the namby-pamby narrative voice that controls the chapter has such a rose-colored view of the trio of girls that it obliterates their true qualities (after all, old Giltrap's dog is far more believable as the mangy cur viewed by the Cyclops narrator than the "lovely dog Garryowen that almost talked, it was so human"—352), it remains preposterous that Edy in Nighttown was the innocent who cavorted on Sandymount beach. The intended contrast between the idle pleasures of the daughters of the bourgeoisie and the children of the slums is emphasized by the shock of viewing not two different girls, but one that presumably is the same person. The two faces of Edy testify—with a vengeance—that Rosie O'Grady and the colonel's lady are sisters under the skin. Everything that had its presumed and unquestioned innocence is reflected in the black mirror of Circe.

The tree that falls in the forest unobserved has its resounding crash. Bloom arrives too late to survey the afternoon maidens in their midnight guises (nor would he necessarily recognize them as the same princesses), but the reader is forced to come to grips with the ugliness of reality even though he can assuage the horror by being allowed to assume that it is someone's temporary hallucination. The printed page, particularly in Circe, lacks the total view afforded by the proscenium stage, where, even if a member of the audience prefers not to look at all, everything that happens on stage is there to be seen by every other member of the audience. Circe, more than any other chapter in *Ulysses,* is subject to the selective camera that determines the image on the cinematic screen. Long shots occasionally light up the larger setting; medium shots limit the range but increase the significance of what is framed; close-ups sacrifice almost everything that surrounds the object in focus for heightened intensity. If it is the reader who hallucinates in Circe, each reader will have to alter the circumstances by which characters are identified and classified and arrive at individual conclusions on fantasy and reality.

Before it settles down to being essentially a psychological repository of the nightmares of guilt and the dreams of glory for the two male principals, Circe is a searing portrait of the dark night of the soul. Those who have been viewed (even ambivalently) in the false light of innocence are the first to be hideously reversed, and of the Nausicaa dramatis personae Cissy Caffrey persists throughout the transformation to be the instrument of Stephen's destruction, corroborating Gerty's envious suspicions of her. Nighttown at midnight is indeed Circe's domain, a domain in which all men except those that carry the magical moly are metaphorically degraded, a degradation they bring into the netherworld with them. Only Bloom is capable of survival and escape, and in this recasting of Homer's setting the hero manages to bring out of the lair with him the badly bruised Stephen Dedalus. Cissy Caffrey makes the transformation from the mythic temptress aloofly singing her obscene song to the flirtatious but malevolent young girl pushing her soldier escort toward the destruction of the helpless Stephen: she plays the Circe role for him that Bella Cohen attempts to enact for Leopold Bloom. An analogue for Cissy is the "elderly bawd" peddling maidenhead on Mabbot Street and cursing the unresponsive Stephen (431, 441–42). She reappears as "THE BAWD" (593) championing the British soldiers against the Irish patriotism of "THE VIRAGO."

Appearance and reappearance form a pattern in Circe, much like the dog that tags after Bloom and undergoes changes of breed along the way. As anonymous as the dog and the bawd, a secretive customer at Bella Cohen's arouses Bloom's suspicions (he suspects that it might be Boylan on a post-Molly binge). The customer is first represented only by his hat and waterproof on the antlered rack (502)—symbolizing Bloom's uneasiness—later makes his exit past the rack as a "male form" and is heard by Bloom as a "male voice" (525), and is finally exorcised by Bloom-Svengali: "A male cough and tread are heard passing through the mist outside" (526). In spirit he is replaced by the "two silent lechers" (585) brought by Corny Kelleher to the red-light district, whom he identifies to Bloom as "Two commercials that were standing fizz at Jammet's" (606)—because they were mourning their losses on a race, the *Topographical Guide* tentatively speculates that they might be Boylan and Lenehan.

Bloom's own metamorphoses are again achieved through name changes. His favorite is undoubtedly "Leopold the First" (482), but most of the others are foisted upon him by his detractors. The sluts and ragamuffins in their combined wisdom label him "Bluebeard," and taking their cue from Mulligan, whom they could not have overheard, also call him "Ikey Mo" (466). Mastiansky and Citron denounce him as "Belial! Laemlein of Istria! the false Messiah! Abulafia!" (497); Bella renames him in her own image, apparently aware of *Ruby, Pride of the Ring,* "Ruby Cohen" (535); and the Man in the Macintosh tries to unmask him, "That man is Leopold M'Intosh. . . . His real name is Higgins" (485). The Higgins name echoes strangely in Circe as that of the whore Zoe Higgins, but it is also Bloom's mother's maiden name (changed by her father from Karoly). Like Bella, the macintosh man is affixing his own name to Bloom, but Bloom had actually been responsible for the misnomer in the first place. In a couple of lists Bloom's name appears surreptitiously indeed: among Miriam Dandrade's violators Bello includes a "Henry Fleury" (536) and among the "mute inhuman faces" is that of "Poldy Kock" (538). Larry O'Rourke might not recognize himself there as "Larry Rhinoceros."

The Martha Clifford identity is made more enigmatic when she appears before Bloom and the watch. Accusing him of breach of promise, she claims that her "real name is Peggy Griffin" (456), opening the possibility alluded to that she too may be engaging in the epistolary romance under an alias. To compound the confusion of identities there is the accusation of THE SINS OF THE PAST: "Unspeakable messages he telephoned mentally to Miss Dunn at an address in d'Olier Street" (537). That Boylan's secretary is named Miss Dunne (misdone?) is coincidence enough, although Bloom's acquaintance with Blazes might be sufficient for him to know the secretary's name. Hart and Knuth note that Boylan's office may be on D'Olier Street (he is seen outside the Red Bank), but that more likely this Miss Dunn is related to the poultry vendor on D'Olier Street, where Simon Dedalus bought his Christmas turkey (P 29).

The face-without-a-name situation worsens in Circe, and the nameless become self-incorporated: among those chasing Bloom to Beaver Street are "Whatdoyoucallhim, Strangeface, Fellowthatslike, Sawhimbefore, Chapwith" (586). The first is the hunchback Bloom saw early in the morning on Dorset Street; "Sawhimbefore" might designate the "nobleman" that Bloom observed returning along the Strand; but

"Fellowthatslike" seems to point forward rather than back, to the cabby in the next chapter who looks like Henry Campbell. "Chapwith" may function in the same direction: it anticipates Corley's comment that the chap Stephen is with (Bloom) was seen by Corley with Blazes Boylan, which means that Bloom himself is among those chasing him. But so is the Nameless One, quite probably from the context the collector of bad debts who narrates Cyclops (the assumption that it might be the Citizen is discarded because the Citizen is also among the pursuers).

A few names in Circe worthy of notice because of their oddity include these: Minnie Watchman listed with the nine Jewish males, presumably to make a minyan, although women are excluded from such participation (perhaps the illegal entry of a woman into the Masons, as Nosey Flynn reports, accounts for Minnie's inclusion); Stephen swearing by "virtue of the fifth of George and the seventh of Edward" (587)—the latter was King of England, but the former would have to wait six years for his father to die (the phraseology suggests statutes, and therefore an earlier George); the imaginary Miss Ferguson conjured up as Stephen's beloved by Bloom mishearing the quotation referring to Fergus. Touches such as these often determine the accidents of denomination in *Ulysses,* as those who echo Stuart Gilbert know regarding the three whores, Zoe, Florry, and Kitty: "Female creature, flower, virgin ore: animal, vegetable, mineral" (p. 294, *n* 1).

Eumaeus

Bracketed by approach to and retreat from the cabman's shelter, Eumaeus has its basic location in the shelter's narrow confines. However, the camera's eye never allows us to view the entire scene at once and enumerate the characters present. Nor are most of them clearly defined individuals, and like the metamorphosing dog in Circe they change identities throughout. The two constants are Stephen and Bloom; two defined variables are the grizzled seaman and the shelter keeper, but they are both shrouded in mystery. Whether the keeper is actually Skin-the-Goat Fitzharris is never determined (he makes no attempt to identify himself as such and certainly no one asks him). On the other hand, the sailor presents himself as W. B. Murphy, an able-bodied seaman, and shows papers to prove it. Bloom at least remains skeptical, speculating that he is sailing under false colors, since the postcard he displays bears the name A. Boudin as addressee. How many casual customers are scattered about is impossible to determine, but the safest assumption is three. At one instance they are labeled "one man," "another," and "another" (629), but their occupations, if any, are unclear. The narrative voice is uncertain, referring to them most often as "cabbies" (at one time noting, "the jarvey, if such he was"—632), but the trio is also detailed on the same page as "longshoreman number one," "loafer number two," and "a third" (the narrative voice simultaneously guessing at a vocation and making a value judgment).

Even as the constants in a sea of variables, Stephen and Bloom do not go unaltered. Stephen's name remains intact, but there are problems of identity and location, since Bloom makes certain assumptions about his piety and patriotism that are fallacious and the newspaper reports his presence at a funeral he never attended. Bloom is reduced by the same newspaper to "L. Boom" (647), a diminution that he does not appreciate, while the first indication of the full name of Dignam's brother-in-law, Bernard Corrigan, also appears in the story. Simon Dedalus, like his son, undergoes a transformation he would have been amazed at: W. B. Murphy advertises him as a circus sharpshooter. Murphy exists as the most unreliable of sources, but his case of mistaken identity nonetheless establishes, within the context of the fiction at least, *two* separate and distinct Simon Dedaluses. Bloom's mind, achieves a similar result when Stephen lauds John Bull the composer and Bloom assumes that it is John Bull "the political celebrity" (662).

Nominal duality is one facet of the ironic confusions; faulty genealogy is another. The John Corley whom Stephen confronts on the street is detailed back to various ancestors because of the Homeric parallel, which affords him the nickname of "Lord John Corley" (616), making him a counterpart to "Don John Conmee" (223, 561). Even if the speculation on his artistocratic family tree were in any way relevant to the presence of the down-and-out sponger, the introduction of below-stairs connections and the uncertainty of the actual line of descent compromise the position of the son of Inspector Corley. This discrepancy between the title and the name of Lord John Corley parallels the comic juxtaposition of Yeats's famous initials and the sailor's surname, the common Murphy, although the latter part does have its connection with the seafaring trade, as a reference to "A Palgrave Murphy boat" indicates (639). That "Shakespeares were common as Murphies" (622) is the core of Stephen's disquisition on naming ("Cicero, Podmore, Napoleon, Mr Goodbody, Jesus, Mr Doyle") and he insists that names are impostures, since they are most often "imposed." Certainly Parnell's aliases, "Fox and Stewart" (649), would exemplify his argument; one may wonder as well about the identity of "the girl in the office" (618) who proved discouraging to Corley when he applied for a job from Boylan, quite probably the same Miss Dunne of other speculations.

Ithaca

Nowhere else in *Ulysses,* with the notable exception of the name-laden Cyclops chapter, are there more catalogues of names than in Ithaca. A tabulation of the categories here once again attests to the balance of absurd accidentals and directed coincidences that marks the name-inclusion techniques of the novel. Even names that have become standard and familiar are capable of interesting surprises: Bloom's middle name, Paula (723), for example. The adopted tone of computerized information, fulsome to a fault, offers information of more sorts than anyone could possibly want or tolerate, so that middle names are supplied for Tweedy and Val Dillon, as well as Gladstone, and middle initials for Bantam Lyons and Nannetti. Even Plumtree is given his given name, along with others to whom additional appellations are added. One such notable is Dunbar Plunket Barton who had hitherto been known only as a judge who dabbled in Shakespeare theory. To offset this identification of two separate characteristics of the same person, there is the allusion to a Moore Street merchant named Henry Price, obviously not to be confused with the Henry Blackwood Price that Deasy claims as kin. Name augmentation will prove to be a trap, however, as is soon realized.

In fleshing out the past for both Bloom and Stephen, Ithaca recalls names from *Dubliners* and *A Portrait* as yet unmentioned. It has been obvious of course that Bloom's Mrs. Riordan had been Stephen's Dante, but we now find that the elderly Morkan sisters were Stephen's aunts. There are two lists of Bloom's past friends, one especially devoted to those already dead and another to the circumstances of his three baptisms. More important is the Bloom family tree and the name changes undertaken by both his father and his maternal grandfather. They changed from names that were palpably Hungarian (Virag and Karoly), but not necessarily Jewish, to such disparate names as Bloom and Higgins, the first unmistakably Jewish, as verified by the dozens of Blooms and Blums in the Clanbrassil Street area of Dublin uncovered by Louis Hyman, and the second unmistakably Irish. The information presented in the genealogical survey of Bloom's background consequently opens more questions than it resolves. From Stephen's list of maternal grandparents, however, we learn only that Uncle Richie bears his father's name and that little Crissie was named after her grandmother, Christina Goulding (682).

Other categories reveal St. Patrick's genealogy, pantomime credits, Jewish dignitaries of historical note, and Irish and British political figures of the nineteenth century, as well as financiers and astronomers. One basic Moses engenders a pair of others—"Moses Maimonides . . . and Moses Mendelssohn" (687)—while one basic Sinbad the Sailor is echoed deep into sleep by fourteen others until even their alliterative names lose their euphony. The most vital catalogue in Ithaca is undoubtedly that of Molly's twenty-five extramarital lovers, a list once accepted at face value but long since partially or totally discredited. The catechism technique of Ithaca lulls the unwary into accepting the validity of the information so scientifically spun out in it, but the source of information remains mysteriously hidden behind a bank of quixotically programmed computers. The source of the twenty-five names has to be Bloom's own mind, but there is no evidence that even he believes his list—or any part of it except the last item, Blazes Boylan. Enough names are already familiar to make the group suspect (Menton's behavior to Bloom at the funeral is hardly that of a successful seducer to the man he has cuckolded; Goodwin and Dollard have already earned Bloom's bemused scorn, an attitude inconsistent with any rivalry; and Lenehan has supplied us gratuitously with information about the extent of his meagre conquest of Molly). That even such vague and indirect figures as the organ-grinder and the bootblack are included attests to the masochistically desperate nature of the cataloguing, while the "unknown gentleman in the Gaiety Theatre" (731) is disqualified by his preexistence in Bloom's thoughts at the Ormond: "Chap in dresscircle, staring down into her with his operaglass for all he was worth" (284). Since that is the extent of Bloom's knowledge about him, it remains the extent of his knowledge half a day later. Lenehan's evidence eliminates an omniscient source of information for the list; Bloom's evidence on the chap in the dress circle proves that these are "admirers" of Molly that he knows about but could hardly consider seriously at any rational moment.

Molly herself will have the last word and cut down more than three-quarters of these contenders with her derisive scorn for their fat legs (Dollard), skinny legs (Goodwin), criticizing ways (Dedalus), dirty eyes (Val Dillon), and "big babyface" (Menton), while her recollection of the dress-circle chap corroborates Bloom's first impression: "that fellow . . . at the Gaiety . . . tipping me there and looking away hes a bit daft I think I saw him after trying to get near two stylish dressed ladies outside Switzers window at the same little game I recognised him on the moment the face and everything but he didn't remember me" (767). Even without Molly's coup de grace, the accuracy of the list is open to question after it is noticed that "Father Bernard Corrigan," probably fictitious, is included (731).

Molly's curiosity about sex with a cleric further destroys the credibility of the list, but she does indicate that she had gone to a Father Corrigan for confession, a fact Bloom had probably been made aware of and remembered in his moments of masochistic jealousy. Molly's reveries, however, give Father Corrigan no first name, and only by tracing Bloom's thoughts during the day can the accident of the first name be realized. Although he observed Dignam's brother-in-law at Glasnevin, the name of the man does not seem to have penetrated into Bloom's consciousness until he reads it in the *Telegraph*. However, long before that he had thought about the sermon given by Father *Bernard* Vaughan and knows that a Father Conroy is assisting at the Star of the Sea Church. If he knows that it is Father *Bernard* Conroy he never betrays that knowledge, but that fact is nonetheless betrayed in *Thom's*. By conflating the confessor with one or two other clergymen named Bernard (plus the recent exposure to Bernard Corrigan's name), Bloom has perpetrated a piece of fictional creation unverifiable by any other set of facts.

Penelope

Molly's thoughts provide both corroboration for a host of names that she shares with her husband and a small world of her own, particularly that of the Gibraltar of her girlhood. The fallibility of Molly's memory can be relied upon to cause lapses and errors parallel to Bloom's. Whereas Bloom on Sandymount Strand thinks of Molly's youthful flirtation with Mulvey ("lieutenant Mulvey that kissed her under the Moorish wall beside the gardens. Fifteen she told me"—371), Molly has difficulty remembering his first name: "what was his name Jack Joe Harry Mulvey was it yes I think" (761). It is apparent that Bloom knows about Mulvey because of Molly's admission (which occurred during their courtship: she remembers a book "I lent him afterwards with Mulvey's photo in it so as he [sic] see I wasnt without"—756) and that Mulvey has been somewhat forgotten by her until this night, the memory spurred probably by the day's tryst with Boylan. Although Mulvey is fixed in Bloom's mind, Gardner is not, and his absence from the list proves that if there is a narrative voice consistent throughout Ithaca, it is not omniscient, and (more likely) that Bloom knows nothing of the existence of "Gardner Lieut Stanley G 8th Bn 2nd East Lancs Rgt" (749). Richard Ellmann assumes that Bartell d'Arcy may be the only party to Molly's adulterousness, but Molly leaves the question vague since she only suggests backstairs spooning; her recollections of Stanley Gardner make him a romantic figure but provide no details of actual adultery.

The residue of Gibraltar days accounts for an interesting cast of new characters, from the Stanhopes and Captain Grove[s] to the Prince of Wales and President Grant, to Spanish servants and Arabs and Jews and the matador Gomez (Bloom had earlier mentally crossed the border into La Linea where "O'Hara of the Camerons had slain the bull"—727). Particularly informative is the name of Molly's mother, Lunita Laredo, and her Jewish origin. An odd touch may be discerned in the person of Molly's friend, Hester Stanhope, a name that gives her almost as much trouble as Mulvey's: she recalls her first as Mrs. Stanhope (and the husband's nickname as "wogger"—755), but a few minutes later she calls her Hester (756). Molly's faulty memory may be playing tricks on her, and the name of Lady Hester Stanhope (if she would be expected to have heard of her) may have intruded to provide a name close enough to the original but possibly not exactly accurate. Her inventiveness with names dates back at least to the mythical *novio* with which she taunted Mulvey, "the son of a Spanish nobleman named Don Miguel de la Flora" (759), who has become metamorphosed into her actual conquest, "Don Poldo de la Flora" (778). There are too many names that are mysteriously alike in Molly's reminiscences, like "Mrs Rubio" (759) and "Captain Rubio" (762)—was the house servant the widow of the captain, and what sort of captain had he been?—especially following her thoughts on Ruby, Pride of the Ring (751). And she admits to a fascination with the "queer names" of Gibraltar, "Delapaz Delagracia . . . father Vial plana . . . Rosales y OReilly . . . Pisimbo and Mrs Opisso" (779), as she becomes drowsy.

THE CRITIC AS CENSUS TAKER

The entries which follow are presented in deliberately condensed form. Only the barest identifications are offered, especially for persons who pre-exist Joyce's fictions: full information is readily available to the reader, either in the sources indicated by the letters A, N, T, etc. (see Legend, pp. xi–xiii) or in dictionaries and encyclopedias. Like other readers of Joyce's works, annotators select reference materials which are consistent with their own interpretation of the text. It is not our intention to impose our interpretations, but to identify concisely and to locate. The format is intended for easy retrieval and reference, like a telephone directory, not an encyclopedia. We feel that the value of such a reference tool is to provide material easily obtained at a glance. The reader is invited to track down persons of special interest in the innermost reaches of their lairs by consulting the pertinent reference books for expanded explanations. In our own quiet way, however, we have imposed certain "corrections" where previous information may have been misleading.

The census-taker, unlike the critic, is forced to look at his materials literally. Every perceptive reader is aware that Joyce takes certain liberties with some familiar and relatively unfamiliar personages and that their names are used connotatively in his works. Where the name pre-exists Joycean coinage the census-taker offers only reference identification, leaving interpretation and application of the information to the critic.

Directory of Names

*"A. E."/"AE" 140 see Russell, George
(Abeakuta, Alaki of/ABEOKUTA, ALAKE OF) African potentate who visited England in 1904 334 A/N
(ABISHAG) Sunamite maiden brought in to keep King David warm 528 A/N
(ABRAHAM) biblical patriarch 76, 340, 437; G 14 A/N
(Abram*) a type of coal 669 N
(ABRINES, R. AND J.) Gibraltar bakers 779 N
*[ABRAMOVITZ, Rev. Leopold/REV. ABRAHAM LIPMAN] one of the circumcised at Bloom's sacrifice 544 N + Hyman, p. 329
(ABULAFIA, ABRAHAM BEN SAMUEL) 13th-century self-proclaimed Messiah 497 A/N
(ACHATES) faithful friend of Aeneas 88, 614 A/N
(ACHILLES) Greek hero of the Trojan War 193, 640, 658, 660 A/N
(ADAM) 47, 137, 297, 779; P 113, 114, 117–18, 134 A/N see Eve
(ADAM KADMON) cabalistic personification of unfallen man 38 A/N
(ADAM, ADOLPHE) 19th-century French composer S 66
(ADAMS, RICHARD "Dick") Cork journalist and attorney for Fitzharris legal luminary 137, 642 N
*ADDERLY, C. in bicycle race 254
(ADDISON, JOSEPH) 18th-century English author P 115 N
(Ades) among those attempting to debag Clive Kempthorpe in Oxford vignette 7
[ADONAI] God of Judgment pronouncing on the blessed and the damned 599–600
(ADONIS) beloved by Venus 191 A/N
(ADRIAN IV/NICHOLAS BREAKSPEAR English pope in 12th century 399–400 A/N see Nicholas, farmer
("Adrianopoli") in Brini's genealogical list 495

(AENGUS) Tuatha de Danaan god of youth and beauty 214, 217, 249 A/N see Dedalus, Stephen
(AESCHYLUS) Greek dramatist S 97, 101, 192–93
(Agatha, Sister) nice nun Bloom remembers from Tranquilla Convent 155, 368, 552 N
("AGENBUYER") the Redeemer 197, 391 A/N
("Agendath") in Brini's genealogical list 495
(AGRIPPA VON NETTESHEIM, HEINRICH CORNELIUS) 16th-century German occultist P 224 N
(AHASUERUS) biblical king named by the Citizen as the Wandering Jew condemned by Christ 217, 338 A/N see Bloom, Leopold
(Ahern/AHERNE, OWEN) character in Yeats's stories S 178
(AJAX) Maffei's horse 454
(ALACOQUE, MARGARET MARY) 17th-century enthusiast of the Sacred Heart, later beatified and canonized 202; D 37 A/N/N
(ALBANY, DUKE OF) dead son of Queen Victoria 85 see Leopold, Duke of Albany
(ALBERT) prince consort of Queen Victoria 102, 255, the German lad 330 A/N
("Albert Edward") one of Bloom's guesses for A. E. 165 see Edward VII
(ALBERT, S.) 12th/13th-century bishop and patriarch of Jerusalem 339 A/N
(ALBINI, ETTORE) Italian socialist G 9
(ALCIBIADES) Greek general and political figure 415 A/N
(ALDBOROUGH, LORD) extravagant 18th-century nobleman 221 A/N/T
(ALDWORTH, ELIZABETH) daughter of Arthur St. Leger of Doneraile, became a Mason 177–78 N
(ALEEL) poet friend of the Countess Cathleen in Yeats's play P 225 N
(ALEXANDER, CHARLES McCALLOM) revivalist who visited Dublin in 1904 151 N
(ALEXANDER, F.) owner of Throwaway 648 N
*[ALEXANDER, REV. DR WILLIAM] Church of Ireland primate 480, 482 N + *Thom's,* p. 1796
(ALEXANDRA, QUEEN) wife of King Edward VII 720 A/N

(ALEYN, SIMON) twice Catholic, twice Protestant vicar of Bray 391 A/n
("ALLFATHER") the heavenly man 185, 423
(ALFONSO XIII) born in 1886 as King of Spain 760 A/N
(ALFRED, S.) 9th-century West Saxon king 339; S 104 A/N see also Bergan, Alfred
("Algebra, Mr") personification of Bloom's method of computation 658
("Algy") 5 see Swinburne, Algernon Charles
("Ali Baba Backsheesh Rahat Lokum Effendi") member of the F.O.T.E.I. 307 A/N
(ALICE) elephant loved by Jumbo 333
("Alice") one of Bello's pet names for Bloom 535 N
(ALICE) heroine in song "Ben Bolt" 624 A/N
(ALICE) heroine being sought in song 649 A/N
(ALLAH) 308, 427 A/N
Alleyne, Mr Farrington's employer D 86–88, (89), 90, 91–92, (93), (94) + nephew (92) see also Crosbie & Alleyne
("Allfours, Mr") in mock parliamentary debate 316
(ALLINGHAM, WILLIAM) 19th-century poet and editor 709 A/N
*(Allsop/ALLSOPP AND SON) brewers 176, 328 N
(ALOYSIUS GONZAGA, S.) Jesuit patron saint of youth 339, 685; P 56, 242 A/N/N
(ALOYSIUS PACIFICUS, BROTHER) follower of St. Francis 339 A/N
("Alphonsus Eb Ed El Esquire") Bloom's possible attribution for A. E. 165
(ALPHONSUS LIGUORI, S.) 18th-century Church missionary P 152 N
("Alphonsus, Mother") recommended by Bloom for the nymph 553 A/N
(ALVAREZ, MANOEL) 16th-century Portuguese grammarian P 179
(AMBROSE, S.) one of the four great doctors of the Church 49 A/N
(AMMON RA) supreme Egyptian deity 143 A/N
("Anderson, Sir Hercules Hannibal Habeas Corpus") in charge of clearing the debris of the quake caused by the Citizen's flying biscuit tin 345 N
(ANDERSON, MARY) actress performing in Belfast on 16 June 1904 93 N

*(ANDERSON, MICHAEL "Micky") watchmaker 246, 253 N/T + *Thom's,* p. 1797
(ANDREW, S.) patron saint of Scotland 482
*(ANDREWS AND CO.) grocers 60, 526 N/T
*(ANDREWS, WILLIAM DRENNAN) Dublin juror 322 N
(ANGUS THE CULDEE/AENGUS) 9th-century Irish ascetic and poet in parade of heroes 297 A/N
(Ann, queen*) a pudding 352
(ANN, widowed) of Prince Edward, wooed by Richard, Duke of Gloster 211 A/N see also Shakespeare, Ann Hathaway
("Anne, Queen") news of her death is proverbially stale news 118 A/N
("Anonymous, S.") in ecclesiastical procession to Barney Kiernan's 339
(ANSELM, S.) 12th-century Italian ecclesiast P 119 N
(ANTHONY, S.) of Padua, 13th-century Franciscan S 57
("ANTICHRIST") personification of evil to be conquered by Christ 505 A/N
"Antichrist, Reuben J." (505), [506] see Dodd, Reuben J.
(ANTISTHENES) Greek philosopher who opposed Plato 148–49, 201, 242, 523 A/N
(ANTONIO) mentioned in song 97, 632 A/N
(Antonio) Greek who tattooed Murphy 631–32, 636, 646
(ANTONIO) one of five Shakespeare characters of that name 636 A/N
("Anycock, Margaret Mary") 202 see Alacoque, Margaret Mary
("Ape Swillale, Mr") 396 see Costello, Francis
(APHRODITE) Greek goddess of love 201 A/N see also Venus
Apjohn, Percy Bloom's boyhood friend (162), [548], (667), (704), (716), (737) N/T
(APOLLO) Greek sun god 113, 419 N/T
(AQUARIUS) water carrier in the Zodiac 553, 671 A see Bloom, Leopold
(AQUINAS, S. THOMAS) 17, 47, 205, 208, 339, san Tommaso Mastino 637; P 127, 154, 176–77, 186, 207, 209–10, 212–13; S 77, 79, 91, 95–96, great doctor of the Church 103, 104, 143, 171, orthodox doctor of the Church 205, 212–13, 241 A/N/N

(ARAM, EUGENE) character in Lord Lytton's novel 756 A/N
(ARAMBURO, ANTONIO) Spanish tenor D 199 N
ARANA Y LUPARDO, JOSÉ Spanish pupil at Clongowes P 13, 54
("Aranjuez") in Brini's genealogical list 495
(ARCHIMEDES) Greek scientist 378 A/N
(ARDEN, ENOCH) sailor in Tennyson poem presumed dead 624 A/N
(ARDEN, MARY) 208 see Shakespeare, Mary Arden
(ARDILAUN, LORD) 79, 425 see Guinness, Arthur Edward
("Aristocrat") 722 see "Aristotle"
(ARISTOTLE) 25, *maestro* 37, 185–86, 192, Stagyrite 204, 212, stagyrite 432, 687 + wife (204); P 176, 187, 204, 208; S 143, 186–87, 220 A/N/N
("ARISTOTLE") author of a book of grotesques, *Masterpieces* 235, 411, 772 A/N
(ARIUS) 4th-century heresiarch 21, 38, 523 A/N
Armstrong pupil in Mr. Deasy's school 24–27 + parents and older brother (24)
Arnall, Father teacher at Clongowes and deliverer of sermon at Belvedere P (11), 12, (26), 47–52, (57), 108–15, 117–24, 127–35
(ARNOLD, MATTHEW) Victorian poet and critic 7, 518 A/N
*(ARNOTT AND CO.) drapers 155 A/N/T
(ARRAH NA POGUE) Boucicault heroine in parade of Irish heroes 297 A/N
(ARTHUR) young prince in Shakespeare's *King John* 208 A
("Arthur Edmund") one of Bloom's guesses for A. E. 165 see also Guinness, Arthur Edward
Artifoni, Almidano Stephen's music teacher 228–29, 249, 255, [518] N/T
Artifoni, Father Stephen's Italian teacher S 169–71, 192–95, (196), (215), (222–23) see Ghezzi, Fr Charles
("Ash, Mrs Poll") participant in forest wedding 327
*(ASKIN, PAUL, AND SON) land agents on dead side of street 95
("Aspenall, Miss Timidity") participant in forest wedding 327
(ATALANTA) legendary Greek heroine D 72 N

(ATHENA, PALLAS) Greek goddess of wisdom greyeyed goddess 191, 208 A/N

[ATHLONE POURSUIVANT] officer of the College of Arms in Bloom parade 480 N

(Athos) Rudolph Bloom's dog 90, 528, 724 N

Athy Stephen's schoolmate in Clongowes infirmary P 23–26, 41–45 + father (24–25)

(Atkinson) voter canvassed for Tierney D 131

*(ATKINSON, F. M'CURDY) Dublin literary figure 216, 519 N

(ATTRACTA/ARAGHT, S.) 5th-century female Irish saint 339 A/N

(Aubrey) in Oxford debagging vignette 7

(AUBREY, JOHN) 17th-century English writer of biography 204 A/N

(AUGUSTINE, S.) 4th-century Bishop of Hippo 142, 339, 391; P 129, 236 A/N/N

(AVERROES) 12th-century Arabian-Spanish philosopher 28, 390 A/N

(AZAZEL) biblical scapegoat-demon 497 A/N

(BACON, SIR FRANCIS) Elizabethan author 195, 208, 634; S 25, 52 A/N

(BACON, FRIAR) in Robert Greene's play 617 A/N

(BAILEY, BILL) wanderer in song urged to come home 774 A/N

*(BAIRD, D. G., AND TODD, J. P.) engineering works 614; P 176 N/T

(BALBUS) protector of Caesar's Rome P 43 N

("Baldhead") Cranly's mock king of Flanders P 230

(BALDWIN I) of the House of Flanders P 229–30 N

(BALDWIN THE FORESTER) claimed to be the Count of Flanders P 229 N

(BALFE, MICHAEL WILLIAM) Dublin composer 162; D 106 A/N/N

(BALL, ROBERT) Dublin-born astronomer 154, 465, 708 + wife (465) A/N

("Ballocky") 216 see Mulligan, Malachi Roland St John

(Balmer) Mrs. Bellingham's coachman 466

(BALOR OF THE EVIL EYE) Formorian giant king in parade of Irish heroes 297 A/N

(BANBA) legendary queen of Ireland, personification of the country 302 A/N

(Bandman Palmer, Mrs/BANDMANN-PALMER, MRS MILLICENT) American actress 76, 92, 198, 446, 729, 735 A/N

Bannon, Alec Mulligan's friend and Milly's admirer from Mullingar (21), young student (62), (65–66), (285), (372), (397), 401–28, [509], (542), (693) + cousin(s) (66), (397)

*(BAPTY, WALTER) Dublin professor of singing 281 A/N + *Thom's,* p. 1902

(BARABBAS) thief spared in lieu of Jesus 94, 245; P 119 A/N/N

(BARBARA, S.) patron saint of armorers 339, 599 A/N

*(BARCLAY AND COOK) bootmakers 683 N/T p. 15

("Barebones, Rev. Ananias Praisegod") translator for the Alaki 334 A/N

("Barleycorn, John") personification of drink 95 N

*(BARLOW, JOHN) mace bearer at the council sessions 247 N + *Thom's,* p. 1802

(BARMECIDES) Persian nobility in Mangan poem 332 A/N

*(BARNARDO, J. M.) furrier P 97 N/T

(Barnes) reputed candidate for Clongowes cricket team captaincy P 41

(Barney, uncle) of Patsy Dignam 250 see Corrigan, Bernard

(BARNUM, P. T.) circus impresario 509; S 133 A/N

*(BARRACLOUGH, ARTHUR) Dublin professor of singing 277, 663 A/N + *Thom's,* p. 1803

*(BARRETT, REV. PATRICK "Paddy") prefect of Clongowes, actually teacher at Belvedere College P 30, 43, 48 + Sullivan, p. 92

(BARRINGTON, JOHN) soap manufacturer 672 N

(BARRINGTON, SIR JONAH) 18th/19th-century Irish legislator and memoirist 241 A/N

(BARROW, MISS) murder victim of the Seddons 593 A/N

*(BARRY, J. M., AND CO.) tailors 289 N/T + *Thom's,* p. 1804

[Barry, Mrs Yelverton] accuser of Leopold Bloom 464–74, 594 + husband (464)

(Bartholomona) bearded lady in the circus 566

("Bartle the Bread") 427 N see M'Intosh
(BARTLETT, SIR ELLIS ASHMEAD) M. P. and political writer S 157
*(BARTON, DUNBAR PLUNKET) judge who wrote on Shakespeare-Ireland link 198, Our judges (see also Madden, Dodgson Hamilton) 203, 679 A/N
Barton, James hackney cab driver who chauffeurs Boylan 279, [563–64]
(BARTON, MAJOR BERTRAM B.) owner of land near Clongowes P 59
(BASS, WILLIAM ARTHUR HAMAR) brewer and owner of Sceptre 325, 416, 417, 426, 648 N
*(BASSI, AURELIO/ or BASSI, JOSEPH) sculptor and figuremaker respectively on Wellington Quay 259 N/T + *Thom's,* p. 1804
(BATEMAN, KATE) American-born actress 76 A/N
*(BATTERSBY) house agent 61 T
(BAWN, MOLLY) title heroine of novel by Margaret Hungerford 756 A/N
("Bays, Miss Daphne") participant in forest wedding 327
(BAZAN, DON CESAR DE) character shot at in *Maritana* 626 A/N
(BEACONSFIELD, LORD/BENJAMIN DISRAELI) English novelist and politician 495 A/N
(BEARE, DON PHILIP O'SULLIVAN) 17th-century Irish-Spanish historian in parade of Irish heroes of antiquity 297 A/N
("Beau Mont") 393 see Beaumont, Francis
(BEAUFORT, DUKE OF/HENRY CHARLES FITZROY SOMERSET) owner of horse Ceylon 32, 573 A/N
("Beaufoy, Mrs") 158 see Beaufoy, Philip; Purefoy, Wilhelmina
BEAUFOY, PHILIP short-story writer (68–69), (158), Matcham (280), (373), [458–60], (647), (685) A/N see also Purefoy, Wilhelmina
(BEAUMONT, FRANCIS) Elizabethan playwright 393 A/N
("Beech, Miss Gladys") participant in forest wedding 327
(BEELZEBUB) the devil that tempts Stephen 40, 571 A/N
*(BEETHOVEN, LUDWIG VON) German composer in parade of Irish heroes 297 A/N

Behan jarvey who brings Kelleher and the two commercials to Nighttown 586, (606), 607–8
Beirne, Miss of the Eire Abu Society staging the concert D 142, 147–48
(BELIAL) devil or object of false worship 497 A/N
Bell, Mr second tenor at Eire Abu concert D 142–43, 146, 147, 148
(Belle) 324 see Tupper, Belle
(BELLEW, LORD) testified on the tattoos of a lost heir in Victorian court case 650 A/N
("Bellicosus, Brother Louis") in procession of saints, real and fabricated 339
[Bellingham, Mrs] one of Bloom's three accusers of sexual misconduct 465–74, 594
["Bello"] 530–44 see Cohen, Bella
("Belluomo") Paris lover in Stephen's vignette 42; G 8
(BELVEDERE, LORD/COL. ROBERT ROCHFORT) jealous husband of Mary Rochfort 223 A/N
("Ben Maimun") in Brini's genealogical list 496
("Ben, Old") 185 see Jonson, Ben
"Benaben, Big" 257, 287 see Dollard, Benjamin
(BENADY, MORDEJAI AND SAMUEL) Gibraltar biscuit manufacturers remembered by Molly 761 N
("Benamor") in Brini's genealogical list 496
(BENEDICT OF SPOLETO, S.) 6th-century monk who founded the Benedictine order 339 A/N
("Beninobenone, Commendatore Bacibaci") doyen of the F.O.T.E.I. 307–8
(BENNETT, JAMES GORDON) American journalist and editor who established an auto race 98, 536, 647 A/N
(Bennett, Sergeant-Major Percy) British soldier stationed in Portobello Barracks who presumably fought Myler Keogh 173, 250–51, 318–19, 451, 603
"Bensoul benjamin" 270 see Dollard, Benjamin
(BERESFORD, SIR JOHN) British admiral accused of condoning flogging 329 A/N
*BERGAN, ALFRED Dublin prankster who worked as assistant to the subsheriff (160), (267), 298–345, [446] N + *Thom's*, p. 1807
*(BERGIN, DANIEL L.) publican 221, 613 N/T + *Thom's*, p. 1807

Bergin, Mr at the Morkans' party D 183–84
(Bergin, Mrs) subject of discussion by students at Clonliffe S 74
(BERKELEY, GEORGE) 18th-century idealist philosopher and Bishop of Cloyne 48 A/N
(BERNARD, S.) 12th-century abbot of Clairvaux 339, 356, 391 A/N see also Kiernan, Bernard (339)
(Bert) liftboy designated by Bello as one of the seducers of female Bloom 536
("Bertie") customer name used by prostitutes as Stephen passes by P 102
(Bessie) servant girl employed by the Conroys D 181
*BEST, RICHARD librarian at the National Library 186–214, douce youngling (215), [509] N
("Betty, Old") typical of those who feel the change of weather in their joints 376
*(BEWLEY AND DRAPER) general merchants 632 N/T
["Biddy the Clap"] harridan in Nighttown 590, 593, 597
(BILLINGTON) apparently an English hangman 303 A/N
("Billy, King") 253; D 208 see William III
("Binbad") 737 see Sinbad the Sailor
(BINGHAM, G. CLIFTON) wrote the lyrics of "Love's Old Sweet Song" 706 A/N
(BISHOP, WASHINGTON IRVING) American mind reader 444 A/N
(BISMARCK, OTTO VON) German chancellor S 74
*(Blackburn/BLACKBURNE, R. T.) Crofton's employer at the Dublin County Council 336
(Blackwhite) reputedly a great salesman D 154
("Blackwood, Mrs Arabella") participant in the forest wedding 327
(BLACKWOOD, SIR JOHN) Deasy's reputed ancestor, whom he erroneously claims voted for the Union with Britain 31, 574 A/N
(Blake Forsters) family which Temple claims to be an offshoot of descendants of Belgian nobility in Ireland P 230
(Blake, Nancy) Floey Dillon's friend who, Molly remembers, died recently 758
(BLAKE, PHIL) presumably the creator of a weekly Pat and Bull story 119

(BLAKE, WILLIAM) English poet and artist 24, 186; P 249; S 32 A/N/N
["Blanca, señorita"] sinister figure who demands from Bloom the password for entrance into Nighttown 436
(BLAVATSKY, MME HELENA P.) Russian-born theosophist 140, H.P.B. 185 A/N
(BLEIBTREU, KARL) theorized that Shakespeare's plays were written by the Earl of Rutland 214 A/N
("Blephen") 682 see Bloom, Leopold; Dedalus, Stephen; "Stoom"
("Blockwell, Philip Augustus") M. P. that Bello claims is one of the seducers of female Bloom 536
("Bloom") penultimate figure in Brini's genealogy 496 see Bloom, Leopold
("Bloom Pasha, von") 455 see Blum, Sir Julius
Bloom, Ellen Leopold Bloom's mother, nee Higgins Mamma poor mamma (111), a mother's thought (413), poor mamma's panacea (435), [438], (555), (682), (708), (721), your dear mother (723), poison himself after her (767)
("Bloom, Lady") 489 see Bloom, Marion
Bloom, Leopold advertising canvasser for the *Freeman's Journal* residing at 7 Eccles Street 54–70, 71–86, 87–106, (106), 107–15, 116–29, (135), (137), 146–47, 151–77, (177–78), 179–83, 200, (201), 217–18, A darkbacked figure 227, 233, (234–35), 235–37, (246), (256), (257), 258–87, 288–91, (297), that bloody freemason (300), (302), 303–33, (335), (336), (337), (338), S. Leopold (339), 341–45, 353, 382, 385–428, 433–609, 612–65, 666–737, (738–48), (750–56), (758), (761), (763–83) see Appendix B.
*BLOOM, MARCUS J. dentist (250), (337), (455), [586] N/T + *Thom's,* p. 1810.
Bloom, Marion "Molly" concert soprano and wife of Leopold Bloom She didn't like her plate full (55), A sleepy soft grunt answered (56), No use disturbing her (57), (60), 61–64, mummy's (66), (67), her voice (68), (69), (74–75), (76), walk into her here (77), (78), (79), (80), (81), (82), her skin (84), (87), (89), the shape is there (92), *Madame* (93), (103), (106), when she disturbed me (107), (108), (115), (123), (135), What was it she wanted? (151), She's right after all (154), (155), (156), (158), (161), (162), She was humming (167), She twentythree (168), (172), (174), she had her hair (176), (177), (181), Afternoon she said

(183), gay sweet chirping whistling within (225), A plump bare generous arm 226, for an invalid (227), reappeared on the windowsash (234), (234–35), she wouldn't like that much (236), At four, she said (260), a friend of mine (265), (268), (270), Night we were in the box (271), (274), when first I saw her (275), And one day she with (277), bought for her (278), She must (279), Her eyes over the sheet (281), (282), She looked fine (284), (288), (289), (290), The fat heap he married (305), (306), (315), (319), a lady friend (325), M. B. (see also Bloom, Millicent) (333), (335), (338), (368), (369), (371), (372), (373), (374), everything she takes off (375), I kissed her shoulder (376), (377), (379), Strange moment for the mother (380), (381), And she can do the other (382), with dear wife (385), (390), (397), the daughter of a gallant major (409), follows her mother (414), their darker friend (422), Know his dona? (425), (426), (430), [439–41], (443), (446), (447), (448), (449), (452), (457), the missus was out shopping (461), (467), A VOICE [473], repudiated our former spouse (483), (489), Somebody would be dreadfully jealous (500), the missus is master (527), person you mentioned (530), I tried her things on (536), offering his nuptial partner (537), (541), I see her! (542), (543), It wasn't her weight (547), [565–67], its own legal consort (627), (632), (635), (637), (652–54), somebody having a temper of her own (657), (658), (661), (662–63), (667), (677), (678), (682), two figures in night attire (692), hostess (695), the instructed (696), (702), (715), (721), (727), 728–37, 738–83

("Bloom, Methusalem") 336 see Bloom, Rudolph

Bloom, Millicent "Milly" daughter of Molly and Leopold Bloom, a photographer's assistant in Mullingar a sweet young thing down there (21–22), a girl with gold hair (61),(62–63), (66–67), (89), (90), (99), She mightn't like (100), (113), (155), (156), All the beef to the heels (168), (172), (175), (181), Wise child that knows her father (see also Goulding, Christina) (273), (278), (285), M. B. (see also Bloom, Marion) (333), the child was sick (335), (368), (372), (379–80), lovesome daughter (385), skittish heifer, big of her age (397), that very picture which he had cherished (404–5), She follows her mother (414), Bold bad girl from the town of Mullingar (425), Photo's papli (427), (448), [542], with his daughter (630), (677), (691), (692), infantile memories had he of her (693), she sustained her blond hair (694), (695), (720), (721), (723), with female issue born (736), (742), (746), (754), (758), (761), a daughter like mine (763), (766–67), answering me like a

fishwoman (768), (770), (773), (775), (779), the mustachecup she gave him (780)
Bloom, Rudolph Leopold Bloom's dead father, born Rudolf Virag Poor papa! (76), my last wish (90), down to the County Clare on some private business (92), Only a pauper (96), Rattle his bones (97), (101), poor papa went away (110), I'll be at his grave (113), Poor papa too (114), Poor papa with his hagadah book (122), Poor papa's daguerreotype atelier (155), Society over the way papa went to (180), that book of poor papa's (284), the son of Rory (297), And his old fellow before him (336), (337), poor papa's father (378), the head of the firm (413), (414), [437–38], My old dad (457), Poor dear papa (528), with poor papa's operaglasses (549), (682), (684), (691), (695), (708), (716), (723–25), (747), (765), (767) see also Virag, Rudolf
Bloom, Rudy dead infant son of Molly and Leopold Bloom (66), My son inside her (89), (96), (111), (151), (168), (285), that son of his that died (338), an only manchild which on his eleventh day on live had died (390), no son of thy loins (413–14), [609], (701), and only male (736), hed be 11 (774), I oughtnt to have buried him (778)
("Bloombella") 578 see Bloom, Leopold; Cohen, Bella
(BLOOMFIELD, LAURENCE) hero of Allingham's long poem 709 A/N
(BLUDSO, JIM) hero of American ballad 458 A/N
(BLUEBEARD) wife-killer in fairytale 466 A/N
(BLUM, SIR JULIUS) extremely wealthy British civil servant in Egypt 719 N
(BLUMENBACH, JOHANN FRIEDRICH) 18th/19th-century German physiologist and anthropologist 418 A/N
("Blumenduft, Herr Professor Luitpold") gives scientific evidence on the hanged man's erection 304 see Bloom, Leopold; Blumenbach, Johann Friedrich
(BLUMENFELD, RALPH DAVID) London newspaper editor 137 A/N
Boardman, baby cared for by sister Edy on Sandymount Strand 346–65, 367, (371), (373), [486]
Boardman, Edy one of Gerty MacDowell's companions 346–65, 367, That squinty one (368), And the others (see Caffrey, Cissy) (369), 372, 431–32
("Boasthard") 395 see Dedalus, Stephen; see also "Young Boasthard"

(BOBRIKOFF, GENERAL NIKOLAI IVANOVICH) Russian general shot by a Finn on 16 June 1904 134 A/N see *Finnegans Wake*

("Bobs") presumed dower duchess of Manorhamilton, touted as one of the violators of female Bloom by Bello 536

("Bobs, Lord") 421 see Roberts, Lord Frederick Sleigh

(BOCCACCIO, GIOVANNI) 14th-century Italian writer of the *Decameron* 207; S 150 A/N

(BODE, JOHANN ELERT) 18th/19th-century German astronomer 700 A/N

(BODKIN, MATTHEW) editor of the *United Ireland,* who turned against Parnell and O'Brien 654 A/N

Boland bullying student at Belvedere P 79–82

(BOLAND) bakers 57

("Bollopedoom") 678 see Bloom, Leopold

(BOLT, BEN) sailor in song separated from Alice for twenty years 624 A/N

*(BOLTON, WILLIAM) grocer 161 N/T

(BOMBADOS) probably a pantomime figure P 105 N

("Bomboost, Hiram Y.") member of the F.O.T.E.I. 307

(BONAVENTURE, S.) 13th-century theologian, general of the Franciscans P 120, 154 N

(BOND, WILLIAM) moribund in poem by William Blake P 249 N

("Boniface") name given to the landlord at Burke's pub, from the patron saint of innkeepers 426–27 A

(BONIFACIUS, S.) 8th-century bishop—in procession 339 A/N

("Boom, L.") 647, 648 see Bloom, Leopold

(BORGIA, LUCREZIA) villainess in Donizetti opera D 199 N

(BORNEO, WILD MAN OF) character in song 380 A/N

(Bos Bovum) a bull 401 N

(BOUCICAULT, DION) 19th-century Irish playwright 167 A/N

(Boudin, A.) presumed recipient of Murphy's postcard 626, 647

(Boulger, Charley) former city marshal of Dublin presumably 165

(Bouverist, Nelly/BOUVERIE, NELLIE) "principal" girl who sang in *Sinbad* 678, 679 N

(BOYCOTT, CAPT. CHARLES CUNNINGHAM) agent in Mayo who enraged his tenants 296 A/N

*(BOYD, SAMUEL) chemist of Boileau and Boyd 259 N/T or BOYD, JAMES N

*(BOYD, WALTER) judge in Dublin bankruptcy court 626 N

*(BOYD, WILLIAM) Dublin Y.M.C.A. general secretary 246 N

(Boylan, "Dirty Dan") father of Blazes Boylan, horse dealer 319, his father made money 749

Boylan, Hugh "Blazes" advertising man and local impresario, Molly's paramour (62–63), (66–67), fair man (75), 92, If he (153), He wouldn't (154), He other side (167), (172–73), He was in the Red bank (175), Straw hat 183, 227–28, 229–30, I'll see him (232), 246, toff's mouth 251, 253–54, Jingle (256), Jingle (257), (261), (262–63), 263–67, He's off (268), 269–71, Jingle (274), He can't sing (274), 276, Jingle 277, young gentleman 279, (281–82), Cockcarracarra 284, Those girls (285), With a cock (286), (318–19), (325), fair gentleman? (333), tie he wore (368), he gave her money (369), He's right (372), about the time he (373), Molly, he (374), He gets the plums (377), Let him (382), If it were he (525), whoever you are (526), That night she met . . . (530), man of brawn (541), [564–67], [579], (618), (619), got a bit of a start (647), (731–34), (740), (741), (742), (744–45), (747), (748), (749–50), (753), (754), (758), (761), (763), (764), (766), (769), (770), (773), (774), (775), (776), (778), (780), (781) (for 740–781 see Appendix B), + 2 sisters (745) T

(Boyle, "Tusker"/"Lady") effeminate schoolmate of Stephen's at Clongowes P 42, 44, 45

(BRACEGIRDLE, MRS ANNE) 18th-century London actress 370, 382 A/N

(BRADDON, MARY ELIZABETH) author of *Henry Dunbar* 756 A/N

Brady, Dr Francis Molly's doctor when Milly was an infant [587], (731), (754)

(BRADY, JOE) member of the Invincibles, hanged for part in Phoenix Park murders 136, 138, 304 A/N

(BRAINE) trainer of Throwaway 648 N

(BRANDES, GEORG) Shakespeare critic 195 A/N

*(BRANGAN, REV. T.) Dublin cleric, Order of St. Augustine 317 N

(BRANSCOMBE, MAUD) actress whom Bloom could have seen perform 370, 720 A/N

(BRANSOME) brand of coffee 136

(BRAY, VICAR OF) cleric in song, known for politically changing his religion 391 see Aleyn, Simon

*BRAYDEN, WILLIAM H. editor of the *Freeman's Journal* 117–18, [586] N/T + *Thom's* p. 1815

Breen, Denis demented victim of "U.P.:up" postcard (157–58), 159–60, Those two loonies (164), (240), 253, 298–99, (320–21), he was passing 321–22, S. Denis (339), See him sometimes (381), [446], [586], dotty husband (744), (773) + father's cousin (321) N + *Thom's* p. 1815? see "Brini, Papal Nuncio"

Breen, Mrs Josephine (nee Josie Powell) wife of Denis, girlhood friend of Molly 156–60, she said (167), (240), 253, 299, 321, (369), (373), [442–49], [586], (722), (742), (743–44), (761), (773)

(BREMOND, J. DE) owner of Maximum II in Gold Cup 648 N

(BRENDAN, S.) 6th-century Irish abbott 297, 339 A/N

*(BRESLIN, EDWARD) Bray hotel proprietor 680 N/T

(BRIAN BORU/BOROIMHE OF KINCORA) Irish king who defeated the Danes at Clontarf, A.D. 1014 public house 99, 296, 678, 679 A/N/T

(BRIDE/BRIGID, S.) patroness of Ireland 339, 726 A/N

(Bridgeman) moneylender, Dignam's creditor 313

(BRIERLY, A.) lover of Mrs. Maybrick 744 A

("Briggs") hypothetical name Molly finds unsuitable 761

(Brigid) servant in Dedalus household P 10, 24

Brigid servant in Rowan household E 16–17, 25–26, (29), 55–56, 89–93, (98), 100

"Brini, Papal Nuncio" elevated characterization of the cousin of Breen's father (321), [495] Appendix A

(BRISTOW, JOHN GOSLING) whose obituary appeared in the *Irish Independent* 298 N

*(BROADBENT, J. S.) fruiterer 254 N/T

(Brophy) lame gardener alluded to by Bloom 553

(Brophy, Katherine) John Corley's mother 616

("Brown, Jemina") woman in doggerel + mother 372

(BROWN, JOHN) Queen Victoria's coachman 330 A/N

*(BROWN, MERVYN) someone Bloom knows 104 N + *Thom's* p. 1817

("Brown, Robinson") names Bloom gives to the "average man" 627
(BROWN THOMAS AND CO.) Dublin store 168; D 138 N/T
(BROWNE, COUNT MAXIMILIAN ULYSSES VON) killed at the Battle of Prague, haunts Clongowes 330; P 19 A/N/N
Browne, Mr Protestant guest at the Morkans' D 182–85, 192–95, 197–206, 206–9, (217)
(BROWNING, ROBERT) Victorian poet D 179, 188, 192 N
(BRUCE'S BROTHER, THE) Edward, brother of Robert—14th-century invader of Ireland 45 A/N
(BRUNETTO, MESSER) 194 see Latini, Brunetto
(BRUNO, GIORDANO—THE NOLAN) 16th-century Italian philosopher and heretic S 170; P 249 N
(BRUTUS) Roman conspirator in Shakespeare's *Julius Caesar* 73 A/N
*(BUCKLEY, JOHN) butcher 56, 764 N/T
(BUDDH) 192 see Buddha
(BUDDHA, GAUTAMA) 80, 192, 297, 508, 771; S 190 A/N
("Buffalo Bill") 624 see Cody, William
(BULL, JOHN) Elizabethan composer whom Bloom confuses with personification of Imperial Britain 662 A/N
(Buller, Captain) presumably a cricketer at T.C.D. 86
(BULWER-LYTTON, EDWARD) Lord Lytton, 19th-century novelist 756 A/N
("Bungardilaun") 299 see Guinness, Arthur Edward
("Bungiveagh") 299 see Guinness, Edward Cecil
(BURBAGE, RICHARD) Elizabethan actor, played Hamlet 188, 201 A/N
Burke, Andrew ("Pisser") whom Bloom knew when he lived at the City Arms Hotel, now a friend of The Nameless One (305–6), (315), (320), (335), (338), [488], [586], (731), (765), N
*(BURKE, DANIEL) wine merchant 137; D 108 T
(BURKE, EDMUND) 18th-century politician and author 139 A/N/T
(Burke, Father) political crony of Dick Tierney D 123
*(BURKE, JOHN) publican 423, 424 N/T
Burke, O'Madden journalist 131–44, 148–50, (230), (263), [490]; D 144–46, 147–48, 149 N/N

(BURKE, COL. RICHARD) Irish-American Fenian 43 A/N
(BURKE, THOMAS NICHOLAS "Father Tom") 19th-century Irish Catholic orator D 165–66 N
(BURNS, GEORGINA) presumably a 19th-century singer D 199
(BUSHE, CHARLES KENDEL) 18th/19th-century Irish jurist 139; P 97 A/N/N
*(BUSHE, SEYMOUR) Irish barrister 100, 139, 410, 465, 690 A/N
Butler, Father teacher at Belvedere College D 20, (21), (22)
*(BUTLER, GEORGE) maker of musical instruments 151 N/T
*(BUTLER, PATRICK) publican D 165 T
Butt, D., S.J. dean of studies and professor of English at U.C.D. (670); S (23), (25), 27–29, (33), (35), (38), 42, 100–5, (108), chalk-faced chap (116), (141), an earnest jesuit (193), 226–27, the priest (228–29), (230); P 184–90, (192), 194, 199, (205), (240), (251) + "wife" (199) see Darlington, Fr Joseph
BUTT, ISAAC founder of the Home Rule Association in Ireland (138), [599] A/N
"Butterly"* a pun on bitterly 17
[Butterly, Maurice] farmer who offers Bloom a turnip 486
"Buzz, Brother" Bloom's name for a typical priest (83), [495], [498]
(BYRD, WILLIAM) Elizabethan composer 662; P 233 A/N/N
*BYRNE, DAVID "DAVY" Dublin publican (170), 171–79, (279), [490], [586], (676); D (93) N/N/T
*(BYRNE, ELIZABETH "BETTY") sweets seller P 7
(Byrne, Father) priest residing in Jesuit house with Artifoni S 170
*(BYRNE, LOUIS A.) Dublin coroner 75, 111; D 158 N/T
(Byrne, Peter) U.C.D. student, answered for by a classmate? P 191 see also Cockburn
*(BYRNE, MME T. LEGGET) Dublin dancing/piano teacher 575 N/T + *Thom's* p. 1819
(BYRON, GEORGE GORDON, LORD) English poet 495, 743, 775; P 70, 81–82; S 26, 33, 148; D 83–84 A/N/N
*(BYRON, PATRICK) Clontarf publican P 164 T

(CADBY) piano in Bloom's home 706
("Caddereesh"!) 319 N
*(CADOGAN, GEORGE HENRY, EARL) lord lieutenant of Ireland at turn of century 659 A/N
(CAESAR, JULIUS) 25, 26, 109, 193, 297, 776; P 43 A/N/N
Caffrey, Cissy friend of Gerty MacDowell 346–65, (366), 367, the others (368), the others (369), the dark one (371), 372, 430–31, 574, 587–603 + father (353) see Introduction
Caffrey, Jacky young brother of Cissy, Tommy's twin 346–65, 366, 367, the children (371), [433], [437]
Caffrey, Tommy young brother of Cissy, Jacky's twin 346–65, 367, the children (371), 372, [433], [437]
("Cahill, Mrs") in anecdote with Mother Grogan 12
*(CAHILL, T.) publican 252 T or printer N
(CAIN) 157
(Cairns) plasterer credited by the gaffer with witnessing a public defecation 450
(CALADRINO) Boccaccio's "pregnant" man 207 A/N
(CALIBAN) monster in Shakespeare's *Tempest* 6, Americanized as "Patsy" 205, 492 A/N
(Callan) presumably employer of Paddy Leopold D 93
(Callan) in *Freeman's Journal* obituary 91, 279, 280, 465
Callan, Nurse at Holles Street Lying-In Hospital (373), 385–87, 406, (408), (410), 423, [522], (722)
*CALLINAN, CHRISTOPHER Ignatius Gallaher's brother-in-law (137), (234–35), [488], [586], (731) N
(CALLISTA) heroine of Cardinal Newman's novel S 194
"Calmer" 395 see Bloom, Leopold
(CALPORNUS) father of St. Patrick 666 A/N
(CALYPSO)* Mulvey's ship 761 A/N
CAMERON, SIR CHARLES 19th-century Irish-born newspaper magnate (234), [586] N
(CAMPANINI, ITALO) 19th-century operatic tenor D 199 N
("Campbell, Dave") member of Elijah's "audience" 507
("Campbell, Foxy") Stephen's prototype of the Jesuit 39; P 161 Sullivan, p. 92; Introduction see Campbell, Rev. J.; Campbell, Rev. Richard
*(CAMPBELL, HENRY) Dublin town clerk whose lookalike is in the cabman's shelter 631, 638, 641, 650 *Thom's*, p. 1825
(Campbell, Rev. J.) preaches Good Friday sermon at Gardiner Street Jesuit church S 119

(CAMPBELL, MRS PAT) English actress D 146 N
(CAMPBELL, REV. RICHARD) master at Belvedere College P 161 Sullivan p. 92
(CAMPBELL, THOMAS) 19th-century English poet; did not write Gray's "Elegy" 113 A/N
("Canebrake, Dorothy") member of the forest wedding 327
(CANICE, S., OF KILKENNY) 6th-century Irish missionary 44, 339 A/N
(CANNON, MORNINGTON "MORNY") jockey on Zinfandel 174, 648 N
("Cantekissem, Father") contemptuous name for a priest 406
(CANTRELL AND COCHRANE) manufacturers of soft drinks 76, 81, 261
(CANTWELL AND M'DONALD) spirits merchants 260 N/T
(CANTWELL, JOHN or THOMAS) pupil at Clongowes Wood P 9
(CAOLTE) long-lived Irish warrior in colloquy with St. Patrick 323 A/N
(CAPULET, JULIET) Shakespearean heroine 333; D 186 N
(CAREY, JAMES/"Peter"/"Denis") member of the Invincibles, turned Queen's evidence; his brother Peter also indicted in Phoenix Park murders 81, 163, 642 A/N
*(CARLISLE, JAMES) manager of the *Irish Times* 160 N
(Carlisle, Lily) possibly made pregnant by Mulligan's friend Seymour + father 22
(CARLYLE, THOMAS) 19th-century English author S 148
(CARMEN) heroine of Bizet's opera 212 A/N
(Carr/CANN, EMMA) in *Irish Independent* obituary 298 N
Carr, Pvt Harry British soldier who knocks Stephen down 430–31, 450–52, 574, 587–603 A/N
*(CARROLL, JOHN) jeweller 258 N/T
(CARTON, SYDNEY) Dickens hero portrayed by Martin-Harvey 767 N
(CARUSO, ENRICO) Italian tenor D 199 N
("CARUSO-GARIBALDI") mock-composite of two famous Italians 317
(CASEMENT, SIR ROGER) exposed atrocities in Belgian Congo, executed by British for gun-running in Ireland 335 A/N
(CASEY, JOHN) 19th-century Fenian poet 624 A/N

Casey, Mr   Parnellite friend of Mr. Dedalus   P (16), 27–39; S (56), 100–105

Cashman, Johnny   97-year-old Corkonian drinking with Mr. Dedalus   P 94–95 + 2 grandchildren P (94)

(CASSANDRA)   gloomy Trojan prophetess doomed to be disbelieved   33   A/N

*(CASSIDY, JAMES)   publican   61, 538   N/T

("Cassidy, Mrs")   quoted in anecdote   D 183

(CASTELEIN, FATHER A.)   author of a book on the "elect" thought of by Conmee   223   A/N

(CASTLETOWN, LORD)   reported on deplorable state of Irish forests   326   N

(Catalani)   from context a castrato, but see Catalani, Angelica 308

(CATALANI, ANGELICA)   19th-century Italian soprano 308   A/N

(CATESBY)   brand of linoleum   355

(CATHERINE OF SIENA, S.)   14th-century mystic   P 123 N

("Cautious Calmer, Mr")   396   see Bloom, Leopold

(CAVALCANTI, GUIDO)   13th-century Italian poet   45; P 176   A/N/N

("Cavil, Mr")   396   see Lynch, Vincent

("Cedarfront, Miss Rachel")   member of the forest wedding 327

(CELESTINE, S.)   pope who presumably sent Patrick to Ireland   339, 666   A/N

(CENCI, BEATRICE)   Italian Renaissance heroine celebrated by Shelley   G 11

*(CEPPI, P.)   framemaker   260   N/T

(CERES)   Roman harvest goddess   504   A/N

CEYLON   horse that won the Prix de Paris in 1866   (32), [573]   A/N

(Chace, Pvt Arthur)   from context a convicted and hanged murderer   303

(CHAMBERLAIN, JOSEPH)   British statesman whose 1899 T.C.D. visit sparked demonstrations   162–63, 457   A/N

Chandler, Annie   wife of Thomas Chandler   D (71), (79), 82, (83), 84–85 + infant (79), 82–85

Chandler, Thomas Malone   law clerk and poet manqué   D 70–85

(Chang, Hi Hung/LI HUNG CHANG) member of the F.O.T.E.I.: Chinese dignitary who visited London in 1896 307 + Hugh Staples, *JJQ* (Fall 1977)
(CHARDENAL, C. A.) author of *The Standard French Primer* 243, 253 A/N
(CHARLEMAGNE) 9th-century Frankish king 297 N
(CHARLES I) of England 243 A/N
(CHARLES II) of England 708 A/N
(CHARLES V) of Spain 328 A/N
Charles, Uncle maternal granduncle of Stephen Dedalus (680), P 7, (11), (16), (18), 27–39, 60–62, 65–66, (87)
"Charley"* Zoe's name for the chandelier 503, 515
[Chatterton, Abraham] presumably a high school friend of Leopold Bloom 548
*(CHATTERTON, HEDGES EYRE) vice-chancellor of Dublin University 124 N
"Chawley" name used by one of the drinkers at Burke's to address one of the others 426
(CHETTLE, HENRY) Elizabethan playwright 204 A/N
("Chickabiddy") mock romantic name from typical breach-of-promise suit correspondent 285
(CHILDS, SAMUEL) accused of murdering his brother Thomas 100, 139, 410, 412, 456 A/N/T
(CHILDS, THOMAS) murdered brother of acquitted Samuel 100, 139, 410, 412, 456 A/N/T
("Chloe") prototypal Grecian shepherdess 416 A
(Chow, Cha Pu) presumably typical beloved 333
("Christ, Bloom") 507 see Bloom, Leopold
("Christ, Florry") 507 see Talbot, Florry
(CHRIST, JESUS) often as expletive (!) 10, 12, 16, 19, 26, 37, 38, 41, 81, 82, 91, 94, 107, 117, 123, 132, 133, 135, 151, 185, 197–98, 216, 237, 238, 292, 293, 296, 300, 301, 302, 303, 314, 323, 330, 335, 342, 345, 349, 385, 391, 424, 427, 462, 485, 498, 508, 520, 524, 536, 579, 582, 584, 591, 622, 643, 703, 742, 743, 752, 769, 771; S 32, 44, 86, 107, 111, 112, 113, 116, 132, 134, 138, 140, 141, 142, 146, One 172, 185, 189, 190, 191, 217, 222, 228, 232, 248, 249; D 166, 173; P 106, 108, 109, 111, 113, 114, 117, 118, 119, 124, 127, 131, 134, 138, 139, 141, 146, 147, 148, 149, 242 A/N
("Christ, Kitty") 507 see Ricketts, Kitty
("Christ, Lynch") 507 see Lynch, Vincent
("Christ, Stephen") 507 see Dedalus, Stephen

("Christ, Zoe") 507 see Higgins, Zoe
(Christbaum) in Brini's genealogy 496
("Christfox") 193 N see Christ, Jesus; Fox, George
(Christicle!) 428
(Christies/CHRISTY) 19th-century minstrels 443 N
("Christine") 3 see Christ, Jesus
(Christopher) a hotelkeeper? P 28-30
(CHRYSOSTOMOS, S. JOHN) 4th-century Greek ecclesiast and orator 3, 494 A/N Introduction
("Chubb, Uncle") hypothetical usurper in the household while sailor is away 624
(Chuechli-Steuerli, Herr Hurhausdirektorpräsident Hans) member of the F. O. T. E. I. 307
(CICERO, MARCUS TULLIUS) 2nd-century B.C. Roman orator 124, 394, 622 A/N
(CIRCE) in the *Odyssey* magical temptress; here mistaken for Ceres 504 A/N
Citron, J./CITRON, ISRAEL Bloom's erstwhile neighbor (60), (122), (156), [497], [544], [586] + wife (754) N/T + Hyman, pp. 174, 329
*(CLAFFEY, M.) pawnbroker, mother of Pat 155 N/T + *Thom's,* p. 1831
(CLAFFEY, PAT) presumably became a nun 155 N/T
*(Claire of LA MAISON CLAIRE) milliner and dressmaker? 167, 246 N/T
(Clancy, Mr) Nationalist friend of Molly Ivors D 189
(CLARA, S.) 13th-century founder of Sisters of St. Clare 339 A/N
(Clarke, Lotty) subject of Bloom's youthful voyeurism 549
*(CLARKE, THOMAS) tobacconist and Irish insurrectionist P 210 see Cooney
(CLAUDIUS) villain in *Hamlet* dull-brained yokel 202 N
(CLAVER, S. PETER) 17th-century Spanish Jesuit missionary 80, 81, 223 A/N
(CLAY, HENRY*) brand of cigars named for 19th-century American politician 247, 471, 485 A/N
*(CLAY, ROBERT KEATING) elected deputy chairman of Richmond Asylum 16 June 1904 534 N + *Thom's,* p. 1932
*(CLEARY, P. J.) Franciscan vicar of Adam and Eve's Church 317 N + *Thom's,* p. 1833
(CLEOPATRA) 208, 297 A/N

(CLERY AND CO.) Dublin drapers 76, 350, 352 N/T

Clery, Emma Stephen Dedalus's beloved Blueribboned hat? 215; P 69–71, (77), (82–83), (115–16), (202), 215–16, (218), (219–23), 232, (233), (234), (238) + mother (248), (249) + brother (250–51), (252); S (44), 46–47, (52), (56), 65–68, Someone (115) + father 152–56, (161–62), (179), 183, 187–89, (190–92), 196–99, (200–201), (203), (210), 215, (216), (230–31), 233–34 Introduction

Clifford, Martha "Mady" Bloom's pen-pal paramour Answered anyway (72), photo perhaps (73), (77–79), her letter (91), (107), she wrote (115), What perfume (123), I called you naughty (160), Are you not happy (168), (256), (262), Are you not happy (263), A lovely girl (271), (274–75), Are you not happy (277–80), lovely name (285), Suppose she were (286), (288), (368), Did I forget to write (269–70), a false name (372), Are you not happy (377), (380), I called you naughty (381), (414), Lady in the case (455), [456–57], (721), (722), (735), some little bitch (739) N

(Clinch, Mrs) acquaintance of Bloom's whom he almost mistakes for a prostitute 370

*(Clohissey/CLOHISEY, M.) bookseller 242, 729; O'Clohissey D 188 N/T

(CLOYNE, BISHOP OF) 48 see Berkeley, George

(Coates/COATS, JAMES & PETER) thread manufacturers 160 N

["Cock of the North"] horse jockeyed by Mr. Deasy 573

(COCKBURN, FRANCES MARY) in *Irish Independent* obituary 298 N

Cochrane pupil in Mr. Deasy's school 24–27, (29)

(CODY, WILLIAM) Wild West impresario 624 A/N

*COFFEY, FR M. chaplain at Glasnevin cemetery 103–4, (105), (277), (284), [473]; S 167 T or COFFEY, FR FRANCIS N

*(COFFEY, WILLIAM) butcher 175 N

(Coghlan, Joe) in Mullingar helps butcher's boy retrieve drowned body S 252

(Coghlan, Mr and Mrs) photographer in Mullingar to whom Milly is apprenticed 62, 66, 156

*COHEN, BELLA brothel-keeper in Nighttown (475), 527–85, (587), (606), (729) N/T

(Cohen, Cuck) Bello claims him as one of her husbands as well as a step-nephew 544

(Cohen, old) former owner of the Bloom bed 772, 780
("Cohen, Ruby"/"Miss Ruby") name given to Bloom by Bello 535, 539
(Coleman) in *Freeman's Journal* obituary 91, 279, 280, 465
(COLERIDGE, SAMUEL TAYLOR) Romantic poet 205; S 148 A/N
(Colgan) candidate opposing Tierney D 121, 124
("COLLEEN BAWN") heroine of Irish novel, play, song—in list of heroes 297 A/N
(COLLINS, ANTHONY/John Anthony) 18th-century English theologian P 197 N
*(COLLINS, DR J. R.) gynecologist consulted by Molly 770–71 N/T
*(COLLINS, KATE) proprietress of North City Dining Rooms 145 N/T p. 63
(COLLINS, LOTTIE) dancer at the Gaiety—no relation to John Anthony Collins P 179
(COLLINS, WILKIE) English Gothic novelist 756 A/N
*(COLLIS AND WARD) solicitors presumably employing Richie Goulding 88, 232, 240, 252, 266, 269, 287, 289, 299, 446 N/T
(COLMAN, S.) first Bishop of Cloyne, 6th century 339 A/N
(Colombus/COLUMBUS, RUALDUS) 16th-century anatomist 512 A/N
*(COLUM, PADRAIC) Irish poet 192 A/N
(COLUMBA, S.) 339 see Columcille, S.
(COLUMBANUS, S.) 6th/7th-century Irish saint 27, 42, 339 A/N
(COLUMBUS, CHRISTOPHER) 297; S 184 A/N
(COLUMCILLE, S.) 6th-century Celtic abbot 339 A/N
*(COMBRIDGE AND CO.) bookseller and art dealer 168 N/T
(Comerford, Mr & Mrs M.) former friends of the Blooms 720, 753
(Comisky, "Bags") arrested for drunkenness, according to Corley 618
Compton, Pvt British soldier in Nighttown with Carr 430–31, 450–52, 574, 587–603
Comyn pupil at Mr. Deasy's school 24–27
("Conacre, Cowe") participant in mock debate 315 A/N

("Confucius, Brian") conflated name in list of "Irish" heroes 297 A/N
("Conifer, Miss Fir") participant in forest wedding 327
("Conifer, Miss Larch") participant in forest wedding 327
("Conifer, Miss Spruce") participant in forest wedding 327
*CONMEE, REV. JOHN rector at Clongowes, then prefect of studies at Belvedere and superior of the residence at St. Francis Xavier's Church (80), (190), 219–24, 225, 226, 242, (246), (415), (416), [561], [579], (690); P (9), (20), (24), (40), (41), (46–47), (48), (53), (54), (55), 56–58, (71–72), (93) A/N/N
(CONN OF THE HUNDRED BATTLES) High King of Ireland c. a.d. 200 296, 323 A/N
(Conneff, Thomas) in list of Irish heroes 296
*(CONNELLAN, REV. THOMAS) Protestant propagandist for conversion of Catholics 180 N/T + *Thom's,* p. 1837
*(CONNERY, W. & E.) owner of pub "The Ship" 199, 696; S 223 N/T + *Thom's,* p. 1837
Connolly Stephen's schoolmate at Belvedere P 168–69
(Connolly, Conny) presumably a friend of Milly Bloom 767
*CONROY, FR BERNARD curate, Star of the Sea Church, Dignam's confessor and Gerty's; Bloom assumes that he's Gabriel's brother (see Conroy, Fr Constantine) (252), 358–65, (377), 382, [469] N + *Thom's,* p. 1837; Introduction
(Conroy, Fr Constantine) Gabriel's brother and senior curate at Balbriggan 377; P 186 N
(Conroy, Ellen) Gabriel's dead mother D 179, 186–87
(Conroy, Eva) daughter of Gabriel and Gretta D 180
Conroy, Gabriel teacher and book reviewer; resident in Monkstown; nephew of the Morkan sisters (125), (377); D 176–82, 184–85, 186–224 N
Conroy, Gretta wife of Gabriel Conroy (69); D 176–77, 179–82, (187), (189), 190–91, 195–96, (206), 209–24 + grandmother (218), (220), (221) N
(Conroy, T. J.) Gabriel's dead father D 179
(Conroy, Tom) son of Gabriel and Gretta D 180
(Conservio) fictitious character in doggerel 524 A/N
*(CONWAY, JAMES) publican 74, 86 N/T
(COOK, THOMAS, AND SON) travel agents 297 A/N
(Cooney) tobacconist and Nationalist agitator S 61, 214 see Clarke, Thomas

(COOPER-OAKLEY, ISABEL) English theosophist 185 N
(Corbet, Jem/CORBETT, JAMES J. "GENTLEMAN JIM") American heavyweight champion 251 A/N
(Corbet, Joey) Cork university crony of Mr Dedalus P 90
(CORDELIA) heroine of Shakespeare's *King Lear* 192 A/N
(Cordoglio*) Italian for "sorrow" 192 see Cordelia
[Cork, Lord Mayor of] in procession honoring Bloom 480
(CORLESS, THOMAS) Dublin restaurateur D 72 T see Jammet Bros.
(Corley, Inspector) father of John Corley 616; D 51 + mother or aunt (616–17)
Corley, John casual seducer and later down-and-out 616–19; D 49–56, (57), (58), 59–60
(Corley, Patrick Michael) John Corley's grandfather 616
(CORMAC MacART) 3rd-century Irish king 169, 323, 667 A/N
*(CORMACK, THOMAS) publican 434 N/T
(CORNELIS CORNELISSEN VAN DEN STEEN/CORNELIUS A LAPIDE) 16th/17th-century Flemish biblical exegete P 233 N
(CORNELIUS, S.) 3rd-century pope 339 A/N see also Kelleher, Cornelius
(CORNWALL, DUKE OF) British Army general 345 N see George V
(CORNWALLIS, MARQUESS) British general, Lord Lieutenant of Ireland during Rebellion of 1798 P 38 N
(CORNWELL, DR JAMES) 19th-century grammarian P 10 N
Corrigan pupil at Clongowes Wood P (44), (45), 54
Corrigan, Bernard Dignam's brother-in-law, Patsy's uncle 101, Him? 102, 104, 112, Uncle Barney (250–51), (647), (704) Introduction
(Corrigan, Fr Bernard) presumed by Bloom to have been Molly's lover 731 see Corrigan, Bernard; Corrigan, Father
(Corrigan, Father) to whom Molly had gone for confession 741
Costello, Francis "Punch" medical student at the Lying-In Hospital 388–428, [493], [506], [509] + father (398–99)
Cotter, old formerly something in a distillery D 9–11, (13)

Courcy, Miss de in second carriage of the viceregal procession 252–55
*(COURTENAY, COL. ARTHUR H.) barrister and judge 322 N
*(COUSINS, JAMES H.) one of Stephen's creditors 31 N + *Thom's,* p. 1841
Cowley, Alderman presumably a Dublin politician 246; D (127)
Cowley, "Father" Bob spoiled priest now in financial straits (76), 239–40, 243–45, Cow (257), 265–91, [586] N
(COX, CHARLES) 18th-century M. P. to whom Bloom's geometry book is dedicated 709 N
"Crab" character in Mulligan's drama (217), [496]
*(CRAIG, GARDNER AND CO.) accountants 534 N/T
*(CRAMER, WOOD AND CO.) sellers of musical instruments 380 N/T
(CRAMPTON, SIR PHILIP) 19th-century Dublin surgeon 92, 170; P 214 A/N/N/T
("Crane, Jack") member of Elijah's congregation 507
Cranly Stephen's companion and later erstwhile friend (7), (32), (184–85), (211); P (178), (191), 194–201, 204, (207), 215, 226–32, (233), 234–47, (247–48), (249), (250); S (39), 105–9, 113–19, 122–30, 136–43, (144–45), (148), (157), (161), 172–75, 179–80, 182–83, 184–87, (195), (202), (203), 207–8, (208–9), 211–14, 215–16, 217–18, 219–26, (229) + father & mother P (248) N; Introduction
("Crawford") 336 see Crofton, J.T.A.
*CRAWFORD, MILES editor of the *Evening Telegraph* (35), (125), 126–44, 146–50, (323), (381), (397), [458], [470], (648)
(CREACH, ARCHBISHOP DAVID) enemy of the 15th-century Earl of Kildare 231 A/N
("Creeper, Miss Virginia") participant in the forest wedding 327
("Creole Sue") member of Elijah's congregation 507
(CRESSID/CRESSIDA) heroine of Shakespeare's *Troilus and Cressida* 208 A/N
*(CRIMMINS, WILLIAM C.) publican 239–40 N/T + *Thom's,* p. 1843
("Croesus") one of female Bloom's violators, named for rich Lydian king 536 A/N
("Crofter") 336 see Crofton, J. T. A.
*CROFTON, J. T. A. employee of the Collector-General's

office (93), 336–45, [489], [586]; D (129–30), 130–35, (165) N
(CROKER, "BOSS" RICHARD) New York politician, Irish-born, in parade of Irish heroes 297 N
(Croly, Police Sergeant) at Mrs. Sinico's inquest D 114
(CROMWELL, OLIVER) Puritan Protector of England 334, 342, 644 A/N
("CRONION, FATHER") personification of Time 421 A/N
(Crosbie and Alleyne) solicitors employing Farrington 91; D 87, 88 n
(Crosby, Dan) tutor and crony of Mr. Dedalus P 164
Crotthers, J. Scottish medical student 388–428, [493], [509]
*(CROTTY) singer at the Gaiety Theatre 230
("Crow, reverend Carrion") the Holy Dove 595
(CRUSOE, ROBINSON) Daniel Defoe's lonely adventurer 109, 153, 495 A/N
(CUCHULIN) hero of the Ulster cycle in parade of Irish heroes 296 A/N
*CUFFE, JOSEPH cattle dealer (97), (294), (315), (399), (409), (465), [586], (680), (731), (752–53), (772) N/T + *Thom's*, p. 1844
(Cullen, James) apparently a draper in Ennis 685
*(CULLEN, M.) bootmaker 302 N/T
(CULLEN, PAUL CARDINAL) 18th-century Irish cardinal P 38; S 173 N
(CULPEPPER, NICHOLAS) 17th-century English physician 418 A/N
(Cummins, Father) director of the sodality at Stephen's university S 182
*(CUMMINS, M.) pawnbroker 320 N/T + *Thom's*, p. 1845
(CUMMINS, MARIA) 19th-century author 363 A/N
Cunningham, Martin employed at Dublin Castle (80), 87–101, 107, 115, (121), (219), 246–48, (303), (313), S. Martin (333), 336–45, [469–70], (568–69), (626), (647), (704), (773); D (155), 156–74 + wife (96), [568–69]; D (157) N
(CUPID) Roman god of love 348
(Cuprani) apparently a printer, naturalized Irishman 119
*(CURRAN, CONSTANTINE) one of Stephen's debtors 31 N
(CURRAN, JOHN PHILPOT) 18th/19th-century Irish barrister and debater 139 A/N

(CURRAN, SARA) beloved of Robert Emmet 305 A/N
*(CUSACK, MICHAEL) organizer of the Gaelic Athletic Association P 180; S 61 N/N see Citizen
(CYMBELINE) title character in Shakespeare's play 218 A/N
(CYR, S.) 4th-century child martyr 339 A/N

("D. O. C.") writer to newspapers on matters poetic 312
(DAEDALUS) Greek labyrinth builder, artificer, and aeronaut 210, grandoldgrossfather 569; P 169–70, hawklike man 225, 253 A/N/N
Daedalus, Isabel Stephen's sister S (101), (109), (126–27), (131–32), (151), (159), (160–61), (163), 164–65, (166), (167), (169), (228)
Daedalus, Maurice Stephen's younger brother S 26, (27), (33), 36, (48), (49), 56–59, (81), 99–100, (105), (112), (122), (126), 144–45, (151), 159–60, (161), 164, (165), 166, 167, (203), (214), 226, 228–30, 230–31
Daedalus, Mrs Stephen's mother S (56), (58), (81), 83–87, (88), (101), (109–11), (126), (127), 131–35, (138), (151), 159–60, (160–61), 162–63, 164–65, 209–10, (214), 216–17, (226), 227–28, (229), (231)
Daedalus, Simon Stephen's father S (48), (56), (70), (85), (87–88), 100, (105), (109–11), 120, (127), (131), (134), (135), (150–51), 159–60, (161), 164, (166), 167–68, (209), (214), 216–17, (222), (226), 227–28, (229), (231)
Daedalus, Stephen S 23–234, 237–53 see also Dedalus, Stephen
("Dainty Dixon, Mr") 396 see Dixon
(Dalton, Captain) under whom seaman Murphy claims to have served 625, 631
("Daly") name used by the Dedaluses when pawning their possessions P 174
(DALY) 18th-century Dublin gambling establishment 241 N/T
Daly, Miss attending the Morkans' party D 182–84, (191), 197–206
*(DALY, TERESA) tobacconist 262, 263, 264, 289 + shopgirl (262), 264 N/T
(Daly, Warden) source of Molly's bit of pessimistic philosophy (?) 772

(DAMASCENUS, JOHANNES/S. JOHN DAMASCENE) 8th-century describer of Christ 689 A/N
Dan Mr. Fulham's cart driver S 238–39, 244–45, 246
(DANA) Irish goddess of the Danaan 194 A/N
Dandrade, Miriam sold her exotic garments to Bloom (160–61), (536), [587]
(DANIEL) adjudicator in the story of Susanna and the elders (here Portia in *Merchant of Venice*) 488 A/N
Daniel, Annie eldest of the Daniel daughters entertaining Stephen at their home S 43, 46, (66), (130), (153), 234
Daniel, Miss Annie's sister (or sisters) S 44, 234
Daniel, Mr whose Sunday evenings at home Stephen attends S (42), 43–46, (61), (89), (130), (155), 156–59 + son 171–74
(Daniel, Mrs) wife of Mr Daniel S 156
("Dannyman") 642 see Mann, Daniel
"Dante" P 7 see Riordan, Mrs
(DANTE ALIGHIERI) 296, 637; P 252; S 41, 92, 158–59, 169, 174; G 11 A/N/N
(DANTES, EDMOND) Count of Monte Cristo in Dumas's novel P 62–63 N
D'ARCY, BARTELL tenor with whom Molly had at least a flirtation (156), (234), [586], (731), (745), he gave (763), (774); D (184), (191), 198–206, (206), a man's voice (209–10), 211–15
("Daremo, Signor Laci") according to Bello, one of Mrs. Dandrade's violators 536
["Dark Mercury"] denounces Bloom 456
("DARK ROSALEEN") in Irish heroes and heroines of antiquity 297 A/N
(DARLING, GRACE) 19th-century rescuer of shipwreck victims, in Wordsworth poem 376, 382 A/N
*(DARLINGTON, FR JOSEPH) dean of studies at U.C.D., wrote on Shakespeare 205 A/N + Sullivan, p. 198 see also Butt, D., S. J.
(DARWIN, CHARLES) 19th-century scientist 407, 716 A/N
(DAVENANT, SIR WILLIAM) Carolingian dramatist, reputed son of Shakespeare 202 A/N
(DAVID, KING) 242, 495, 504, 528, 689?, 700 + messianic successors 495, 689; P 210 A/N
(DAVID, S.) patron saint of Wales 482

Davin Stephen's friend from Limerick at U.C.D. P. (180–83), (195), 200–204, (228), (238), (250) see also Madden
(Davin, Fonsy) Davin's cousin P 182
(DAVIN, MAT) Davin's uncle, Irish athlete P 181 N
(DAVIS, THOMAS OSBORNE) 19th-century Irish Nationalist poet and editor 317 A/N
(DAVITT, MICHAEL) organizer of the Irish Land League 599, 657, 681, 716; P 7, 15 A/N/N
*(DAVY, J. AND T.) publicans 137, 696 N/T
("DAVY, MEDICAL") in scurrilous song 209, 217, 428 A/N
*DAWSON, DAN baker and politician (91), (123–26), (234), [586] + daughter and her fiance (126) N
("Deadhand") taunts Bloom 496
("DEADWOOD DICK") 19th-century black American sheriff, hero in pulp fiction 328 A/N
(DEANE, SIR THOMAS) architect of National Library and National Museum 183 A/N
Deasy, Garrett headmaster of Dalkey school employing Stephen (27), 29–36, (37), his letter for the press (38), (48), (132), He's from beyant (189), (199), (518), [573–74], (617), that first epistle (648) + wife (132) N
("Dedalo, Stephano") 242 see Dedalus, Stephen
Dedalus, "Boody" Stephen's sister 225, 226–27, (620), 2 Dedalus girls (747); P (18?), 86?, 163–64, 174–75
Dedalus, Delia "Dilly" Stephen's sister 151–52, (226), 237–39, 243, 253, [579], (581), (620), sister (645?), (670); P (18?), 86?, 163–64?
(Dedalus, John Stephen) Stephen's great-grandfather P 94–95
Dedalus, Katey Stephen's sister 225, 226–27, (620), 2 Dedalus girls (747); P (18?), 86?, 163–64, 174–75
Dedalus, Maggy Stephen's sister 226–27, (243), (620); P (18?), 86?, 163–64, 174–75
Dedalus, Mary/May Goulding Stephen's mother (5), (6), (8), Her door was open (9–10), She was no more (27–28), ghostwoman (38), (41), (42), could not save her (46), her mouth's kiss (48), Her grave (105), (134), (151), (190), *Amor matris* (207), (238), his wife (274), (415), the vision (421), (422), [579–83], (609), (663), (670), (680), (682), (695), (774), (778); P 7–8, (9), (10), (13), (14–15), (16), (18), (20), (23–24), (26), 27–39, 65, (67),

71–72, his family 86?, 96–97, (98), (151), (163), (164–65), 174–75, (224), (238), (240–42), (248), (252)

Dedalus, Maurice Stephen's brother (211); P (18), (71), 72, his family 86?, 96–97, (98), 163–64 N

Dedalus, Simon Stephen's father Kinch the elder (18), (38), (42), (43), (58), 87–100, 102–3, 104–7, (117), 123–27, Your governor (131), (136), Chip of the old block (144), (151), he comes out with (152), (165), (199), your old fellow (201), your old fellow (207), (226–27), 237–39, 239–40, 252, De (257), 261–91, (380), (388), his friend's (390), Pa Kinch (425), [470], Imitate pa (517), [572], [579], (604), (605), (616), (619–20), (623), (645), (647), (659), (661), (663), (670), (680), (682), (704), (731), (735), (768), (773), (774); P 7, (9), (11), (16), (17), (18), (20), (23), (26), 27–39, (52), 60, (61), 62, (64), 65–66, (70), 71–72 (76–77), (83), (84), 86–95, 96–97, (162), (163), (164), 175, (184), (228), (241), (250) + father P (30), (38)

["Dedalus, Simon Stephen Cardinal"] 523–25 see Dedalus, Simon; Dedalus, Stephen

Dedalus, Stephen 3–51, 88, 131–50, 228–29, 241–43, (248–49), (260), (262), 388–428, 430–33, following him (452), He's inside (475), 503–83, 587–609, 613–65, 666–704, (711), (735), (768), (773), his son (774–75), young poet (776), hes running wild (778), he could easy (779); P 7–253 + youngest brother P 163–64; + sister P 163–64 + grandfather P (91–92), (94) + sister P (98) + cousin P 96–97

("Deephen") S 165 see Daedalus, Stephen

Delacour, Miss client of Crosbie & Alleyne D (89), 90–92, (93)

(Delagracia) a name Molly remembers from Gibraltar 779

*(DELAHUNT, JOSEPH & SYLVESTER) publicans 234 N/T

*(DELANY, REV. WILLIAM) president of U. C. D. 317 N + Sullivan, p. 199

(Delapaz) a name Molly remembers from Gibraltar 779

(DEMETER) Roman earth goddess 504 A/N

(DEMIURGOS, LOS) creator of the physical world 37 A/N

(DEMOSTHENES) 4th-century B.C. Athenian orator 139 A/N

(DE MURZKA, ILMA) 19th-century soprano D 199 N

(DENIS, S.) 3rd-century bishop of Paris; patron saint of France 339, 357 A/N see also Breen, Denis

*(DENNANY, THOMAS H.) dealer in graveyard sculpture 99 N/T
(Dennehy, Francis) chemist in Ennis from whom Virag bought aconite 685
(Dennehy, Captain Slogger) polo player admired by Mrs. Talboys 467
(DENNY, HENRY, AND SON) meat manufacturers from Limerick 59 N
(DENVER) title hero of 1882 play, *The Silver King* 728 A/N
(DERMOT) one of the "twelve tribes" 323 A/N see MacMurrough, Dermot
*Derwan/DERWIN, JAMES building contractor (450), [484] N see also Kerwan
(DESMOND, EARL OF) 328 see Fitzgerald, James Fitzmaurice
(Devan, Harry) son of Tom Devan who was a friend of Milly's 766
*(Devan/DEVIN, TOM) sanitary department employee 252 + two sons 766 N
(Devine) one of Eveline's childhood playmates D 36
(Devlin, Miss) D 136 see Kearney, Mrs
(DEVORGHIL) faithless wife of Teirnan O'Rourke 34–35, 324 N
(DE WALDEN, LORD HOWARD) 174 see Eelis, Thomas Evelyn
(DE WET, CHRISTIAN RUDOLPH) Boer general and statesman 163, 593, 649 A/N
("Dewey-Mosse, Mrs Kitty") member of the forest wedding 327
("Dick") 650 see Tom, Dick and Harry
("DICK, DOCTOR") doctored Dublin pantomimes 685 A/N
("DICK, MEDICAL") in scurrilous Gogarty song 209, 217, 428 A/N
(DICKENS, CHARLES) English novelist S 86
*(DICKINSON, EMILY MONROE) sister of Charles Stewart Parnell 165A/N
("Diet, Doctor") Bloom's prescription for newborn Purefoy child 423
Dignam, Alice one of the Dignam orphans Five young children (101–2), [568], 5 children (774)

Dignam, baby one of the Dignam orphans Five young children (101–2), [568], 5 children (774)
Dignam, Freddy one of the older Dignam children Five young children (101–2), (355), [568], 5 children (774)
Dignam, Mrs widow of Paddy Dignam the poor wife (102), ma (250), ma (251), (313), (349), (355), (373), she wants the money (380), (473), [568] + children (774)
Dignam, Patrick Aloysius "Patsy" oldest son of deceased Dignam the boy 101–4, 110, 112, that boy's name (219), 234, 250–52, 254, (302), (355), a boy (379?), [568], (704), 5 children (774)
Dignam, Patrick T. "Paddy" Dubliner buried in Glasnevin 16 June 1904 (58), (64), (70), (73–74), poor fellow (84), (91), (95), (98–99), the stiff (101), her husband (102), the father (103), (104), (109), his soul (111), (118), (122), (157), (164), (171), poor little . . . (232), (240), (247), (251–52), (277), (279), (288), (289), (300–304), (313), (354–55), (370), (372), (373), (380), (396), Padney (427), [472–74], (647), (655), (704), (705), (711), the funeral (728), (739), (773), (774) N
Dignam, Susy one of the Dignam orphans Five young children (101–2), [568], 5 children (774)
Dignam's brother-in-law 101 see Corrigan, Bernard
(Dilectus/DELECTUS*) collection of favorite Latin pieces P 94
(Dillon, Atty) daughter of Mat Dillon 377, 422, 758
(Dillon, Floey) married daughter of Mat Dillon 115, 377, 422, 743, 758 + husband 770
(Dillon, Hetty) daughter of Mat Dillon 377
Dillon, Joe Wild West enthusiast at Belvedere D 19, (21)
*(DILLON, JOSEPH) auctioneer 129, 151, 237, 539 N/T
Dillon, Leo Belvedere pupil, brother of Joe Dillon D 19–21, (22) + parents (19)
(Dillon, Louy) daughter of Mat Dillon 377
(Dillon, Maimy) daughter of Mat Dillon 377, 780
(Dillon, Mathew "Mat") old friend of Bloom and Tweedy, at whose house Bloom met Molly 106, 115, 275, 376, 377, 542, 667, 680, 707, 731, her father 758, 774, 775 T
(Dillon, Tiny) daughter of Mat Dillon 377, 422
*DILLON, VALENTINE BLAKE former Lord Mayor of Dublin, brother of Mat Dillon (155), (234), (371), (465), [586], (731), (750) N + *Thom's*, p. 1851
Dillon, Rev. Dr W., S. J. president of Stephen's university S

(23), (66), (89), 90–98, (99), (119), 120, (153), 171–74, (227), (230) see Delaney, Rev. William
(DIMSEY, DAVID/"Davie") surviving husband of Martha Elizabeth Dimsey 298 N
(DIMSEY, MARTHA ELIZABETH) in *Irish Independent* obituary 298
(DINA) in song 443
("Dinbad") 737 see Sinbad the Sailor
*(Dineen/DINNEEN, FR PATRICK S.) compiled Irish-English dictionary 211, priesteen 215 N
(DINORAH) heroine of Meyerbeer opera D 199 N
(DIONYSIUS THE PSEUDO-AREOPAGITE) 5th/6th-century Christian writer, identity and authenticity disputed G 1
(Diplodocus*) extinct reptile 514 A/N
("Disabel") S 165 see Daedalus, Isabel
("Dix") 424 see Dixon
Dixon young medical at Lying-In Hospital Nice young student (97), (163), 386–407, junior medical officer (410), [493–94], [509]; P 226–32, 234–37, (250)
Dlugacz, Moses presumably Jewish pork butcher (56), 58–60, (68), (279), [464], (763?)
("DOADY") name applied to Mr. Purefoy from Dickens's *David Copperfield* 421 A/N
*(DOCKRELL, THOMAS, AND SONS) glass and paper merchants 155, 462 N/T
*DODD, JR. son of Reuben J. Dodd (94–95), (152), [497–98], [506] N
*DODD, REUBEN J. legal accountant and moneylender 93–94, (94–95), (183), gombeen man (244), (252), Judas Iscariot's (267), (288), (322), (474), [497–98], [506] a/N/T + *Thom's,* p. 1852
("Doggerina") 755 see Stanhope, Hester
(Doherty) an acquaintance of Cranly's P 245 see Mulligan, Malachi Roland St John
*(DOHERTY, REV. WILLIAM) Catholic priest at the Pro-Cathedral 317 N
Dolan, Father prefect of studies at Clongowes Wood See it in your face (135), [561]; P (44), 48–51, (52), (54), (55), (57), (59), (72) N
Dollard, Benjamin solicitor, basso, crony of Mr. Dedalus (91), (154), (174), (234), (241), 244–45, (256–57), 267–91, [488–89], [521–23], [586], (731), (774)

*(DOLLARD, J.) printer (252–53) N/T
("Dolling") D 169 see Döllinger, Johannes Josef Ignaz von
(DÖLLINGER, JOHANNES JOSEF IGNAZ VON) theologian who broke with the Catholic Church over papal infallibility D (169–70) N
(DOLMETSCH, ARNOLD) English musician 661 N
(DOLORES) song heroine 256, 264, 265, 267, 275, 286 A/N see also Idolores
(DOMINIC, S.) 13th-century founder of Dominican order 339, 358 A/N
(Donnelly, Alphy) Joe Donnelly's estranged brother D 100, 102, 104
Donnelly, Alphy Joe Donnelly's young son D 103–6
Donnelly, Joe Maria's host on Halloween D (100), (102), 103–6 + mother (100)
Donnelly, Mrs Joe Donnelly's wife D (100), 103–6
*(DONOHOE AND SMYTH) publicans 345 N/T
Donovan student at U.C.D. P 210–11, (212) + sister P (211)
(Doran) whose ass becomes a mistaken lover—in song 537 A/N
Doran, Bob resident at Mrs. Mooney's boarding house, married to Polly Mooney (74), 167, 246, the drunk 251, 298–345, [454]; D (63–65), 65–68, (69) N; Introduction see also Mooney, Polly
*(DORAN, MICHAEL) publican 182 N/T
Douce, Lydia barmaid at the Ormond 246, 252, bronze (256–57), 257–91, [564–66] N
*(DOWDEN, EDWARD) professor at Trinity College 204, 214 A/N/T
DOWIE, DR JOHN ALEXANDER evangelist from Zion, Illinois, self-proclaimed Elijah (151), (428), [492], [507–8], (690) A/N
(DOWLAND, JOHN) Elizabethan composer 661; S 155; P 233; G 9 A/N/N
("Dowling") D 169 see Döllinger, Johannes Josef Ignaz von
*(DOWNES, SIR JOSEPH) baker and confectioner D 102, 103 N/T
("Doyle") a common name 622
(DOYLE, SIR ARTHUR CONAN) author of the Sherlock Holmes stories 708 A/N
(Doyle, Caroline) wife of Luke Doyle, friend of the Blooms from their courtship days 707, all the Doyles 771

DOYLE, FR CHARLES in charge of the theatrical at Belvedere P (83), plump freshfaced jesuit 84–85 Sullivan, pp. 87, 92
(Doyle, Henny) friend of the Blooms from their courtship days 377, 747, all the Doyles 771
*(DOYLE, J. C.) baritone with whom Molly is scheduled to sing 63, 93 N
Doyle, Jimmy son of wealthy butcher D 42–48
*(DOYLE, LUKE) building surveyor, friend of the Blooms from their courtship days 158, 377, 705, 707, all the Doyles 771 T
*(DOYLE, MME) dressmaker and milliner 250 N/T + *Thom's*, p. 1856
(Doyle, Mr) Jimmy Doyle's father, merchant prince of butchers D 43, 45–46
*(DRAGO, A.) hairdresser 68, 180, 275 N/T + *Thom's*, p. 1857
(DRAKE, SIR FRANCIS) Elizabethan navigator 188 A/N
*(DRIMMIE, DAVID, AND SONS) insurance agents who once employed Bloom 370, 586, 769, 772 + managing clerk [586] N/T
Driscoll, Mary former servant at the Blooms a female domestic (409), [460–61], (463–64), (739–40) + aunt (739)
(DRUMMOND, WILLIAM—OF HAWTHORNDEN) 17th-century Scottish poet 194 A/N
(DRUMONT, EDWARD) French journalist 43, 50 A/N
(DRYDEN, JOHN) 17th-century poet and playwright the poet D 168 N
[Dubedat, Gwendolen] who kisses Bloom 486 see Dubedat, Miss
"Dubedat, Miss" a name Bloom conjures with (175), [586] see *Thom's*, p. 1858 for du Bedat see Dubedat, Gwendolen
[Dubedatandshedidbedad, Miss] 586 see Dubedat, Miss
(DUBLIN, EARL OF) 331 see Edward VII
(DUBOSC) 18th-century train robber 456 N
(du Boyes, H.) presumably a typewriter salesman whose ad appears in the *Telegraph* 647 N
*DUDLEY, EARL OF/WILLIAM HUMBLE WARD Viceroy, Lord Lieutenant of Ireland (183), viceregal cavalcade 239, 241, 248, 252–55, 257, (270), (307), (526), [579] A/N
*DUDLEY, LADY vicereine in viceregal cavalcade (138), (160), 239, 241, 248, 252–55, 257, (307), (526), [579] A/N

*Dudley, Nicholas/DUDLEY, J. C. curate at St. Agatha's R. C. church 222 N
(DUFF, HARVEY) police informer in Boucicault's *The Shaughraun* 163 A/N
Duffy, James bank employee residing in Chapelizod D 107–17 + father D (112)
Duggan, Mr bass D 142–43, 147 + father D (142)
(Duggan, Mrs) whose husband was a drunkard; Bloom knew her at the City Arms 373
(DULCINEA) beloved of Don Quixote 192 A
("Dullman, Darby") sentimentalized old man—in song 423 A/N
(DUMAS, ALEXANDRE) father and son, 19th-century French authors 212 A/N
(DUN, SIR PATRICK) 17th/18th-century physician 332; P 209 N/N/T, p. 69
(DUNBAR, HENRY) title character in novel by Mary Elizabeth Braddon 756 A/N
("DUNDEE, THE BONNY") S 215 see McCann, Philip
*(DUNLOP, DANIEL H.) member of Dublin Theosophical Society 185 A/N
*(DUNN, JOSEPH) poulterer P 29 N/T
(Dunn, Miss) possibly related to Joseph Dunn 537
(Dunn, Tizzie) childhood playmate of Eveline Hill D 36, 37 + sibling D 36
("Dunne") 320 see O'Molloy, J. J.
Dunne, Miss Boylan's secretary 229–30, girl in the office (618)
(Dunne, P.) railway porter testifying at Sinico inquest D 114
(DUNPHY, THOMAS) publican 98; S 168
(DUNS, JOHN/SCOTUS) medieval theologian 42; E 68, 108 A/N
(Dwenn, Mrs) old friend of Molly 758
Dwyer Stephen's schoolmate at Belvedere P 168–69
(Dwyer, Father—of Larras) presumably Cranly's parents' parish priest P 248
(DWYER, MICHAEL) leader in the 1798 rebellion 296 A/N
(Dyas, Bob) university friend of Simon Dedalus P 90
(DYMPNA, S.) 6th-century Irish saint, patroness of lunatics 339 A/N

(E——— C———) P 70 see Clery, Emma
(EDISON, THOMAS ALVA) American inventor 634 A/N
("Edith") hypothetical name for sort of girl Stephen assumes associates with his Dalkey pupils 25
(EDMUND) villain in Shakespeare's *King Lear,* as well as name of his brother 209, 211 A/N
(EDWARD II) first Prince of Wales 297 N
EDWARD VII King of England 1901–10 Albert Edward (31), princely presence (32), Never see him (73), Her son (102), His Majesty (116), (151), (165), Edward Guelph-Wettin (330–31), gracious prince (409), His Majesty's (471), (589), [590–91], (593), [594], occupant of the throne (646), prince of Wales (751), H. R. H. (752); a German monarch D (121–22), (124), (131–32) A/N/N
(EDWARD, S.) Edward the Confessor, 11th-century English king 339 see also Lambert, Edward J.
(EDWARDS) soup manufacturer 175
(EELIS, THOMAS EVELYN, LORD HOWARD DE WALDEN) owner of Zinfandel in the Gold Cup 175, 325, 648 N
(Egan) through whom Bloom hopes to get a train pass 626
(EGAN, JOHN "BUCK") 18th-century politician and duellist P 184 N
*(EGAN, JOHN J.) publican D 58
Egan, Kevin Fenian exile in Paris (41–44), (49), (325), [592] + brother (43) N
(Egan, Mrs) estranged wife of Kevin Egan 43–44
Egan, Patrice French-born son of Kevin Egan (41–44), [592]
"EGLINTON, JOHN" 184 see Magee, William K.
(EKDAL, HEDVIG) daughter in Ibsen's *Wild Duck* S 86
("Elderflower, Miss Priscilla") participant in forest wedding 327
(ELEPHANTIS) Greek writer of erotica 516 N
("Elephantuliasis") 516 see Elephantis
(ELIAS OF CORTONA) 13th-century disciple of St. Francis S 176
ELIJAH the prophet whose second coming will herald the Messiah (151), (152), (227), (240), (249), (250), (279), (339), (345), (428), [507–8], (550), (676) A/N
(ELIZABETH) mother of John the Baptist P (248) N
(ELIZABETH I) queen of England Eliza Tudor 201, 205 A/N

Ellen Stephen's senile relative P 68
(Ellis, Mrs) mistress of school Bloom attended 77, 712 + husband (77) N
(ELLIS, WILLIAM) author of book on Madagascar owned by Bloom 708 A/N
("Ellpodbomool") 678 see Bloom, Leopold
("Elmshade, Lady Sylvester") participant in forest wedding 327
(ELSTER-GRIMES) Grand Opera Company, played in Dublin 92, 627 a/N
*(ELVERY, J. W.) proprietor of the Elephant house, seller of waterproofs 94, 272 N/T
(ELVIRA) heroine of Balfe's *The Rose of Castille* 297 A/N
(Emery, Robert) whose grave Bloom sees in Glasnevin 114
(Emma) S 44; P 219 see Clery, Emma
(EMMANUEL) 496; S 172 see Christ, Jesus
(EMMET, ROBERT) Irish martyr executed 1803 114, 240, My eppripfftaph 257, 290–91, 305 A/N
(EMPEDOCLES) 5th-century B. C. physiologist 418 A/N
Ennis dull student at Belvedere P 104, 105, 168–69
(ENO) purveyor of fruit salts S 52
(EPICTETUS) Greek philosopher 1st/2nd-century A.D. P 187, 194 N
(EPIPHANIUS, S.—THE MONK) 4th-century theologian 689 A/N
(EPPS) manufacturer of cocoa 657, 675, 676, 677, 775
(ESAU) son of Isaac, brother of Jacob 211, 473 A/N
(ESCHYLUS) S 97 see Aeschylus
(ESSEX, EARL OF/ROBERT DEVERAUX) Queen Elizabeth's paramour and victim 185 A/N
(ETERNAL, THE) G 14 see Jehovah
("Ethel") typical name assumed by Stephen for female acquaintances of his Dalkey students 25
(EUCLID) Greek mathematician D 9 N
("Eunuch") in Brini's genealogical progression 495
*(EUSTACE, DR HENRY M.) from whose private asylum Bloom is accused of escaping 493 N/T
Evans noiseless attendant at the National Library 184, 200, 211
(EVE) wife of Adam 38, 199, 297, 391–92, 514, 516; P 114, 117–18, 134 A/N

(EVERARD, COLONEL N. T.) tobacco experimenter in Ireland 640 A/N
("Everyman") personification of mankind 727 see Bloom, Leopold

(FABRINACCI, LEONARDO) 13th-century Pisan mathematician 637 a/n
(FACHTNA, S.) 8th-century Irish saint 339 A/N
*(FAGAN, REV. PETER) Marist Father at Catholic University School 317 N
(FAHRENHEIT, GABRIEL DANIEL) 18th-century German physicist 704
(FAIR REBEL) horse recalled by Stephen from his race track visit 32 A/N
*(FALCONER, JOHN) printer and publisher 95 N/T
*FALKINER, SIR FREDERICK RICHARD jurist, Recorder of Dublin (138), 182–83, (322–23), (344), [470–71] A/N/T; Introduction
(FALLON, WILLIAM) pupil at Belvedere P 163
("False Franklin, Mr") 396 see Lenehan, T.
(FALSTAFF) Shakespeare's foolish knight 204, 206 A/N
Fanning, "Long" John subsheriff of Dublin, "the long fellow" (119), (244), (245), 247–48, (252), (267), (282), (289), (299), (314), (375), [471]; D (123), (126), (127), (129), 172–74 N
("Fanny, Mad") 165 see Parnell, Frances Isabel
Farley American friend of Rivière D 46–48
Farley, Father priest whom Bloom tried to convince to take Molly into the choir (80), [490] N
(FARNABY, GILES AND RICHARD) father and son, 17th-century English composers 662 A/N
(Farrel, Pat) newsboy at the *Telegraph* 128
*FARRELL, CASHEL BOYLE O'CONNOR FITZMAURICE TISDALL Dublin eccentric, nicknamed "Endymion" 159, two loonies (164), 215, 244, 249–50, 254, (286), [511] N
(FARRELL, SIR THOMAS) Irish sculptor who executed the statue of Smith O'Brien 93 A/N
Farrington clerk at Crosbie & Alleyne D 86–98
(Farrington, Ada) Farrington's wife D 97
(Farrington, Charlie) Farrington's son D 97
Farrington, Tom Farrington's son D 97–98
("Fashion, Dame") personification of fashion 350

(FAUNTLEROY, "LITTLE" LORD) title hero of children's book S 88
(FAURE, FÉLIX) president of France toward end of the 19th century 43 A/N
(Fawcett) in *Freeman's Journal* obituary 91, 279
*(FAY, P.) cattle salesman, layman in clerical procession 318 N + *Thom's*, p. 1868
(FEHRENBACH) former butcher 234, 250 see Mangan, P.
(FELIX DE CANTALICE, S.) 16th-century Italian saint 339 A/N
(FELL, DOCTOR) 17th-century Oxford dean, subject of antipathetical epigram 354 A/N
(FENIUS FARSAIGH) progenitor of the Phoenicians and Milesians, according to Geoffrey Keating 688 A/N
(FERGUS) from song in Yeats's *Countess Cathleen* 9, 323, 608 A/N
("Ferguson, Miss") imagined beloved of Stephen 609, 656 see Fergus
(FERRANDO) in Verdi's *Il Trovatore* 39 A/N
(FERREOL, S.) early Christian martyr 339 A/N
(FESTE) clown in Shakespeare's *Twelfth Night* S 28–29
(FIACRE, S.) 7th-century Irish saint 42, 327, 339 A/N
*(FIELD, WILLIAM) M. P. and cattle traders' president 35, 314–15 N
*FIGATNER, AARON jeweler (259), [586] N/T + *Thom's*, p. 1869
("Finbad") 737 see Sinbad the Sailor
(FINBARR, S.) 7th-century bishop, founder of Cork 339 A/N
*(FINDLATER, ADAM S.) Dublin businessman, son of Alexander Findlater 58 A/N + *Thom's*, 1869
(FINDLATER, ALEXANDER) founder of provisions firm and church restorer 781; P 160 N/T
(FINGALL, LADY) 663 see Plunkett, Elizabeth Mary Margaret
(Finlay, H. B. Patterson) railway representative at Sinico inquest D 114
*(FINN, M. AND R.) 254 hotel proprietors
(FINN MacCOOL) 3rd-century leader of the Fianna 317, 323 A/N
(FINTAN, S.) 6th-century Irish monastic 339 A/N

*(FINUCANE, THOMAS D.) Dignam's doctor 472 N + *Thom's,* p. 1870
(FIONNUALA) daughter of Lir, turned into a swan 192 A/N
(FITTON, MARY) Queen Elizabeth's maid of honor, putative Dark Lady of the Sonnets 201 A/N
"Fitz" friend of Temple S 173–74
("Fitzedward, Lord Gerald") 599 see Fitzgerald, Lord Edward
*(FITZGERALD, D. AND T.) solicitors 125 N/T
(FITZGERALD, LORD EDWARD) a leader of the 1798 rebellion 241, 599 A/N
(FITZGERALD, GERALD) 8th Earl of Kildare, burned down Cashel cathedral 231 A/N
(FITZGERALD, JAMES FITZMAURICE) 10th Earl of Desmond, conspired against Henry VIII 328 A/N
(FITZGERALD, LORD THOMAS, "Silken Thomas") rebelled against Henry VIII 45, 230, 344, 628 A/N
*FITZGIBBON, GERALD Lord Justice of Appeal, debated against John Taylor (141–42), (397), [586] N/T
*FITZHARRIS, JAMES, "Skin-the-Goat" drove decoy car after Phoenix Park murders (136), (138), Periplepomenos (416), 621–60 A/N
(Fitzpatrick, James) boyhood friend of Bloom 682
Fitzpatrick, Mr secretary of the Eire Abu Society D 139–41, (141–42), (144), 146–49
*(FITZSIMON, H. O'CONNELL) superintendent of Food Market 294 A/N + *Thom's,* p. 1349
(Fitzsimons/FITZSIMMONS, ROBERT L.) English heavyweight champion toward end of the 19th century 251 A/N
(FLAHERTY, NELL) owner of drake—in song 524 A/N
(Flanagan) friend of Temple S 225–26
*(FLANAGAN, REV. JOHN) curate in charge of the Pro-Cathedral 318 N
(FLANDERS, MOLL) Defoe heroine 756 A/N
*(FLAVIN, REV. J.) curate at the Pro-Cathedral 317 N
FLEMING, ALOYSIUS Stephen's classmate at Clongowes P 13, (15), (16), 21, 40–45, 47–53
(Fleming, Jack) embezzler Bloom remembers who fled to America 86
Fleming, Lizzie employed at Dublin by Lamplight laundry D 101

(Fleming, Mrs) cleaning woman in the Bloom household 87, 89, 93, 675, 764, 768
(FLETCHER, JOHN) Elizabethan playwright 393 A/N
(Fleury, Henry) one of Mrs Dandrade's violators, according to Bello 536 see Flower, Henry
("FLIPPERTY JIPPERT") a fiend 519 A/N
*(FLINT) in marriage announcement in the *Irish Independent* 298 N
(FLOOD, HENRY) 18th-century Irish statesman 139; P 97 A/N/N
("Flor, Senhor Enrique") 327 see Flower, Henry
(FLORA) heroine in song 266 A/N
("Flora, Don Miguel de la") Molly's pretended Gibraltar novio 759 see Flower, Henry
("Flora, Don Poldo de la") 778 see Bloom, Leopold; Flower, Henry
["Florry-Teresa"] 509 see Talbot, Florry
("Florryzoe") 578 see Higgins, Zoe; Talbot, Florry
(FLOTOW, FRIEDRICH VON) composer of *Martha* 278 A/N
*(FLOWER AND M'DONALD) coal merchants 670 N/T + *Thom's*, p. 1475
"Flower, Henry" Bloom's pen name (72), (77–79), (91), (279–80), (285), (288), (290), false name (372), (455), (456), (492), [517–23], (544), (627), (721), (722), (735)
(Flowers) master at Clongowes Wood P 41
Flynn, Eliza sister of the dead priest D 14–18
(Flynn, James) dead priest D 9–18
Flynn, Mike Stephen's track coach P 61, 64
Flynn, Nannie sister of dead priest D 14–18
Flynn, "Nosey" acquaintance of Bloom and habitué of Davy Byrne's pub 171–79, 232, 253, (325), (370), [470], [487–88], [491], longnosed chap (765) N
Fogarty, Mr grocer friend of Power, Kernan, and Cunningham (99); D (155), 166–74 N
(FOOT, LUNDY, AND CO.) 253 tobacco wholesaler n/t
("Forrest, Mrs Liana") participant in the forest wedding 327
(FORREST, REV. DR) Dean of Worcester, performed wedding recorded in the *Irish Independent* 298 N
(Forster, Captain Francis) "Irish chieftain" presumably related to the ruling house of Belgium P 229–30 N

(FORTUNATUS, VENATIUS) 6th-century bishop and poet P 210 N
(Forty Warts) presumably predecessor of the visiting Alaki 334
(FOSTER, VERE HENRY LEWIS) 19th-century author of copybooks 720 A/N
(Foster/FORSTER, WILLIAM E. "BUCKSHOT") Irish chief secretary 1880–82 656 A/N
*FOTTRELL, GEORGE clerk of the crown and peace (344), [461] N + *Thom's,* p. 1874
(FOUTINUS, S.) 3rd-century bishop of Lyon 389 A/N
(FOX, GEORGE) Quaker founding father 193 A/N
("Fox, Mr") 492, 649; P 36 see Parnell, Charles Stewart
("Fraidrine") 214 see Ryan, Fred
(FRANCIS XAVIER, S.) 16th-century Jesuit missionary 670; P 56, 107–11 A/N/N
(FRANCIS, S.) 13th-century founder of Franciscan order 339; S 176 A/N
"François" Gallaher's appellation for the barman at Corless's, probably Frank D 74–82
(François, Master) 751 see Rabelais, François
Frank Eveline's sailor love D (37), (38–39), 40–41
(FRANKLIN, BENJAMIN) American statesman and inventor 297 A/N
*(FRANKS, DR Hy/HENRY JACOB) Dublin doctor with cure for clap 153, 523 see Hyman, p. 168.
("Frederick the Falconer, sir") 323 see Falkiner, Sir Frederick Richard
(FREEMAN, EDWARD AUGUSTUS) 19th-century English historian S 26
(FREYTAG, GUSTAV) 19th-century German novelist 709 A/N
(FRIDAY) Robinson Crusoe's man 109 N
*(FRIERY, CHRISTOPHER) solicitor 768 N
(FRIGIDIAN, S.) 6th-century Irish hermit 339 A/N
*(FROEDMAN, FRANCIS) pharmacist 668 N/T
(FRY) brand of chocolate 711
(Fulham, Mr) corn factor living below the Morkans D 176
Fulham, Mr Stephen's godfather in Mullingar S (48), (169), (216), (226), (228), (238–39), 240, 241–44, (245), 246–50, (253)
*(FULLAM, JOHN) ship's chandler 618 N/T + *Thom's,* p. 1876

(Furey, Michael) Gretta's adolescent love D 218–21, 223
Furlong, Miss guest at the Morkans' party D 182–84, 197–206
FURLONG, TOM pupil at Clongowes Wood P 49
(FURSA, S.) 7th-century Irish monk 297, 339 A/N
(FURSEY, S.) 339 see Fursa, S.

(GABLER, HEDDA) Ibsen heroine G 8
(GABRIEL) archangel of the Annunciation 358, 385; P 217 A/N/N
*(GAHAN, H. T.) competing bicyclist 237 N
(GALATEA) statue brought to life by Pygmalion 176 A
Galbraith, Mrs acquaintance of the Blooms [586], (751)
(GALILEO GALILEI) Italian astronomer 634, 700 A/N
(GALL, S.) 7th-century Irish monk 339 A/N
(Gallagher, Michael) carpenter who originally owned Bloom's geometry book 709
*(GALLAGHER, WILLIAM) grocer 221 N/T + *Thom's*, p. 1877
GALLAHER, FRED/Ignatius Dublin journalist on London press (88), (135–37); D (70–74), 74–82 N/N
*GALLAHER, GERALD pupil at Belvedere 220 n
*GALLAHER, MRS JOE acquaintance of Molly's, mother of Gerald (449), [586], (768) N
(GALLE, JOHANN) 19th-century German astronomer 700 A/N
(GALVANI, LUIGI) 18th-century Italian scientist P 213 N
[Galway, Mayor of] in procession honoring Bloom 480
*(GAMBLE, MAJ. GEORGE FRANCIS) director of Mt. Jerome cemetery 108 N
(Gann, Joe) hanged by Rumbold 203 A/N
(Gardner, Lt Stanley G.) British army officer involved with Molly 746, 747, 749, 762–63
(GARIBALDI, GIUSEPPE) 19th-century Italian nationalist 163 A/N
("Garry, Owen") 311 see Garryowen
Garryowen Giltrap's dog in the Citizen's care 295–345, 352 A
("Garth, Miss Olive") participant in forest wedding 327
Garvey, Mr journalist in Mullingar S (246), 250–53 + wife S (251)

(GATHERER, MAISTER) collector of entrance fee at the Globe 209 N
(GAUTAMA) 508 see Buddha, Gautama
(GAUTIER, THEOPHILE) 19th-century French poet 44 A/N
(Gavan, Miss) Eveline's superior at the Stores D 37
*(GEARY, JAMES W.) sexton at Glasnevin cemetery 99 N/T p. 66 + *Thom's*, p. 1876
(GEA-TELLUS) Greco-Roman personification of the earth 737 A/N
(GEORGE THE ELECTOR) King George I of England a gracious prince 330 A/N
(GEORGE IV) of England, visited Ireland in 1821 409, 628 A/N
(GEORGE V) Duke of York, then King of England 587 (here a statute of a previous King George), 679 A/N
(GEORGE, S.) patron saint of England 482, 597 A/N
*GERAGHTY, MICHAEL E. plumber who cheated Moses Herzog (292–93), (294), [586] N/T
["Gerald"] a moth, object of Virag's solicitousness 516–17
(Gerald) a boyhood confrere of Bloom's 536–37
(GERARD, JOHN) Elizabethan author on history of plants 202, 280, 661 A/N
(GERTRUDE) Hamlet's mother, the lustful queen 207
("Gerty") typical name that Stephen associates with the girl friends of his Dalkey pupils 25
(GERVASIUS, S.) 2nd-century Christian martyr 339 A/N
(GHERARDINO DA BORGO SAN DONNINO) 13th-century reformer of the Franciscan order P 220 N
*(GHEZZI, FR CHARLES) professor of Italian at U.C.D. P 192, 249 N
(GILBERT, WILLIAM SHWENK) writer of comic libretti with Arthur Sullivan P 192 N
(GILBEY, WILLIAM A.) bottler of gin and port 675
*(GILL, M. H., AND SON) Catholic booksellers 95, 186, 198 N/T
*(GILLEN, P.) hairdresser 433 N/T
(Gillespie, Miss) like Molly a visitor at the Dillons' who played the piano 758
(GILLETT, GEORGE ALFRED) deceased father of the bride in *Irish Independent* announcement 298 N

(GILLETT, ROSA) mother of bride in *Irish Independent* announcement 298 N
(GILLETT, ROTHA MARIAN/Marion) whose marriage is announced in the *Irish Independent* 298 N
(Gilligan, Philip) boyhood friend of Leopold Bloom fellow that died 114, 155, 682, 704 N
(Giltrap) Gerty MacDowell's maternal grandfather 312, 348, 352, 355 N
(GIOVANNI, DON) lover-hero of Mozart's opera 179, 180, 496 A/N
(GIRALDUS CAMBRENSIS) 12th/13th-century Welsh chronicler 326; P 230 A/N/N
(GIUGLINI, ANTONIO) 19th-century Italian tenor 374; D 199 A/N/N
(GLADSTONE, WILLIAM EWART) 19th-century British prime minister 80, 434, 716, 721; P 249; S 74, 157, 172 A/N/N
(GLAUBER, JOHANN) 17th-century German chemist 450 N
(GLAUCON) dialoguist in Plato's *Republic* 415 A/N
(GLEESON, MR WILLIAM) prefect at Clongowes P 40, 44, 45, 48, 54 Sullivan, pp. 34–41
("Glens of The Donoghue") 599 see O'Donoghue of the Glens
(Glory Alice!) 444
("Glory Allelujerum") 408 see Purefoy, Theodore
("Glycera") traditional Grecian pastoral female name 416 A/N
Glynn clerk in Guinness's and student at U.C.D. P 234–37; S 117–18, 129–30, 148, (159), (182), (202) + sister S (148), (182)
Glynn, Joseph presumably organist at Church of St. Francis Xavier (82), (288), [499]
Glynn, Mme superannuated singer at Eire Abu concert D 143, 147
(GODIVA, LADY) rode naked through Coventry to protest her husband's tax 297 A/N
(GOERZ) German optical manufacturers 166 N
(GOETHE, JOHANN WOLFGANG VON) 184, 196; P 211; S 41, 43, 201 A/N/N
*(GOFF, JAMES) tax official 39 *Thom's*, p. 98
*(GOGARTY, OLIVER ST JOHN) friend of Joyce in Dublin G 15 see Mulligan, Malachi; Doherty; Goggins

Goggins drinking companion of Lynch P (204), 229–32, (235)
(Gold Stick in Waiting, Lord Walkup on Eggs) presents the cotton magnates to the Alaki 334
(Goldberg, Mr) of the Liffey Loan Bank D 159
*GOLDBERG, OWEN Bloom's childhood friend (162), [548], (667) N
("Goldfinger") one of the yellow children to whom Bloom gives birth 494
(GOLDSMITH, OLIVER) 18th-century Irish-born author 228 A/N/T
*[GOLDWATER, JOSEPH] one of Bloom's minyan 544 N + Hyman, p. 328.
(GOLIATH) Philistine giant killed by David 296 A/N
(GOMEZ, FERNANDO) Spanish torero 755 A/N
*(GONNE, MAUD) militant Irish nationalist 43, 72 A/N
("Goodbody") a common name 622
(GOODRICH, SAMUEL G.) 19th-century American publisher P 53 N
Goodwin, Professor doddering pianist who once accompanied Molly (63), (155), (156), (268), (284), [575], (731), (745), (747), (775) N
(GORDON, GEN. CHARLES GEORGE) 19th-century British military hero 757 A/N
(GORDON, DR W.) with wife & child in births column of the *Irish Independent* 298 N
(GORGIAS) 4th/5th-century B.C. Greek philosopher 148, 201 N
*(GORMAN, REV. BERNARD) provincial, St. Teresa's R.C. church 317 N
*(GORMAN, REV. TIMOTHY CANON) parish priest of SS Michael & John's R. C. church 318 N
(GOUGH, GEN. HUGH) Anglo-Irish military leader 457 A/N
(Goulding, Christina "Crissie") daughter of Richard and Sara Goulding 39, 88, wise child 273
(Goulding, Christina Grier) mother of Richie Goulding 682
("Goulding, Collis and Ward") 88 see Collis and Ward; Goulding, Richard "Richie"
Goulding, John brother of Richie Goulding (38), (237); S (134), 166 + wife S (166)
(Goulding, Richard) father of Richie Goulding 682
Goulding, Richard "Richie" Mr. Dedalus's brother-in-law, cost

drawer for Collis & Ward (38–39), (88), (160), 232, 252, 265–91, (370), [446–47], [528] T
(Goulding, Sara "Sally") wife of Richie Goulding 38–39, 41, 88
(Goulding, Walter) son of Richie Goulding 38–39, 273
(GOUNOD, CHARLES) 19th-century French composer 745 A/N
(GRANT, ULYSSES S.) U.S. general and president 757 A/N
(GRANUAILE/GRACE O'MALLEY) Irish sea captain and piratess 330 A/N
(GRATTAN, HENRY) 18th/19th-century Irish statesman 139, 228, 599; P 97 A/N/N/T
[GRAY, DOLLY] song heroine 589 A/N
(GRAY, EDMUND DWYER) owner of *Freeman's Journal,* son of Sir John Gray D 170 N
(GRAY, SIR JOHN) owner of *Freeman's Journal,* M. P., Irish patriot 94, 150, 276; D 170 A/N/N/T
*(GRAY, KATHERINE) confectioner 180 N/T
(GREATRAKES, VALENTINE) 17th-century Irish healer 297 A/N
*GREEN, M. C. in bicycle race 254
*(GREEN, REV. T. R.) Free Church preacher 220 N + *Thom's,* p. 1855
(GREENE, ROBERT) Elizabethan playwright 187 A/N
*(GREENE, ROGER) solicitor 252, 372 N/T + *Thom's,* p. 1886
("Greene, Mrs Rowan") participant in forest wedding 327
*(GREGORY, LADY AUGUSTA) Irish writer and patroness 216 A/N
*(GREY, GREGOR) artist 137 N + *Thom's,* p. 1886
(Griffin) student at U.C.D. P 210
("Griffin, Peggy") name "Martha Clifford" claims is her real one 456 + brother 456
*(GRIFFITH, ARTHUR) Nationalist editor and founder of Sinn Fein 43, 57, 72, 163–64, 334, 335, 599, 748, the little man 772; S 61 A/N
(Grimes) canvassed by O'Connor D 123–24
(Grimes, Mary) character in anecdote D 183
Grimes, Michael Dublin pawnbroker D 172–74
(GRIMM, JACOB AND WILHELM) 19th-century collectors of fairy tales 210–11 A/N

(GRISELDA) patient heroine in Boccaccio and Chaucer 201 A/N
Grogan, old mother character in Irish song (12–13), (217), (404), [490–92] N
*(GROGAN, R.) tobacconist 221 N/T
(Grove[s], Capt.) Gibraltar comrade of Brian Tweedy 755, 756, 757, 782
(GRUNDY, MRS) barometer of British propriety, from 1798 play 646 A/N
(GUELPH-WETTIN, EDWARD) 330 see Edward VII
("Guggenheim") in Brini's genealogical list 495
(GUGGENHEIM, MEYER) founder of wealthy American family 719 A/N
(Guido) 45 see Cavalcanti, Guido
*(GUINNESS, ARTHUR EDWARD, LORD ARDILAUN) son of brewer Benjamin Lee Guinness 79, 81, 117, 131, 240, Bungardilaun 299, 332, 382, 425, two ardilauns 425, 492, 532, 534; S 193 A/N/T
*(GUINNESS, EDWARD CECIL, LORD IVEAGH) son of brewer Benjamin Lee Guinness 79, 81, 117, 131, 240, Bungiveagh 299, 332, 382, 425, 492, 532, 534; S 115 A/N/T
Gumley down-and-out friend of Mr. Dedalus, night watchman for Dublin Corporation (136), 615–16, 618, 639, 660
("Gummy Granny") 595 see Old Gummy Granny
*(GUNN, MICHAEL) 19th-century impresario at the Gaiety Theatre 284, 636, 678, 769 + wife (678) A/N
("Gutenberg, Murtagh") composite name in list of Irish heroes 297 A/N
(GWYNN, NELL) actress, mistress of Charles II 204, 370 A/N

(H. P. B.) 185 see Blavatsky, Mme Helena P.
("H_2O") medical columnist in McCann's review S 182
*(HACKETT, FELIX) Stephen's classmate at U.C.D. P 199 Sullivan, p. 187
*(HACKETT, REV. M. A.) parish priest, St. Margaret's R. C. church 318 N
(HADES!) Greek god of the underworld 464
(HAGAR) Sarah's handmaid, Abraham's concubine 409 A/N

(HAINAU, HERR HAUPTMANN) Austrian army captain, suggested as possible blond ancestor for Milly 693

Haines English friend of Mulligan (4), (7), The Sassenach (9), 11–16, 17–23, (25), His seacold eyes (30), the panthersahib (44), he woke me up (47), (186), (192). (198), (215), 248–49, 253, 412, English tourist friend (620) + father (7) N

[HAINES LOVE, REV. MR HUGH C.] 599 see Haines; Love, Rev. Hugh C.

(HALL, ELIZABETH) Shakespeare's granddaughter 203, 213 A/N

*(HALL, JACK B.) journalist 130 N

(Halliday) athletic pupil at Mr. Deasy's school 29

*(HALLIDAY, JACOB) grocer and wine merchant 323 N + *Thom's,* p. 1889

(Halpin) student at U.C.D. P 210

(Halpin, Dr) medical testimony at Sinico inquest D 114

(HAM) son of Noah 171, 497 A/N

*(HAMILTON, LONG AND CO.) pharmacists 84, 551 N/T

(HAMLET) prince of Denmark 16, 17, 18, 28, 47, 76, 126, 152, 184–88, 194, 195, 197, 198, 204, 207, 208, 212, 213, 215, 394, 561, 595; G 10

(HAMLET) deceased king of Denmark He died in his sleep 139, 152, 188–89, 197, ghost's 202, 213, 394, sleepin in hes bit garten 425, List, list 473, 561 A/N

(Hampton Leedom's) 543 see Leedom, Hampton, & Co.

(Han, Li Chi) prototypal oriental lover 333

(Hancock) acquaintance from whom Bloom hopes to get a pass to the Guinness brewery 152

Hand, Robert journalist, friend of Richard Rowan E (19), (20–22), 25–45, (47–51), (52–55), 57–72, (72–75), 76–88, (94–101), (104), 104–10, (112) + mother (21), (26), (30), (36), (50)

*(HAND, STEPHEN) illegally steamed open telegram for horse race information 426 N

(HANDEL, GEORGE FREDERIC) whose *Messiah* was premiered in Dublin 183 A/N

("HANDY ANDY") 530 see Rooney, Andy

*(HANLON, MICHAEL "MICKY") fishmonger 175 N/T + *Thom's,* p. 1890

*(HANLON, S.) milkman 56 N/T

(HANNIGAN) in Percy French song 42 A/N
(Harakiri, Hokopoko) member of the F. O. T. E. I. 307
Harford money lender, one of Kernan's drinking companions D (150), (159–60), 172–74
Harford, Mr master at Clongowes Wood P 46
(HARMSWORTH, ALFRED C.) British publisher 139 A/N
*[HARRINGTON, TIMOTHY] former Lord Mayor of Dublin 479 N
(HARRIS, FRANK) English writer and editor 196 A/N
(HARRIS, JOHN) translator of Bloom's geometry book 709 A
*(HARRIS, MORRIS) art dealer and jeweler 166 N/T + Hyman, p. 148
*(HARRISON AND CO.) confectioners 157, 159 N/T
("Harry"!) the devil 39 N
(Harry) 202 see Henry VIII
("Harry") 650 see Tom, Dick, and Harry
("Harry, Lord") 400–401 see Henry II; Henry VII; Henry VIII
(HART, MICHAEL) dead Dubliner, known to Bloom 705 N
*(HARTY, SPENCER) engineer for Dublin waterworks 671 N + *Thom's*, p. 1893
(HARVEY) in litigation against insurance company 236 N
(HARVEY, MARTIN) 357, 767 see Martin-Harvey, Sir John
(HASTINGS, LORD) 32 see Rawdon-Hastings, Henry Weysford
(HAUCK, MINNIE) American opera singer 527 A/N
(HAUPTMANN, GERHART) German dramatist D 108; P 176 N
(HAWKINS, SIR JOHN) English explorer credited with bringing the potato to England 478 A
("Hawthorne, Miss May") participant in forest wedding 327
(HAYE, MARY CECIL) 19th-century English novelist 229 A/N
(Hayes) in list of Irish heroes 297 N
*[HAYES, COL. BAXTER] Railway police chief inspector 586 n
(Hayes, Mrs) acquaintance of Molly Bloom 448
("Hazeleyes, Mrs Holly") participant in forest wedding 327

(Healy, Father) of Adam and Eve's church D 195
Healy, Father brother of Mrs. Daniel S 156–59, (233)
(HEALY, REV. JOHN "WADDLER") archbishop of Tuam 297 A/N
Healy, Miss contralto, friend of Kathleen Kearney D 143, 145–49
*HEALY, TIMOTHY MICHAEL Irish politician, Parnell's lieutenant who turned against him (141), (397), [586]; S (207) A/N + *Thom's,* p. 1895
(HEBER/EIBHEAR) legendary Milesian settler of Ireland 688 A/N
("HEBLON") 685 see O'Connor, Joseph K.
(HEENAN, JOHN C.) 19th-century American boxer 242, 318 A/N
Heffernan, Mr Mullingar neighbor of Stephen's godfather S 246–50
(Heffernan, Pat) son of Mr. Heffernan S 246–47
(Hegarty, Aunt) presumably Bloom's maternal aunt or great-aunt 542
(HELEN OF TROY) a woman who was no better than she should be 33–34, 132, 148, 149, 201 A/N
(HELMER, NORA) heroine of Ibsen's *A Doll's House* S 86
*HELY, CHARLES WISDOM stationer and printer, former Bloom employer (106), (114), (154–55), (227), (229), (253), (263), (364), (446), (465), [586], (720), (731), (753), (772) N/T + *Thom's,* p. 1895
(HELY-HUTCHINSON, JOHN) 18th-century Irish statesman P 97 N
(Henchy, John) political canvasser for Tierney D 122–35
Hendrick, Mr *Freeman's Journal* reporter D 144–45, 172–74
(HENGLER, ALBERT) 19th-century circus proprietor 64, 624, 696 A/N
[Hennessy, Don Emile Patrizio Franz Rupert Pope] composite personification of the Irish Wild Geese 592 A/N see also Hennessy, Sir John Pope
*[HENNESSY, SIR JOHN POPE] anti-Parnell politician 592 A/N
(Henry) mourned in newspaper obituary commemoration 91 see also Flower, Henry
*(HENRY AND JAMES) clothiers 253 N/T see also James, Henry

(HENRY II) 12th-century king of England during annexation of Ireland 400–401 A/N
(HENRY VII) 15th/16th-century king of England 400–401 N
(HENRY VIII) 16th-century king of England 202, 328, 400–401 A/N
*HENRY, JAMES J. "JIMMY" assistant town clerk 246–47, [487], [586] N + *Thom's,* p. 1896
(HERBERT, WILLIAM, EARL OF PEMBROKE) possible rival for Shakespeare's dark lady 196, spurned him for a lord 202 A/N
(HERCULES) 326, 345 N
(HEREMON/EIREMHON) one of the legendary Milesians, brother of Heber 688 A/N
(HERMAN-JOSEPH, "S.") 12th/13th-century German mystic, beatified 339 A/N
(HERMES TRISMEGISTOS) occultic pseudo-author 510 A/N
(HEROD) Roman pro-consul in Judea 423 A/N
(HERODOTUS) 5th-century B.C. Greek historian 297 N
Heron, Vincent Stephen's antagonist and later friend at Belvedere P 75–78, 79–83, 105–6, 125
(HERPYLLIS) Aristotle's mistress 204, a light of love 432 A/N
(HERSCHEL, SIR WILLIAM) 18th/19th-century English astronomer 700 A/N
(HERTWIG, OSCAR) German embryologist 418 A/N
*HERZOG, MOSES grocer (292–93), trading without a licence (335), [544], [586] N/T + Hyman, p. 329.
*(Hesseltine, lieutenant colonel H. C./HESELTINE, LT-COL C.) aide-de-camp to the Lord Lieutenant 252–55 N
("Hickey, Brother") typical Christian Brother P 166
*(HICKEY, REV. LOUIS J.) provincial at St. Saviour's Dominican Priory 317 N
*(HICKEY, MICHAEL) bookseller D 188 T
*(HICKS, CECIL) scenery designer for Gaiety Theatre pantomime 678 N
("Hielentman, Jock braw") 425 A/N see Crotthers, J.
Higgins fellow employee of Farrington D (92), 93–94
("Higgins") 485 see Bloom, Leopold
(Higgins, Fanny) Bloom's maternal grandmother 682

(HIGGINS, FRANCIS) betrayer of Lord Edward Fitzgerald that sham squire 241, 296 A/N
(Higgins, Julius) Bloom's maternal grandfather 682
Higgins, Miss guest at the Morkans' party D 197–206
Higgins, Zoe prostitute at Bella Cohen's 475–78, 499–586
(Hill, Ernest) Eveline's dead brother D 36, 38, 39
Hill, Eveline young girl employed at the Stores D 36–41 + father & mother D (36–37), (38), (39), (40) + two younger siblings D (38)
(Hill, Harry) Eveline's older brother D 38, 39
("Hinbad") 737 see Sinbad the Sailor
(HIRSCH, MAURICE, BARON DE) wealthy Jewish philanthropist 719 A/N
[Hobgoblin] celestial croupier 506
*(HODGES, FIGGIS AND CO.) booksellers 48 N/T
(Hogan) crony of Gallaher and Chandler D 75–76, 77, 78
(Hogan, Dan) whose nephew is present at the Gardiner Street Jesuit retreat D 172–74
*(HOLE) defendant in 1901 libel case 321 A/N
[Hollybush*] one of Bloom's accusers 496 N
(HOLMES, SHERLOCK) 495, 636 A/N
Holohan, "Hoppy" lame pub crawler, works for the Eire Abu Society (73–74), (136), [491], [586]; D (58), 136, 138–40, (141–42), 143–49 N
("Holyoake, Mrs Norma, of Oakholme Regis") participant in forest wedding 327
(HOMER) 187, 216 A/N
("Honeysuckle, Miss Bee") participant in forest wedding 327
*(HOOPER, ALDERMAN JOHN) politician and father of Paddy Hooper, old friend of the Blooms 113, 707, 731 N
*(HOOPER, PATRICK "PADDY") *Freeman's Journal* reporter, son of Alderman Hooper 130, 137 N + *Thom's,* p. 1900
*(HOPKINS AND HOPKINS) jewelers P 177 T
(HORACE) Roman poet P 179 N
(Horan) drinking companion of Lynch P 204
*(HORNE, SIR ANDREW JOHN) doctor in charge of the National Maternity Hospital 159, Horhorn 383, 385, 388, 392, 395, 397, 403, 407, 417, 420, 423 A/N + *Thom's,* p. 1901
(HORTENSIO) character in Shakespeare's *Taming of the Shrew* 191 A/N
(HORUS) Egyptian god, son of Isis & Osiris 142 A/N

(HOSEA) 8th-century B.C. Hebrew prophet G 10
Howard, Miss niece of Stephen's godfather S 239–41, (242), 248–50, 253
(Howth, Ben*) the Hill of Howth 297 N
(HOZIER, COL. SIR HENRY MONTAGUE) author of book on Russo-Turkish War in Bloom's library 709 A/N
(HUBBARD, OLD MOTHER) nursery rhyme provider 326 A/N
*HUGGARD, W. C. in bicycle race 254
(HUGH) presumably one of the 12 tribes, probably 6th-century Irish king 323 N
(HUGH, RED) S 63 see O'Donnell Magnus, Hugh Roe
(HUGHES, HARRY) victim of Jew's daughter—in medieval ballad 690–92 A/N
*HUGHES, REV. JOHN of St. Francis Xavier's church 354, (356), 382, [469] N + *Thom's,* p. 1902
Hughes, Mr Gaelic League teacher S 59–60, (63), (82–83), 103–5, (107–8), (115–16), 155–59, (176), (181), (182) + father (60)
(HUGHES, WILLIE) presumably boy actor in Shakespeare's company 198 A/N
(HUGO, VICTOR) 19th-century French author P 156 N
("Human Ostrich") carnival freak S 133
*HUMBLE, WILLIAM 252 see Dudley, Earl of
(HUNGERFORD, MARGARET) 19th-century English novelist 756 A/N
(Hunter, Mabel) presumably an actress P 67 N
*(HURLEY, REV. WALTER) curate at St. James's R. C. church 318 N + *Thom's,* p. 1903
*HUTCHINSON, JOSEPH Lord Mayor of Dublin in 1904 (247), [480] N + *Thom's,* p. 1903
*(HYDE, DOUGLAS) Irish writer and Gaelic revivalist 186, 198, Little Sweet Branch 312 A/N
(Hynes) medical graduate of U.C.D. P 126
Hynes, Joseph M'Carthy "Joe" newspaper reporter and sentimental Parnellite (90), 100, 111–13, 118–19, (180), 292–345, (375), (381), [471–72], [486], [488], [586], (647), (704), (739); D 120–24, (124–25), 133–35 N
(Hynes, Larry) father of Joe Hynes D 124

(IAGO) villain in Shakespeare's *Othello* 30, 209, 212, 567 A/N
(IAR) one of the sons of the legendary Milesius 323 N
(IBSEN, HENRIK) Norwegian dramatist 614; P 176; S 40–41, the person 45–46, 52, 84–88, 91–96, 102 A/N/N
(ICARUS) airborne son of Daedalus 210 A/N
("Ichabudonosor") in Brini's genealogical list 495
(ICHTHYOSAURUS*) extinct creature rather than a person 514 N
("Idolores") 256, 261, 265, 269 see Dolores
(Ignat, F.) presumably author of Bloom's geometry book 709 A/N
("Ikey Mo") 466 see Bloom, Leopold; Ikey Moses
("Ikey Moses") 201 N see Bloom, Leopold
(IMOGEN) character in Shakespeare's *Cymbeline* 197 A/N
(Ines) old servant in Gibraltar remembered by Molly 760
(INGERSOLL, ROBERT G.) 19th-century American agnostic 508 A/N
(INGOMAR) hero of German melodrama P 97
*(INGRAM, JOHN KELLS) Irish writer 241 A/N
(INNOCENT II) pope who sent the first cardinal to Ireland S 53
(INNOCENT III) 12th/13th-century pope P 128
(Inverarity, John Duncan) previous co-owner of Stephen's copy of Horace P 179
(Inverarity, William Malcolm) previous co-owner of Stephen's copy of Horace P 179
(IOPAS, HAIRY!) bard of Apollo in the *Aeneid* 315 A/N
(IREMONGER) cricketer for Nottingham 659 N
(IRVING, HENRY) 19th-century English actor 495; S 97 A/N
*(IRWIN, T. CAULFIELD) Irish poet 192 A/N
(ISAAC) son of Abraham, father of Jacob & Esau 340 A/N
("Isaacs") 424 see Bloom, Leopold
(ISAACS, RUFUS) Jewish-British political figure 690 A/N
("ISCARIOT") 497 see Dodd, Reuben J.; Judas Iscariot
(ISIDORE ARATOR, S.) 12th-century Spanish saint, patron of Madrid 339 A/N
(ISIS) Egyptian goddess 142 A/N

(ISOLDE) betrothed to Mark, beloved of Tristan 297, 332 A/N
(ITA, S.) 6th-century Irish female saint 339 A/N
*(IVEAGH, LORD) 79; S 115 see Guinness, Edward Cecil
*(IVERS, REV. JOHN MICHAEL) curate of St. Paul's R. C. church 317 N + *Thom's,* p. 1910
(IVES, S.) 13th-century Breton lawyer 339 A/N
Ivors, Molly Nationalist friend of the Conroys D 187–90, (190–91), (192), 195–96, (203), (219)

Jack the boy's uncle in "The Sisters" D 10
(JACK) the boy made dull by too much work—in aphorism D 34
("Jack") hypothetical lover in Bloom's thoughts 169
(JACK) housebuilder—in nursery rhyme 391, 394 A/N
("Jack") possible first name for Mulvey, rejected by Molly 761
(JACK THE GIANTKILLER) in nursery rhyme 297 A/N
(JACK THE RIPPER) London murderer of prostitutes 470 A/N
Jack, old caretaker in Tierney's headquarters D 118–35 + son (119–20) + wife (120)
("Jack-in-the-Box, Father") the proverbial confessor S 209
(Jacko) in colloquial expression 245 A
*(JACKSON, GEORGE A.) scene designer for Gaiety Theatre pantomime 678 N
*JACKSON, J. A. winner of bicycle race 237 N
(JACOB) son of Isaac, brother of Esau 122, 340, 413, 437, 517, 698 A/N
*(JACOB, WILLIAM AND R.) biscuit manufacturers 305, 343, 473; P 220 A/N/T
(JACOPONE/JACOPO DEI BENEDETTI DA TODI) 13th-century mad Italian poet S 178
(JACQUARD, JOSEPH MARIE) 19th-century French inventor of a loom 326 A/N
(Jakers!) 324 N
(James!) 427
(JAMES OF COMPOSTELLA, S.—THE GREATER) apostle 29, 339 A/N
(JAMES OF DINGLE, S.) 339 see James of Compostella
(JAMES I) first Stuart king of England 185, Scotch philophaster 205; P 233; G 9 A/N/N

("James, Barton") 279 see Barton, James
*(JAMES, CHARLES A.) hardware dealer & waxworks owner 636, 683 N/T
(JAMES, HENRY) American author 253 N
(JAMES, S.—THE LESS) apostle, bishop of Jerusalem 339; P 106 A/N
*(JAMESON, JOHN, AND SON) Dublin whiskey distiller 179, 341, 775 N/T
(Jamesy!) James Joyce himself 769; G 15
*(JAMMET BROS.) restaurateurs 371, 606 N/T
("Jane, Plain") name used by Bloom to describe Monks' daughter 122
(JAPHET) son of Noah, in Marryat title 18 A/N
(JARLATH OF TUAM, S.) 6th-century Irish bishop 339 A/N
("Jasperstone") in Brini's genealogical list 496 N
(Jay!) 424
(Jays!) 450 see Christ, Jesus
("JAYSUS") S 113, 138 see Christ, Jesus
(JEEP, JOHANNES) 17th-century German composer 663 A/N
*JEFFS, J. B. in bicycle race 254
(JEHOVAH) collector of prepuces 13, shout in the street 34, 201; S 135, 147, 188; G 14 A
(JEHU) a coachman 613 A/N
(JENATZY, CAMILLE) Germano-Belgian auto racer 427; driver of the winning German car D 42 A/N
("Jenny") 324 see Tupper, Belle
("Jerry") slang expression 591 N
(JESU) 387 see Christ, Jesus
("Jersurum") in Brini's genealogical list 495 N see Christ, Jesus
(JESUS) see Christ, Jesus
(Jesusjack!) 742
(JEYES) British manufacturer of cleaning supplies 485 N
(JIM) James Joyce himself G 15
("Jinbad") 737 see Sinbad the Sailor
(JOACHIM OF FLORA/FLORIS) 12th-century Italian theologian 39, 243; S 176–77; G 1 A/N
(JOAN) superannuated wife in song 423 A/N
(JOAN OF ARC/JEANNE D'ARC) S 152
("Joe") in colloquial expression 160

(Joe) fat boy in Dickens' *Pickwick Papers* 188 A/N
("Joe") possible first name for Mulvey, rejected by Molly 761
(JOHN BERCHMANS, S.) 17th-century Jesuit, patron of youth 339; P 56 A/N/N
(JOHN NEPOMUC, S.) 14th-century Bohemian martyr 339 A/N
(JOHN OF GOD, S.) 16th-century founder of the Order of the Brothers Hospitallers 293, 339 A/N
(JOHN O'GAUNT) horse in the 1904 Derby 174 N
(JOHN THE BAPTIST) 728; S 151–52 A/N
(JOHN THE EVANGELIST, S.) disciple and gospeler P 248 N
John, uncle Stephen's maternal uncle (237); S (134), 166 see Goulding, John
("John, uncle") in scurrilous song 776
(Johnny) grandson of old peasant in story about the west of Ireland S 243
("Johnny") in popular expression 124 N
("Johnny") archetypal soldier in Civil War song 378 A/N
(Johnny Magories*) fruit of the hawthorn tree 174 N
(Johnson, Georgina) Stephen's favorite prostitute 189, 433, 559–60 N
(JOHNSON, REV. JAMES "JIMMY") 19th-century Presbyterian minister whose name became a popular expression 320 N
(Johnston, Gilmer) Protestant minister who baptized Bloom 682
(Johnston, R. G.) scheduled to write music for Bloom's Brian Boru song 678
*JOLY, CHARLES JASPER Astronomer Royal of Ireland (167), [586] N + *Thom's,* p. 1913
("Jones") figure in Bloom's projected advertisement 154
("Jones") hypothetical writer of letter exposing illicit lovers 655
("Jones, Davy") personification of the briny deep 379, 624 A/N
("Jones-Smith") in Brini's genealogical list 496
(JONSON, BEN) Elizabethan writer 185; P 176, 189 A/N/N
(JOSÉ, DON) Carmen's lover 212 A/N
(JOSEPH) whose Messiah will precede the Messiah Ben David 495 A/N

(Joseph) horse that figured in young Milly's dream 694
(JOSEPH, S.) husband of Mary 19, 41, 82, 339 (see also O'Molloy, J. J.), his uncle 342, 349, 391, 653; P 147; S 232 A/N
(Josephine) a relative of Stephen's P 68
(JOVE!) S 246
(JUAN, DON) legendary Spanish seducer 467 A/N see also Giovanni, Don
(JUBAINVILLE, MARIE HENRI D'ARBOIS DE) professor of Celtic in Paris 186 A/N
(JUDAS IACCHIAS) 520 see Judas Iscariot a/N
(JUDAS ISCARIOT) betrayer of Christ 213, 217, 267 (see Dodd, Reuben J.), 247 (see Bloom, Leopold), 520, 600 (see Lynch, Vincent), 615 (see Lynch, Vincent) A/N
(JUDGE, WILLIAM QUAN) Dublin theosophist, 19th-century 185 a/N
(JUGGERNAUT) Hindu god whose vehicle crushes those who hurl themselves beneath 452; G 7
(JULIAN HOSPITATOR, S.) penitent patron of hospitality 339 A/N
(JULIET) 333; D 186 see Capulet, Juliet
("JUNIUS") anonymous writer of public letter satirizing George III 337 A/N
(JUNO) Roman goddess 176, 202, oxeyed goddess 322, 415 (!) A/N
(JUPITER PLUVIUS) Roman god, bringer of rain 614 A/N
Justice, Beatrice friend of Richard Rowan, and his son's piano teacher E 16–30, 44–45, (53–55), (74), (75), 93–102, (103), (109) + father E (30)
(Justice, Jack "Doggy") Beatrice Justice's cousin E 105, 108
(JUVENAL) Roman satirist 326 A/N

(K. H.) 185 see Koot Hoomi
*(KANE, MATTHEW F.) Dubliner drowned 10 July 1904 704–5 N + *Thom's*, p. 1915
(Karamelopulos, Count Athanatos) member of the F.O.T.E.I. 307
[Karini] apparently part of a dancing duo 545
(Karoly) 682 see Higgins, Julius
[Kate, Cunty] denizen of Nighttown 590, 597

(KATHERINE) heroine of Shakespeare's *Taming of the Shrew* 191 A/N
(KATHLEEN NI HOULIHAN) personification of Ireland 184–85, 330 A/N
*(KAVANAGH, J.) farrier 613 N/T
*(KAVANAGH, JAMES) publican 246–47, 253; D 126 N/T + *Thom's,* p. 1915
(KAVANAGH, MICHAEL) accomplice in Phoenix Park murders 136 A/N
*(KAVANAGH, P. J./PATRICK FIDELIS) Irish priest, writer and orator 317 N + *Thom's,* p. 1915
Keane, Mr professor of English at U.C.D. and writer for *Freeman's Journal* S (27), 100–105
*(KEARNEY, JOSEPH) bookseller 65 N
Kearney, Kathleen singer and pianist (748), (762); D (137–38), 139, 141, 143, (144), 145–49, (189) + sister D (137) N
Kearney, Mr Kathleen's father, a bootmaker, and Bloom's library guarantor? (65), the noble lord, his patron (409); D (137), 141, 143, 145–46, 148–49 see also Kearney, Joseph
Kearney, Mrs (nee Devlin) Kathleen's mother D 136–49
"Kearns, Anne" one of Stephen's fictional midwives 37, two maries 45, (145–50), Two old women 242, two sanded women 254, two trickies [579]
(KEATS, JOHN) English Romantic poet 509; S 148 A/N
(Keegan, Pat) porter at the Mansion House D 128
(Keevers, Johnny) university crony of Mr. Dedalus P 90
Kelleher, Cornelius "Corny" undertaker's assistant (71), (89–90), (98), 100–101, 103–9, (163), 221, 224–25, (301–2), (320), 321–22, (324), S. Cornelius (339), [579], 585–86, 603–8, (614), (647) N
*(Kellet/KELLETT, DANIEL) draper 529 N/T
(Kelly) disappearing man—in song 97, Key ee double ell 112 A/N
Kelly, Bridie Bloom's boyhood seductress (413), [441]
(Kelly, Dan) from whom Dilly Dedalus received her bracelet 243
(KELLY, DOMINIC) pupil at Clongowes Wood P 46
*(KELLY, DUNNE AND CO.) tanners 47 T
(Kelly, Mary) loved by Constable 14A 333
(KELLY, PADDY) name given to a 19th-century Irish humor weekly 139 A/N

*(KELLY, TERENCE) pawnbroker D 92–93 + clerk D 93 T
(KELLY, TIM) implicated in Phoenix Park murders 136 A/N
(Kempthorpe, Clive) Oxford student being ragged—in incident visualized by Stephen 7
(KENDAL, WILLIAM HUNTER) with wife, English acting duo 769 A/N
(KENDALL, MARIE) English actress and singer 229, 232, 251 A/N
*(KENNEDY, JAMES AND CHARLES) wine merchants 245 N/T + *Thom's,* p. 1920
Kennedy, Mina barmaid at the Ormond 246, 252, gold (256–57), 257–65, (266), 268–91, [564–66] N
(Kennedy, Miss) two sisters mentioned by students at Clonliffe S 74
*(KENNEDY, PETER) hairdresser 240 N/T
[Kennefick, Mrs] one of Bloom's pursuers 586
(Kenny/KENNEY, REV. PETER) Jesuit who founded Clongowes Wood College P 56 N
*(KENNY, DR ROBERT D.) surgeon who attended Mrs. Dedalus 207 N + *Thom's,* p. 1921
(Keogh) Eveline's childhood playmate D 36
("Keogh, Brother") Stephen's designation for typical Christian Brother P 166
("Keogh, Katey") name used by Bloom in verse for Milly 63
Keogh, Mrs presumably the cook at Bella Cohen's [533–34], (539)
*(KEOGH, MYLER L.) Dublin boxer 173, 250–51, 318–19 A/N
*(KEOGH, THOMAS) grocer + clerk 268 N
Keon, Father black-sheep priest D 125–26, (126–27) N
(KEPLER, JOHANN) 17th-century German astronomer 700 A/N
Kernan, Mrs wife of Tom Kernan D 154–58, 161–62, 166, 170–72
Kernan, Tom tea salesman and gin drinker (71), (90–91), 100–102, 105–7, (161), (172), 238, 239–41, 252, Ker (257), 276–91, [470], [483], (647), (704), (729), (773); D 150–54, 156–74 + two older sons D (156) + 3 younger children D (154) N

Kerrigan, Mr guest at the Morkan's party D 183–84
("Kerry Boy") in *Mr Dooley in Peace and War* P 95 N
*(Kerwan/KERWIN, MICHAEL) builder 164 N
(KEVIN, S.) Glendalough monk, patron saint of Dublin 323, 339 A/N
*KEYES, ALEXANDER tea merchant from whom Bloom solicits advertisement (107), (116–17), (119–22), the boss (128), (129), (146), (180), (183), (260), (323), (381), House of Keys (474), [489], [586], (647), (683), (728), an advertisement (729), (775) N/T
(KIAR) son of Queen Maeve 295 N
(KICKHAM, ALEXANDER) brother of Rody Kickham and schoolmate at Clongowes Wood P 40
KICKHAM, RODOLPH/Roderick "Rody" pupil at Clongowes Wood P 8, 11, (70) + brother P (40) Sullivan, p. 48
(KIERAN, S.) 6th-century bishop of Ossory 339 A/N
*(KIERNAN, BERNARD "BARNEY") publican 280, 293, 295, 298, 312, Brian O'Ciarnain's 316, S. Bernard 339, 340, 372, 380, 657, 662, 676, 729, 735 N/T + *Thom's,* p. 1923
(KILDARE, EARL OF) 231 see Fitzgerald, Gerald
(Kildbride) engine driver, escort of Edy Boardman 432
(Kilkelly, Mr) acquaintance of Molly Ivor D 189
("Kinch") 3, 4, 5, 6, 7, 8, 9, 10, 11, 12, 14, 16, 17, 18, 22, 38, 50, 214, 215, 217, 556, 580 N; Introduction see Dedalus, Stephen
("Kinch, Pa") 18, 425 see Dedalus, Simon
("King Willow"*) cricket bat personified as batsman 659 N
*(KING, WILLIAM) printer 252 N/T
(KINGSLEY, CHARLES) 19th-century English author and Anglican clergyman S 93
(KINO, J. C.) tailor 153, 523, 683 N/T
(KINSELLA, PAT) proprietor of Harp Music Hall 167 N
("Kirschner, Abe") member of Elijah's congregation 507
(Kirwin) of the firm of Bodley and Kirwin D 87
Kitty Lynch's afternoon paramour a young woman 224, The young woman 231, (405–6), my queen (415–16)
[Kitty-Kate] 508 see Ricketts, Kitty
("Kittylynch") 578 see Lynch, Vincent; Ricketts, Kitty
(KNAPLOCK, R.) printer of Bloom's geometry book 709
"Knickerbockers" S 39, (216), (231) see McCann, Philip

("Knowall, Mister") 315 see Bloom, Leopold
(Kobberkeddelsen, Olaf) member of the F. O. T. E. I. 307
(KOCH, ROBERT) German bacteriologist 33 A/N
(KOCK, CHARLES-PAUL DE) 19th-century French novelist 64, 269, 282, 465, Poldy Kock 538, 765 A/N
("Kock, Poldy") see Bloom, Leopold; Kock, Charles-Paul de
*(Kohler/KELLER, T. G.) one of Stephen's creditors 31 N
("KOOT HOOMI") Madame Blavatsky's "master" 185 N
(KOSSUTH, LOUIS) 19th-century Hungarian revolutionary 495 A/N
(KRAMER, MICHAEL) title character of Hauptmann's play D 108 N
("Kranliberg") S 119 see Cranly
(Kratchinabritchisitch, Goosepond Prhklstr) member of the F. O. T. E. I. 307
(KRUGER, JOHANNES PAULUS) South African statesman oom Paul 749 A/N

(L. B., Doctor) authority on sexology, according to Virag 515 see Bloom, Leopold
(La Aurora) presumably a partner in a dancing duo 545
(LABLACHE, LUIGI) 19th-century Italian basso 287 A/N
(Lacy, Mick) singing crony of Mr. Dedalus from university days P 88–89, 90
(LAEMLEIN, ASHER) 16th-century Messiah, self-proclaimed 497 A/N
*(LAFAYETTE, JAMES) Dublin photographer 418, 652 A/N/T + *Thom's,* p. 1925
(LALAGE) traditional name for beautiful woman 415 A/N
(LALOR, JAMES FINTAN) 19th-century advocate of land nationalization 716 A/N
*(LALOUETTE) mortician and carriage hire 8 N/T
*(LAMBE, ALICIA) florist 781 N/T
(Lambe, Mr) Londoner who presumably married Georgina Johnson 560
(LAMBERT) presumed progenitor of fatty offspring 569 A/N
Lambert, Edward J. "Ned" grain store employee and friend of Mr. Dedalus (90), 100, 102–3, 106–7, 110, 123–27, (225),

230–32, (240), (241), (276–77), 320–45, S. Edward (339), [470], (647), (704)
(Lambert, Sam) brother of Ned Lambert 240
(Landy) student at U.C.D. S 131
(LANE, W.) jockey who rode Throwaway 415, 648 N
(LANGTRY, LILLIE) English actress and paramour of Edward, Prince of Wales 751, Jersey lily 770 A/N
(LANIGAN, JAMES) Bishop of Ossory at time of Act of Union P 38 N
(LANNER, KATTI/Katty) London ballet mistress 575, 745 A/N
(LAPIDE, CORNELIUS) P 233 N see Cornelis Cornelissen
*[LARACY, SUPERINTENDENT] headmaster of Hibernian Marine School 586 N
*(LARCHET) hotel/restaurant 518 N/T
(Laredo, Lunita) Molly's Spanish-Jewish mother 746, 761, 763, 771 N
(Larkin) pawnbroker S 223
(Larry) hanged man—in song 307 A/N
(LASSALLE, FERDINAND) 19th-century Jewish German socialist 687 A/N
(LATINI, BRUNETTO) 13th-century Italian writer 194; G 15 A/N
(LATTEN, JOHN/"JACK") danced 20 miles to Dublin 468 A/N
(LAURENCE O'TOOLE, S.) 12th-century archbishop of Dublin 339 A/N
*(LAVERY, REV. JOHN) priest at St. Peter's Presbytery 317 N + *Thom's,* p. 1927
Lawless pupil at Clongowes Wood P 107
(LAWRENCE, S.) 3rd-century Roman martyr 700 A/N
("Lawson, Lewy") in Brini's genealogical list 495
LAWTON, JOHN "JACK" pupil at Clongowes Wood P 10, 12, 47–52, (70) Sullivan, p. 48
("Lay, Maureen") typical Irish name in version of song used by the narrator 311 A/N
(LAZARILLO) assailant in operetta *Maritana* 626 A/N
(LAZARUS) brother of Martha and Mary whom Christ raised from the dead 105 A/N
("LAZARUS, SIMON") presumably actual name of Sidney Lee 195 A/N

(LAZENBY, F.) London salad-dressing manufacturer 354 N
(LEARY/LAOGHAIRE) 3rd-century Irish king 667 A/N
*(LEASK, H. M.) linseed dealer 71 N/T
("Lecher") 393 see Fletcher, John
(LECKY, WILLIAM EDWARD) 19th-century Anglo-Irish historian S 149
(LEDA) seduced by swan Zeus 299 A/N
("Ledwidge") 636 see Ludwig, William
*(LEE, EDWARD) draper 752 A/N
*(LEE, PADDY) with whom young Stephen almost boarded a train inadvertently, according to his mother's ghost 581 N + *Thom's,* p. 1928
(LEE, SIDNEY) Shakespeare biographer 195 A/N
*(LEEDOM, HAMPTON AND CO.) hardware dealers 543 N/T + *Thom's,* p. 543
("Le Hirsch") in Brini's genealogical list 495 see Hirsch, Maurice, Baron de
(LEITRIM, LORD) Connaught landlord murdered in 1877 P 33 N
*(LEMON, GRAHAM) candy merchant 151, 272, 676 N/T
Lenehan, T. Dublin wag, racehorse punter, and sponge (125), 128–44, 147–50, (174), gentleman from *Sport* (229–30), 232–35, 252, rose of Castille (256–57), 261–67, (307), 324–45, 387–428, [470], [490], [509], [564–65], (617), (648), (731), (750); D 49–60 N
(Lennon, James) driver of train that killed Mrs. Sinico D 113, 115
(LENTULUS ROMANUS) presumably governor of Judea and describer of Christ 689 A/N
(LEO XIII/GIOACCHINO PECCI) pope 1878–1903 old man Leo 426; D 167–68, 194 A/N/N
(LEONARD, F.) grocer 435, 667 T (or LEONARD, ANNIE newsagent N)
(Leonard, Mr) Catholic wine merchant and employer of Bob Doran D 65–66, 68
Leonard, Paddy habitué of Davy Byrne's pub (90), 178–79, (314), [470], [487], [491]; D (91), 93–96
(LEONARDO DA VINCI) S 33
(LEONARDO PISANO) 637 see Fabrinacci, Leonardo
("Leopold the First") 482 see Bloom, Leopold
(LEOPOLD, ARCHDUKE) of Bavaria 1886–1912 175 N

(LEOPOLD, CHRISTIAN GERHARD) German embryologist 418 A/N
(LEOPOLD, DUKE OF ALBANY) dead son of Queen Victoria 85 A/N
(LEOPOLD, S.—THE GOOD) 12th-century Austrian founder of monastaries 339, 714 A/N see also Bloom, Leopold
(LEPIDUS) one of the triumvirate after the death of Julius Caesar P 250 N
(LESSING, GOTTHOLD EPHRAIM) German classical dramatist and critic 559; P 211, 214; S 33 A/N/N
(LESURQUES, JOSEPH) executed for crime, later exonerated 456 A/N
(LEUGARDE, S.) 7th-century Irish abbot 339 A/N
*(LEVENSTON, MRS K.) piano teacher 182 A/T
*LEVENSTON, MRS PHILIP M.) dancing instructor 182, 575 N/T
(LEVER, CAPT. JOHN ORELL) shipping company owner 639, 640, 642 A/N
(Le Verrier/LEVERRIER, URBAIN JEAN JOSEPH) 19th-century French astronomer 700 A/N
(Leverett, Mr) coroner in Sinico case D 113
(Levinstone) 575 see Levenston, Mrs. Philip M.
*(LEWERS, R. G.) tailor 750 N/T
*(LIDWELL, GEORGE) solicitor Lidlyd (256) (see also Douce, Lydia), Lid (257), (261), He was in at lunchtime (262), 270–91, [586] N + *Thom's*, p. 1931
("Lilac, Lilian") participant in forest wedding 327
("Lilac, Viola") participant in forest wedding 327
(LILITH) female demon, apocryphal first wife of Adam 390, 497 A/N
("Lily") typical name of girl associating with Stephen's Dalkey students 25
Lily servant at the Morkans', daughter of their caretaker D 175, (176), 177–79, (181), 197–98 + father D (175–76), 182 N
(LILY OF KILLARNEY) heroine of operetta based on *The Colleen Bawn* 92, 297 A/N
[Limerick, Mayor of] in procession for Bloom 480
("Linbad") 737 see Sinbad the Sailor
(LIND, JENNY) 19th-century Swedish soprano 274 A/N
(LIONEL) hero of Von Flotow's *Martha* 275, 276, Lionelleopold 288 (see also Bloom, Leopold), Simonlionel 289 (see also Dedalus, Simon), 290, 456, 661 A/N

"Lionelleopold" 288 see Bloom, Leopold; Lionel
[Lipoti, Virag] 511 see Virag, Lipoti
(LIPTON, SIR THOMAS) merchant, grocer 297, 781 A/N
(LIR) Danaan god, father of Mananaan and Fionuala 192 A/N
(LISZT, FRANZ) Hungarian Romantic composer 256, 282 A/N
("LITTLE SWEET BRANCH") 312 see Hyde, Douglas
(LITTLE, PETER STANISLAUS) Clongowes pupil who died at school P 24
(LIVERMORE BROS.) minstrels 443 A/N
(Livingstone) contestant in probated will case 323
(LOBENGULA) 19th-century African king 245 A/N
(LOCKHART, JOHN GIBSON) whose biography of Napoleon is on Bloom's shelf 708 A/N
LOGUE, MICHAEL CARDINAL Archbishop of Armagh and anti-Parnellite [480], [482]; P 33 N/N
(Lohan, Father) Mullingar parish priest S 245–46
("Long John") 119 see Fanning, "Long" John
*(LONG, JOHN P.) publican 180 N/T + *Thom's*, p. 1933
[Longhand and Shorthand] stenographers at Bloom's trial 462
*(LONGWORTH, ERNEST V.) editor of the *Daily Express* 192, 216 A/N
(LOPEZ, RODERIGO) Queen Elizabeth's Spanish doctor 204 A/N
*(LORÉ, PROSPER) hat manufacturer 259 N/T + *Thom's*, p. 1933
(LORETO, OUR LADY OF) 354 see Mary, Blessed Virgin
(LOS) 37 see Demiurgos, Los
(LOT) saved from Sodom + wife who was turned into a pillar of salt 640 A/N
("LOTHARIO") classic seducer D 52 N see Corley, John
(LOUT, SIR) a giant 44 A/N
Love, Rev. Hugh C. Anglican cleric and landlord, interested in Irish history a visitor (225), the clergyman's 230–31, 245, 252, your landlord (270), The landlord (282), [579] N
("Lovebirch, Mrs Barbara") participant at forest wedding 327
(LOVEBIRCH, JAMES) writer of pornographic novels, presumably *Fair Tyrants* 235, 465 A/N

*(LOW, GAVIN) livestock agent 399, 680 N/T + *Thom's,* p. 1933
(Lowry) obituary in the *Freeman's Journal* 91
("Lowry") in Irish curse 312 see Lowry, Dan
*(LOWRY, DAN) impresario at the Empire Theatre 232 N/T p. 52
(LOYOLA, S. IGNATIUS) 16th-century Spanish soldier, founder of Jesuit order 9, 188, 399; P (55–56), (107), (127), (186), (190); G 5 A/N/N
(LUCAS, DR CHARLES) 18th-century pioneer for Irish liberty 139 A/N
(LUCIE) 767 see Manette, Lucie
(LUCIFER) the devil, and also a match* 50, 558; P 117–18, 121, 133–34 A/N/N
(LUCRECE) whose rape is celebrated in Shakespeare's poem 197 A/N
(Lucy) a girl Stephen knew S 230–31
(LUCY, S.) 4th-century virgin martyr, patroness of eyes 339 A/N
(LUCY, SIR THOMAS) English lord from whom Shakespeare presumably stole deer 215 A/N
(LUDWIG, WILLIAM) baritone with the Carl Rosa company, born Ledwidge 636 A/N
(Luigi) old Genoese fisherman in Gibraltar, remembered by Molly 765
(LUNDY, FOOT AND CO.) see Foot, Lundy 253
(LUSK, WILLIAM THOMPSON) 19th-century American obstetrician 418 a/N
(LUTHER, MARTIN) parson who founded the protestant error 523 A/N
(LYCIDAS) drowned hero of Milton's poem 25 A/N
*(LYNAM) bookmaker 233 T
Lynam, Brunny pupil at Belvedere, possibly son of bookmaker 220 N
(LYNCH OF GALWAY) famous family, one of the 14 tribes 328 A/N
(LYNCH, ANNE) brand of tea 675 N
(LYNCH, JAMES) 16th-century warden of Galway who had his son hanged 332 N
Lynch, Vincent Stephen's acquaintance from U.C.D. flushed young man 224, 388–428, 430–33, 502–83, 587–600, Judas

(615); P 201, 204–16, (248), (250), (251); S 136–37, (151–52), (155), (161), 177–78, 190–92, 200–203, (214), (229), 232–34
("Lynchehaun") 245 see Walshe, James
*(LYON, ABRAHAM) Dublin councillor 246 N + *Thom's,* p. 1935
(LYON, JACQUARD DE) 326 see Jacquard, Joseph Marie
Lyons, Frederick M. "Bantam" punter and habitué of pubs (74), 85–86, 178–79, (233), (303), (335), 426, [495], (586), (648), (676); D (65), 130–35
(Lyster, Miriam) presumably Lyster's wife 196
*LYSTER, THOMAS WILLIAM Quaker librarian at the National Library 184, 190–200, 208–11, [509], [598] N
(LYTTON, LORD) 756; D 25 see Bulwer-Lytton, Edward

(Mac) a friend of Lenehan's friends D 58
(Mac) student at U.C.D. S 224
MacAlister student at U.C.D. P 193–94, 199, (209)
("MacAnaspey, Ditto"*) seconding a drink order 295 N
("MacArdle, Brother") typical name given by Stephen to a Christian Brother P 166
*(MacARTHUR AND CO.) estate agents 61 N/T
(MACBETH) Shakespeare villain S 103
(MacCABE, EDWARD CARDINAL) 19th-century archbishop of Dublin 101 N
("MacCabe, Florence") one of Stephen's fictional midwives 37, two maries 45, (145–50), Two old women 242, two sanded women 254, two trickies [579]
("MacCabe, Patrick") putative dead husband of Florence MacCabe 37
MacCann political student at U.C.D. P (177), 194–99, (208–9), (242) see also McCann, Philip
("MacChree, Ben") 522 see Dollard, Benjamin; Macree, Ben
*(MacCONNELL, ANDREW) pharmacist 225 N/T
(MacCONSIDINE, DONALD) 19th-century Gaelic poet 312 N
*(MacCORMACK, JOHN) Irish tenor 93 N
(MacCullagh) student at U.C.D. P 210
(MacDERMOTT, RED JIM) Fenian turncoat 296 A/N
*(MacDONNELL, SIR ANTHONY) undersecretary to the Lord Lieutenant of Ireland 659 A/N

(MacDONOGH, MANUS TOMALTACH OG) 331 see O'Duigenan, Manus
(MacDowell, Charley) Gerty MacDowell's brother 354
MacDowell, Gerty 21-year-old resident of Sandymount 253, (333), 346–67, give her an odd dig (369), limping little devil (370), She must have been thinking (371), 372, down to her (373), That's her perfume (374), Bad for you, dear (376), Sad about her lame (377), that female (381), Goodbye, dear (382), some faded beauty (409), [442], (722), feminine exhibitionism (729), (735)
(MacDowell, Mr) Gerty's father 253, 354–55
(MacDowell, Mrs) Gerty's mother 250, 354–55, 442
(MacDowell, Tom) Gerty's brother 355
("Macduff") from Shakespeare's *Macbeth* 144
("MacEvoy") name used by the Dedaluses when pawning their possessions P 174
(MacFadden, Constable) restores order at fracas before hanging 308
("MacFlimsy, Flora") typical clotheshorse 346 N
(MacHALE, JOHN) bishop of Tuam, early opponent of doctrine of papal infallibity D 167–70 N
(MacHALE, LANTY) owner of ecumenical goat—in Charles Lever's poem 336 N see also McHale, Lanty
("machree, Ben") 287 see Dollard, Benjamin; Macree, Ben
MacHugh, Prof. Hugh scribe and editor 123–50, (263), [462]
("MacKay") in Brini genealogical list 495
*(MacKENNA, STEPHEN) Irish writer 187 N
(MacLIR, MANANAAN) 510 see Mananaan MacLir
(MacMAHON, MARSHALL PATRICK) 19th-century president of France 297 A/N
(MacMANUS, TERENCE BELLEW) 19th-century Irish nationalist P 173; S 38 N
(MacMurragh/MacMURROUGH, ART) 15th-century king of Leinster 296 A/N
(MacMURROUGH, DERMOT) 12th-century king of Leinster, husband of Devorghila 35 A/N
(MacNally) presumably rector of Belvedere, with brother at U.C.D. S 35–36
(MACREE, BEN) hero of drama at the Gaiety 287, 522
(MacSWINEY, ANTHONY) pupil at Clongowes Wood P 70
("MacTrigger, Rev. Mr") missionary—in limerick + "nigger" 171–72

Magee respondent to Stephen's paper S 102–5
(MAGEE, JIMMY) pupil at Clongowes Wood P 13, 54
Sullivan, p. 35
*(MAGEE, MATTHEW) father of William Magee 206–7
A/N
*MAGEE, WILLIAM K. author and librarian at National Library 184–215, (216), chinless Chinaman (410), [509–10] A/N
*(MAGENNIS, WILLIAM) professor at U.C.D. 140 N
*(M'ARDLE, JOHN) surgeon at St. Vincent's Hospital 165 N + *Thom's,* p. 1936
*(M'AULEY, THOMAS) publican 58; D 162 N/T + *Thom's,* p. 1393
(M'CANN, JAMES) recently deceased chairman of the Grand Canal Co. 99 A/N
(M'Carthy) flutist—in song 86 A/N
(M'CARTHY, DENIS FLORENCE) 19th-century Irish poet 708 A/N
("M'Carthy, Jakes") fourth member of the Holy Trinity 135 N
(M'CARTHY, JUSTIN) novelist-politician who broke with Parnell 599 A/N
McCann, Philip friend of Stephen's at U.C.D. and later a creditor 31; S (39), (42), 43–46, 49–52, (67), 88–90, (99), 100–105, 112–15, 130–31, (141), (153), 157–59, 169, (175), 181–82, 183, (187), (191), (214–15), (216), (231), 234 see also MacCann
(McCloud) whose name is applied to a musical reel D 105
McGlade prefect at Clongowes Wood P (11), 22–23, (48)
(McHALE, LANTY) owner of ecumenical goat—in Charles Lever's poem 336 N see also MacHale, Lanty
*(McKERNAN, Mrs) Stephen's former landlady 31 N
(M'Conachie) friend of Corley 617
("M'Conifer of the Glands") participant in the forest wedding 327 see O'Donoghue of the Glens
M'Coy, C. P. "Charlie" clerk in Midland Railway and/or assistant to the Coroner, formerly an ad man for the *Freeman* (67), 73–76, (80), (111–12), (167), 232–35, 252, (282), (368), [470], [586], (627), (647–48), (773); D 156–74 N
(M'Coy, Fanny) wife of Charlie M'Coy 75–76, 234, 282, 368, 627, 773; D 158, 160
(M'CRACKEN, HENRY JOY) executed as rebel in 1798 296 A/N

*(M'GLADE, B.) advertising agent 154 N/T
*(M'GUCKIN, BARTON) Irish tenor with the Carl Rosa Co. 272 A/N
*M'GUINNESS, ELLEN pawnbroker 220, (226), [586] N/T + *Thom's,* p. 1943
"M'Intosh" anonymous thirteenth at Dignam's burial lankylooking galoot 109–10, 112, pedestrian in a brown macintosh 254, chap at the grave (290), man in the brown macintosh (333), fellow today at the graveside (376), yon guy in the mackintosh (427), [485], (647–48), (729)
("M'Intosh, Leopold") 485 see Bloom, Leopold; M'Intosh
(M'Keown, Christ!) 303
*(M'MANUS, MONSIGNOR MILES) vicar general, parish priest at St. Catherine's R. C. church 318 N + *Thom's,* p. 1946
(M'SWINEY, PETER PAUL) 19th-century merchant and politician, whom Mr. Dedalus claims as a cousin 88 N

(M. B.) in love with a fair gentleman 333 see Bloom, Milly; Bloom, Molly
(MAAS, JOSEPH) 19th-century English tenor 272 A/N
(MACAULAY, THOMAS BABINGTON) English historian and essayist P 148; S 156 N
(MACHIAVELLI, NICOLO) 16th-century writer and politician S 194
*(MACK, MRS A.) noted Monto madam 475 N/T
(Mack, Janey!) 11
("Mackerel") 162, 548 A/N see Bloom, Leopold
*(MACKEY, SIR JAMES W.) nurseryman and politician 714 N/T + *Thom's,* p. 1585
Madden Nationalist student at U.C.D. and friend of Stephen S 24–25, (39), (42), 52–56, (61), 62–65, 81–83, 105–9, 115–16, (214) see also Davin; Madden, William
*(MADDEN, DODGSON HAMILTON) jurist and vice chancellor of Dublin University 200 A/N
(MADDEN, O.) jockey who rode Sceptre 128, 233, 415, 426 N
(Madden, Stephen) brother of Stephen's U.C.D. friend S 81
Madden, William medical student and possibly the same as Stephen's U.C.D. friend 388–428, [493], [509]
(Madeleine) Parisienne that Stephen imagines having breakfast 42

(Madeline) the mare—in song 37
("Mady") 279 see Clifford, Martha
(MAETERLINCK, MAURICE) Belgian dramatist 213, 215; S 39–40, 91 A/N
Maffei, Signor villain in Molly's book (64), [454]
*MAGINNI, DENIS J. professor of dancing (153), 220, 235, 253, [575–77] N/T + *Thom's,* p. 1948
(Magnall/MANGNALL, RICHMAL) English schoolmistress and writer of children's textbooks P 53 N
(Magrane, Daniel) boyhood friend of Leopold Bloom 716
(Maher, Father) priest performing marriage service—in song 665 A/N
*(MAHER, REV. T.) at church of St. Francis Xavier 317 N
("Mahogany, Mrs Maud") participant in forest wedding 327
Mahony pupil at Belvedere out on a day's miching D 21–28 + sister D (21)
("Mahound") name for Mohammed or the devil 387 A/N
(MAIMONIDES, MOSES) 12th-century Jewish philosopher and Aristotelian 28, 390, 495, 687 A/N
("Maindorée") one of Bloom's golden children 494
("Mairy") 279, 368 see Mary, who lost her pin
(MALACHI II) 10th/11th-century High King of Ireland 45, 296 A/N
(MALACHI, S.) 12th-century Irish prelate 340, 398 N
(MALAHIDE, LORD TALBOT DE) 223, 402, 616 see Talbot de Malahide, Lord Richard
(Malaria, Señor Hidalgo Caballero Don Pecadillo y Palabras y Paternoster de la Malora de la) member of the F.O.T.E.I. 307
Malins, Freddy inebriated guest at the Morkans' party D (176), 181–82, 184–85, (190), 191, 193–95, 198–206, (206), 208–9, (216–17)
Malins, Mrs Freddy's mother D (185), 190–91, 193, 200–206, 206–9 + daughter D (190) + son-in-law D (191)
(MALLARMÉ, STÉPHANE) 19th-century French symbolist poet 187 A/N
*(MALLON, JOHN) assistant commissioner of Dublin Metropolitan Police 646 N
*(MALONE, REV. CHARLES) curate in charge of the Church of the Three Patrons, Rathgar, who presumably baptized both Stephen and Bloom 682 N
(Maloney, Mrs) boardinghouse keeper 617

(Malony) police magistrate, possibly Daniel Mahony 615 N
(MAMMON) Old Testament devil, personification of material greed D 174
MANANAAN MacLIR Irish sea god (38), (189), (412), [510] A/N
(MANETTE, LUCIE) for whose happiness Sydney Carton goes to the guillotine 767 N
Mangan friend of the protagonist of "Araby" D (30), 32 + sister D 30–32, (33) N
*(MANGAN, P.) pork butcher 234, 250 N/T
(MANN, DANIEL "DANNY") informer in *The Colleen Bawn* 642 A/N
*(MANNING LTD) furriers and costumers on Grafton Street 752 T
*(MANNING, T. J.) publican 163 N/T
(MANNINGHAM, JOHN) Elizabethan diarist 201 A/N
(Manola) in Molly's recollection of an Andalusian singer 750
*(Mansfield/MANFIELD & SONS) bootmakers 529 N/T + *Thom's,* p. 1951
("Manuo, Joseph") 314 see Doran, Bob
(Mapas/MALPAS, MR) 18th-century donor of an obelisk for the Hill of Killiney 332 N/T
("Maple, Blanche") participant in forest wedding 327
(MAPLE, FREDERICK) hotelier P 237 T
(Marcella) midget in circus 636
(MARCELLO, BENEDETTO) 18th-century Italian composer 503 A/N
(MARCELLUS II) 16th-century pope 21 A/N
(MARGARET) Byron's cousin, for whom he wrote his early poem D 83–84 N
Maria spinster employed by Dublin laundry D 99–106
(MARIA THERESA/TERESA) 18th-century Empress of Austria 330, 724 A/N
(MARIANA DE TALAVERA DE LA REINA, JUAN DE) 16th/17th-century Spanish theologian and historian P 246
(MARIES, two) Mary Magdalene and Mary, mother of James and Joses 45, babemaries 142 N
(MARINA) newborn daughter in Shakespeare's *Pericles* 195 A/N
(MARIO, GIUSEPPI MATEO, CAVALIERE DE CANDIA) 19th-century Italian tenor 117, 517 a/N

(Marion/MARIAN) heroine of Wilkie Collins's *Woman in White* 229 A/N
("Marion Calpensis, S.") 339 A/N see Bloom, Marion
("Marionette") 448 see Bloom, Milly
(MARIUS, SIMON) 17th-century German astronomer 700 A/N
*(MARKS, EPHRAIM) owner of penny bazaar 683 N/T + *Thom's,* p. 1502
*(MARKS, LIONEL) antique dealer and framemaker 290 N/T + *Thom's,* p. 1951
(MARRYAT, CAPT. FREDERICK) 19th-century English adventure novelist P 80 N
(MARS) Roman god of war 561, 700 A
Marsh, Charles Alberta one of Bella Cohen's horsey customers (539), [540]
(MARSH, ARCHBISHOP NARCISSUS) founded Marsh's Library in 1707 39; S 176 N/T
(Marshall, Capt.) putative owner of Sir Hugo, horse that won the 1892 Derby 647 N
(MARTHA) heroine of Flotow's opera 117, 256, A lovely girl 271, she went to him 273–75 A/N
(MARTHA AND MARY) sisters of Lazarus 79, 117, 368, 535-36 A/N
(MARTHA OF BETHANY, S.) 339 see Martha and Mary
(MARTIN OF TODI, S.) 7th-century pope and martyr 339 A/N see also Cunningham, Martin
(MARTIN OF TOURS, S.) 4th-century soldier-monk-bishop 339 A/N see also Cunningham, Martin
*(MARTIN, T. AND C.) merchants and manufacturers 344 N/T + *Thom's,* p. 1952
(MARTIN-HARVEY, SIR JOHN) English actor 357, 767 A/N
(Martino/MARTIN, FERNANDO WOOD) 19th/20th-century American chemist P 192–93 N
*(MARTYN, EDWARD) playwright and co-founder of the Irish Literary Theatre 192 A/N
(MARX, KARL) exponent of Communism 342; P 197 A/N/N
Mary servant at the Mooneys' D (64), 67
(MARY) lost her pin—in song 78 A
("Mary") servant in Bloom's fantasy 163

(Mary) to be wooed—in song sung by Mr. MacDowell 354 A/N
(Mary Ann) uninhibited urinator—in song 13 A/N
("Mary Ann') Molly's contemptuous name for overdressed female 764 N
Mary Jane niece of the Morkan sisters, music teacher D 175, (176), 183–84, 186–87, 192–96, 197–206, 206–9, 210–12
(MARY MAGDALENE) reformed by Christ two maries 45, babemaries 142; S 117 A/N
(MARY OF EGYPT, S.) 5th-century penitent prostitute 339; S 117 A/N
(Mary Patrick, Sister) nun who aids the Dedalus children 226 N
(Mary, aunt) in scurrilous song 776
(MARY, BLESSED VIRGIN) My mother's a jew 19, *vous* 41, marybeads 47, 83, His blessed mother 88, 145, madonna 207, 333, 346, 349, 356, 358, Queen of angels 359, 364, 385, 389, our holy mother 390, woman's womb 391, bride, ever virgin 414, 438, Mary Shortall 520, *vous* 521, 741, 746, 752, Santa Maria 759; D 98, 166; P 118, 242; S 112, 117, 232 A/N
(MARY, QUEEN OF SCOTS) antagonist of Queen Elizabeth 220 A/N
("Mary, shady") prostitute 428
(MASETTO) in Mozart's *Don Giovanni* 780 A/N
*(MASSEY, MRS DE) proprietress of the Ormond Hotel 258 N/T p. 64 + *Thom's,* p. 1850
*(MASSEY, EDWARD) bookseller D 188 T
*Mastiansky, Julius/MASLIANSKY, P. friend of the Blooms in their early married days (60), (108), [497], [544?], [586], (667), (731) + wife (749) N/T + Hyman, p. 329
[Mastiansky, O.] one of the circumcised, perhaps same as above 544 N/T
("Matcham") title character in Beaufoy's titbit 68, 69, 158, 280, 458 A/N
(MATTHEW) disciple of Christ P 189 N
(MATTHEW, FR THEOBALD) 19th-century temperance campaigner 95, 276 A/N/T
(MATTERSON AND SONS) victualers from Limerick 532 N
MAXIMUM II French horse in Gold Cup (85), [573], (648) N

*(MAXWELL, LADY) a visitor to Father Conmee 220, (224) N/T + *Thom's,* p. 1954
*(MAY AND CO.) music sellers 69 N
(MAY, O SWEETHEART!) heroine of song 744 A/N
(MAYBRICK, FLORENCE E. C.) murderess of her husband 744 A/N see also Brierly, A.
(MAYBRICK, JAMES) murdered by his wife 744 A/N
(Mayers, Freddy) presumably proprietor of an opera company 774
*(MEADE, MICHAEL, AND SONS) builders 77, 91, 344 N/T + *Thom's,* p. 1954
(Meade, Mr) resident at Mrs. Mooney's boarding house D 65, 138
*(MEAGHER, P.) publican 119, 375 N/T
(MEISSEL, "Pimply") resident in Trieste G 6
(MELCHIZEDEK/MELCHISEDEK) king of righteousness in Genesis 729; P 159 A/N/N
*(MELDON, AUSTIN) physician 403–4 A/N + *Thom's,* p. 1955
(MELNOTTE, CLAUDE) romantic hero of Lytton's *The Lady of Lyons* P 99 N
(MENANDER) classical Greek comic dramatist S 97
(MENDELSSOHN, FELIX) Romantic composer of Jewish descent 342, 661, 687 A/N
(MENDELSSOHN, MOSES) 18th-century German Jewish philosopher 495, 687 A/N
(MENDOZA, DANIEL) Jewish boxing champion of England, 1792–95 687 A/N
(MENELAUS) husband of Helen of Troy 34, 132, 201 A/N
*MENTON, JOHN HENRY solicitor, former employer of Dignam 102, 106–7, 115, he clapped on his topper (121), (158), (160), (240), (245), (247), 253, (299), (455), [470], (473), (498), [586], (647), ornament of the legal profession (655), (704), (731), (739) N/T + *Thom's,* p. 1955
(MERCADANTE, GIUSEPPE SAVERIO) 19th-century Italian composer 82, 282, 342, 661 A/N
(MERCALLI, GIUSEPPE) Italian seismologist 344 N
(MERCATOR, GERHARDUS/GERHARD KREMER) 16th-century Flemish geographer 671 A/N
(MERCEDES) heroine of *The Count of Monte Cristo* P 62–63, 64–65, 66, 99 N

Mercer, Mrs visiting neighbor in "Araby" D 33
(MERCURY/HERMES) messenger of Zeus 19 A/N
(MEREDITH, GEORGE) 19th-century English novelist 211, 425 A/N
[Meredith, Jack] high school friend of Leopold Bloom 548
*MESIAS, GEORGE ROBERT tailor for both Bloom and Boylan (110), (279), (476), [497], (732) N/T + *Thom's*, p. 1955
("Messenger") conceived in Stephen's mind as a figure in a literary vignette 140 Introduction
("MESSIAH BEN DAVID") expected to resurrect the new world 495 A/N
("MESSIAH BEN JOSEPH") expected to collect the Israelites in Jerusalem 495 A/N
(METCHNIKOFF, ILYA) Russian bacteriologist 521 A/N
(METHUSALAH) superannuated patriarch in Old Testament 336 (see also Bloom, Rudolph), 679 A/N
(MEYERBEER, GIACOMO) 19th-century German operatic composer 168, 290, 661 A/N
(MICHAEL) archangel 21, 83; P 113, 118 N/N
Michael, Brother infirmarian at Clongowes Wood (670); P 22–25, (26), (27), (109) N
(MICHAN, S.) 10th/11th-century Danish-Irish saint 240, 293, 297, 339, 344 A/N
(MICHELANGELO BUONAROTTI) 16th-century Italian painter and sculptor 139, 297; S 33 A/N
(MICHELET, JULES) 19th-century French historian 41 A/N
("Mickey") stereotypical Irish peasant S 64
(Mike!) 778
(MILESIUS) whose descendants are the legendary progenitors of Ireland 328, 393 A/N
(MILLER, GEORGE CLARK) in *Irish Independent* obituary 298 N
(MILLER, JOE) 18th-century English comic 134 N
*(MILLER, WILLIAM) plumber 179 N/T + *Thom's*, p. 1957
(MILLEVOYE, LUCIEN) French editor 43 A/N
Mills, Aubrey Stephen's boyhood friend at Blackrock P 63–64
("Mimosa San, Miss O.") Japanese participant in forest wedding 327
("Minbad") 737 see Sinbad the Sailor

(Minette*) French argot for oral sex 201 N
(MIRANDA) Prospero's daughter in *The Tempest* 195 A/N
(MIRANDOLA, PICO DELLA) 15th-century Italian scholar 40 A/N
("Miriam") Quaker wife 196 see Lyster, Thomas William
(MITCHEL, JOHN) 19th-century Irish nationalist and writer 716 A/N
*(MITCHELL, SUSAN) Dublin satirical writer 192 A/N
(Mogg/HOGG, PHOEBE) famous murder victim 593 N
(MOHAMMED) 77, 297, Mahound 387 A/N
*MOISEL, M./NISAN greengrocer, father of Philip Moisel (60), [544] N/T + Hyman, pp. 190, 329
(MOISEL, MRS) wife of one of the sons of Nisan Moisel 162 Hyman, p. 190
(MOISEL, PHILIP) Bloom's Jewish acquaintance, now dead, son of Nisan Moisel 705 N + Hyman, p. 191
(MOLESWORTH, LORD) father of Mary Rochfort—in Conmee's musings 223
(MOLINOS, MIGUEL DE) 17th-century Spanish mystic G 1
("Molldopeloob") 678 see Bloom, Leopold
*(MOLLOY, REV. GERALD) rector of U.C.D. 317 N
(MOLLOY, JAMES LYMAN) Irish lawyer and composer 706 A/N
("Molly bawn") 756 see Bawn, Molly
Moloney student at U.C.D. S 24
(MONA) heroine in song 427 A/N
(Mona*) a ship 638 A/N
("MONA LISA") figure in Leonardo's *La Gioconda* P 214
(MONACHUS, EPIPHANIUS) 689 see Epiphanius, S.
(Monica) Annie Chandler's sister D 82
("Monica, Sister") Mr. Dedalus's contemptuous name for a nun, based on St. Monica's Widow's Almhouse 239 N
(MONK, MARIA) whose *Awful Disclosures* presumably exposed life in a nunnery 235 A/N
Monks dayfather in printing office of the *Freeman's Journal* (121), 122, (156), (647) + wife and daughter (122)
(MONTAGUE, ROMEO) Shakespearean hero 108, 333; D 186 A/N/N
(MONTE CRISTO, COUNT OF) P 62–63–see Dantes, Edmond
(MONTEFIORE, SIR MOSES HAIM) English philanthropist and Zionist 59, 719 A/N
(MONTMORENCY) ? a member of either an ancient French

family or a distinguished Anglo-Irish family—more likely the latter 508 A/N
*(MONYPENNY, R. W.) needlework designer 229 N/T
(MOODY, DWIGHT L., AND SANKEY, IRA DAVID) collectors of sacred songs 661 A/N
(MOODY, FANNY, AND MANNERS, CHARLES) soprano and bass who formed the Moody-Manners Opera Company 627 A/N
(Moonan) successful graduate of U.C.D. although a late-starter P 190 see Moonan below; Moonan, Simon
(Moonan) passed his exams at U.C.D. P 210 see Moonan above; Moonan, Simon
Moonan, Simon cloddish pupil at Clongowes Wood P 11, 14, 41–42, (44), (70)
*(MOONEY, GERALD) publican of Mooney's *sur mer* 262, 518 n/T
Mooney, Ginger employed in Dublin by Lamplight laundry kitchen D (99–100), 100, 101
*(MOONEY, J. G., AND CO.) publicans of Mooney's *en ville* 144, 148, 262, 518 N/T
Mooney, Jack Polly Mooney's brother (173), (314); D 62, 68 N
(Mooney, Mr) bumbailiff, former butcher; Polly Mooney's father (303); D 61–62, 63, 66
Mooney, Mrs boardinghouse madam, Polly's mother (303), (314); D 61–65, (66), (67), (78) + father D (61)
Mooney, Polly wife of Bob Doran (303), (314), [586]; D 62–69
("MOONLIGHT, CAPTAIN") pseudonym of an Irish Land Leaguer 296 A/N
*(MOORE, GEORGE) Irish novelist 191–92, 211, 214, 397, 405 A/N/T
(MOORE, THOMAS) 19th-century Irish popular poet 162, 305; D 25; P 180 A/N/N/T
Moran, Father Nationalist priest and friend of Emma Clery P (202), priest to flirt with (216), (220), (221); S 65–66, (67), (154)
[Moran, Mmes Gerald and Stanislaus] possibly transvestites pursuing Bloom 586 see Gerald (the boy)
(MOREAU, GUSTAVE) 19th-century French painter 185 A/N
(MORGAN, JOHN PIERPONT) American financier and philanthropist 719 A/N

(Moriarity, Maurice) "the Frenchman"—crony of Mr. Dedalus's university days P 90
Morkan, Julia Gabriel Conroy's aunt, sister of Kate Morkan (162), (670); D 175–77, 179–83, 184–85, (186), (192), 192–95, 197–206, 210–12, (220), (222–23) N/T
Morkan, Kate Gabriel Conroy's aunt, sister of Julia Morkan, and Stephen Dedalus's godmother (670); D 175–77, 179–82, 183–85, 186–87, (190), (192), 194–95, 196–206, 206–9, 210–12, (220), (222–23)
(Morkan, Pat) dead brother of Julia and Kate D 176
(Morkan, Patrick) dead father of Julia and Kate D 207–8, 222
(MORLEY, JOHN) Liberal politician, chief secretary for Ireland in the 1880s, and biographer of Rousseau 717; S 40 A/N
(MORPHEUS) god of dreams 639, Murphy 660 A
*MORPHY, G. N. in bicycle race 254
("Morris") in colloquial expression—cow-kisser with unique taste 380
(MORRIS, WILLIAM) 19th-century English writer S 26
(MOSENTHAL, SOLOMON HERMANN VON) 19th-century German dramatist and librettist 76, 437 A/N
(MOSES) safe among the bulrushes 45, 139–40, 142–43, 149, 232, 242, 322, 345, among bulrushes 394, 459, 470, 495, 687, 729 + mother! (232) + mother & sister (142); P 238 A/N
*(MOSES, "DANCER") daughter of Marcus Tertius Moses 449
*(MOSES, MARCUS TERTIUS) tea merchant and political figure 233, 449 N/T + *Thom's,* p. 1963
(MOST, JOHANN JOSEPH) 19th-century German anarchist 197 A/N
*(MOULANG, DANIEL) jeweler and optician 258 N/T + *Thom's,* p. 1963
("Mount, Dolly") based on place name, Dollymount, in northeast Dublin 297
(Mountain, Jack) university crony of Mr. Dedalus P 90
("Mountcashel, Lady") type of horsewoman that Bloom reads about in *Irish Field* 160 N
(MOUNTJOY) Huguenot with whom Shakespeare reportedly resided 188 A/N
(Moya!) 328, 333
Moynihan student at U.C.D. P 191–95, 197–99, (235); S 148–50, (158–59), 171–74, 233–34
(MOZART, WOLFGANG AMADEUS) 82, 661; S 109

("Mud, Mickey") Mr. Dedalus's name for typical Christian Brothers' pupil P 71 see Stink, Paddy
(MUHAMMAD) 297 see Mohammed
(Mulcahy, Terence) splendiferously interred in Glasnevin 107
(Mulhall, Reverend Canon) whose death Richard Rowan reads about E 99
*(MULLET, JOHN) publican 613 N/T
*(MULLIGAN, JAMES) publican of John Mulligan's of Poolbeg Street D 94–96 T + *Thom's,* p. 1964
*(MULLIGAN, JOHN) manager of Hibernian Bank 240 N/T
Mulligan, Malachi Roland St John "Buck" medical student and befriender of Stephen Dedalus 2–9, 10–23, (31), (36), his boots (37), The Ship, half twelve (38), He has the key (44), He saved men (45), a buck's castoffs (49), his my sandal shoon/He threw it (50), (88), (134), (185), (192), (194), 197–218, 248–49, 253, (260), select company (262), (307), (388), (389), (397), 401–28, [493], [509], [580], (620–21), a certain budding practitioner (664–65), (706) + brother (21), (397) + mother (8), (88), *Ma mère* (424) + aunt (4), (5), (6), (88), (199), (425) + father (88) Introduction
(MULLINS, JAMES "JEM") self-taught physician and Irish patriot 641 N
(Mulrennan, John Alphonsus) Gaelic speaker who reports conversation with old man in the West P 251
(Mulvey, Harry) British naval lieutenant, Molly's "lover" in Gibraltar 371, 382, 693, 731, 759–62, 782, he kissed me 783
("Mumpsypum") name given to chorus girl 285
*(MUNRO, A.) in bicycle race 237
(MURATTI) manufacturer of cigarettes 730 N
"Murphy" pseudonym given to Mahoney D 26, 28
("Murphy") 660 Morpheus
*(MURPHY, D. J.) hotel proprietor 735 N + *Thom's,* p. 1408
(Murphy, Danny) presumably son of W. B. Murphy 631
*(MURPHY, REV. JAMES F.) provincial of Church of St. Francis Xavier 317 N + *Thom's,* p. 1966
(MURPHY, FATHER JOHN) leader of 1798 uprising 296 A/N
Murphy, W. B. able-bodied seaman in cabman's shelter 622–60 + wife (624), (631)

*(MURPHY, WILLIAM MARTIN) contractor, *Irish Independent* owner, anti-Parnellite, anti-trade unionist 298 A/N
(Murray girls) friends of Milly Bloom, presumably related to Red Murray and/or Willy Murray 766 N
(MURRAY, JOHN FISHER) 19th-century Irish political writer 716 A/N
*MURRAY, JOHN "RED" employed at *Freeman's Journal* 116–17, [586] N
(MURRAY, LINDLEY) 18th/19th-century English grammarian 653 A/N
*(MURRAY, WILLY) Joyce's uncle, employed at Collis & Ward 300–301 N
(Murren, Dr) presumably a dead physician 113, 162
*[MYERS, LT. JOHN J.] commander of Dublin fire brigade 498 N
("Myrtle, Miss Myra") participant in forest wedding 327
(MYRTO) presumed to be Socrates' first wife 190 A/N

*(NAGLE, JAMES JOSEPH "JOE") publican 297, 618 A/N/T + *Thom's,* p. 1968
*(NAGLE, JOHN JOACHIM "ACKY") publican 297 A/N/T + *Thom's,* p. 1968
(Nagle, Susy) acquaintance of Miss Dunne, possibly related to the Nagle brothers 229
*NANNETTI, JOSEPH PATRICK M. P. and member of the Dublin Corporation, foreman at the *Freeman's Journal* 118–22, (146), he couldn't remember (156), 246, (260), Nannan (314–15), (381), [550], [586], (684) N/T + *Thom's,* p. 1968
(NAPIER, LORD ROBERT CORNELIUS) English general and Governor of Gibraltar during Molly's residence 772, 782 A/N
(NAPOLEON BONAPARTE) 297, 445, 526, 568, 622, 708; D 13, 154; P 47, 63 A/N/N
(NARCISSUS) Greek youth turned into a flower; a statue of him is in the Bloom bedroom 543, 710, 728, 766, 775–76 A
Nash bullying student at Belvedere P 79–82; S 245–46, 250–53
(Nash/NASHE, THOMAS) Elizabethan lyricist and journalist P 233–34 N
("Nasodoro") one of Bloom's golden children 494

(NASR-ED-DIN) 19th-century Shah of Persia who visited England 284, 290 N
(NATHAN) villain in Mosenthal's *Deborah* 76 A/N
("Nature, Dame") personification of nature 405, 627
(Naumann) in *Freeman's Journal* obituary 91
*(NEARY, EDWARD) tailor from whom Kernan bought his coat 240 N/T + *Thom's,* p. 1968 (or NEARY, JOHN, Mary St. tailor)
("Neaulan, Jean Wyse de") 327 see Nolan, John Wyse
(NEAVE) brand of tinned food 338
(NELL, LITTLE) character in Dickens' *Old Curiosity Shop* S 86
(Nelly) in bawdy song 430
("Nelly, Fresh") prostitute incorporated into Mulligan's lampoon 214, 217; P 102 A/N
NELSON, ADMIRAL LORD HORATIO British victor at Trafalgar, paramour of Lady Hamilton (95), (116), (145), (147–50), (276), (325), (433), (492), (495), [579]; S 99 A/N/T
(NEMO, CAPTAIN) hero of Jules Verne's *Twenty Thousand Leagues under the Sea* 297 A/N
(NEPTUNE) Roman god of the sea 123
("Nero") S 136 see Lynch, Vincent
(NERVAL, GÉRARD DE) 19th-century French poet S 179
("Netaim") in Brini's genealogical list 495
(Nevil/NEVILLE, HENRY) English actor and drama teacher 424 N
(NEWCOMBE) coffeehouse proprietor in Cork P 93
(NEWMAN, JOHN HENRY, CARDINAL) 19th-century Anglican convert to Catholicism P 80, 164, 165, 176, 188; S 27–28, 92–93, 148, 173 N
(NIALL OF THE NINE HOSTAGES) 4th/5th-century High King of Ireland 296 A/N
(NICHOLAS II) 11th-century Pope of Rome 399–400 N
(NICHOLAS II) Czar of Russia, sponsor of peace petition 589; S 112–15; P 194, 196, 198 N/N
("Nicholas, farmer") 399–400 see Popes Adrian IV, Nicholas II
*(NICHOLAS, REV. FR.) vicar of Franciscan Capuchin Monastery, St. Mary of the Angels 317 N
*(NICHOLS, J. AND C.) undertakers 71 N/T
("NICK, OLD") the devil 637 A

(NICKLEBY, NICHOLAS) title character of Dickens novel S 124
(NIETZSCHE, FRIEDRICH WILHELM) 19th-century German philosopher D 122 N
("Ninbad") 737 see Sinbad the Sailor
(NOAH) 495, 569, 688 A/N
*(NOBLETT, LEONARD) confectioner S 223
("NOBODADDY") Blake's god of wrath 205, 395 A/N
(NOIR, JESSIE) choreographer of *Sinbad the Sailor* at the Gaiety 678 N
Nolan, John Wyse a crony of Martin Cunningham (177), 246–48, 253, 324–45, [484], [547], [586]
Nolan, Mrs John Wyse proprietress of a dairy store (177), [586]
("Noman") negative personification 727 see Bloom, Leopold
(NORA) wife of James Joyce G 15
*(NORMAN, Conolly/CONNOLLY) superintendent of the Richmond Lunatic Asylum 6 N/T p. 67 + *Thom's,* p. 1971
*(NORMAN, HENRY FELIX) editor of the *Irish Homestead* 192 N
*(NORTH, JAMES H.) estate agent 61 T + *Thom's,* p. 2069

("O. P.") theosophical designation for ordinary person 185 N
(Oakley, Mrs Cooper) 185 see Cooper-Oakley, Isabel
*(O'BEIRNE BROS.) publicans 436 N/T + *Thom's,* p. 1972
("O'Bergan") 300 see Bergan, Alfred
("O'Bloom, the son of Rory") 297 see Bloom, Leopold; Bloom, Rudolph
(O'BRIEN, J. P.) reputed to have helped James Stephens get away 68 N
(O'BRIEN, JAMES) early 19th-century political thinker P 197
(O'BRIEN, JAMES FRANCIS XAVIER) American surgeon who became an Irish Fenian 716 A/N
(O'BRIEN, LORD PETER) Lord Chief Justice of Ireland, known as Peter the Packer 297, 488 A/N
(O'BRIEN, SIR TIMOTHY) innkeeper known for his short measures, using a battered naggin 424

*[O'BRIEN, VINCENT] Irish composer and conductor 499 N + *Thom's,* p. 1973
(O'BRIEN, WILLIAM) editor of *United Ireland,* author of *When We Were Boys* 654, 708 a/n see also Bodkin, Matthew
O'BRIEN, WILLIAM SMITH 19th-century Irish nationalist (68), (93), [599] a/n
"O'Callaghan" a former lawyer, now bootlace vendor; Bloom either "names" him from the character in *His Last Legs* or uses the title to refer to him because of the coincidence of names 93, bootlaces a penny [538]
(O'CALLAGHAN) reputedly a Dublin eccentric (645)
O'Callaghan, Miss guest at the Morkans' party D (206), 211–15
O'Carroll friend of Tom Kernan D 172–74
(OCCAM, DAN) 40 see William of Occam
("Ocean, Old Father") 50 see Proteus
("O'Ciarnain, Brian") 316 see Kiernan, Bernard
(O'Clohissey) D 188 see Clohissey
(O'CONNELL, DANIEL) The Liberator; agitator for Catholic emancipation in Ireland 31, 93, 104–5, 108, Hosts at Mullaghmast 143, 599; P 26; D 214 A/N/N/T
*O'CONNELL, JOHN K. superintendent at Prospect Cemetery, Glasnevin 106–7, how he had the gumption (108), 109–11, [473–74]; S 167 + wife (107–8) N/T p. 66 + *Thom's,* p. 1973
(O'Connor) Wexford transport company 231
(O'Connor) whose family died of poisoned mussels, remembered by Bloom 381
(O'Connor, James) boyhood friend of Leopold Bloom 682
*(O'CONNOR, JOSEPH K.) Dublin solicitor and author of *Studies in Blue* 685 A/N
O'Connor, Mat canvasser for Tierney D 118–35
*(O'CONNOR, THOMAS POWER "TAY PAY") Irish journalist and politician 137, 330 A/N
("O'Dignam") 302 see Dignam, Patrick T.
(O'DONNELL, LEOPOLD) Duke of Tetuan, 19th-century Spanish prime minister 330 A/N
(O'DONNELL, MAXIMILIAN KARL) Count of Tirconnell, 19th-century aide-de-camp to the Emperor of Austria 132 A/N
(O'DONNELL MAGNUS, HUGH ROE/RED HUGH) 16th/17th-century leader of the O'Donnell clan 296, 495; S 63 A/N

(O'DONOGHUE OF THE GLENS) Celtic Catholic family of gentry in County Kerry 599 A/N see M'Conifer of the Glands

*(O'DONOHOE, M. "RUGGY") publican 250 N/T

*O'DOWD, ELIZABETH proprietress of the City Arms Hotel she called it (171), (306), (315), [586], (680) N/T p. 47 + *Thom's,* p. 1975

(O'DROMA, SOLOMON) 14th-century scribe, responsible for the Book of Ballymote 331 A/N

(O'DUIGENAM, MANUS) 14th-century scribe, responsible for the Book of Ballymote 331 A/N

(ODYSSUS) presumably the great-grandfather of St. Patrick 666 A/N

(O'Farrell) apparently a local storekeeper in the Royal Exchange Ward D 128

(O'Flynn) student at U.C.D. P 210

(O'FLYNN, FATHER) priest in ballad 170, 340 A/N

["O'Flynn, Father Malachi"] conducts Black Mass 599 see Malachi, S.; Mulligan, Malachi

("O'Gargle, Doctor") Lynch's appellation for a doctor at the Mater Misericordiae 406

(O'GAUNT, JOHN/JOHN OF GAUNT) dying Duke of Lancaster in Shakespeare's *Richard II* 210 A/N

(O'Grady) to whom Dignam owed three shillings, according to Bloom's conjecture 103

(O'GRADY, ROSIE) sweet heroine in song P 244–45 N

(O'Grady, Tom) university crony of Mr. Dedalus P 90

(O'GROWNEY, FR. EUGENE/SOGGARTH EOGHAN) professor of Irish at Maynooth and one of the founders of the Gaelic League 296; S 56, 60 A/N

(O'HAGAN, THOMAS) 19th-century Irish jurist 138 A/N

O'Halloran habitué of Davy Byrne's pub D (91), 93–96

("O'Halloran") in Brini's genealogical list 495

*O'HANLON, CANON JOHN parish priest of Mary, Star of the Sea Church 358–65, them all (377), 382, [469] N

*(O'HARA, FRANK) manufacturer of window blinds 702 N/T + *Thom's,* p. 1977

(O'HARA, JOHN/DON JUAN) English torero from Gibraltar 727 A/N

*(O'HARA, MATTHEW) on the *Irish Times,* old crony of Gallaher D 75–76

(O'HARE, DR) of the Lying-In Hospital, now deceased 373, 305–86 N
(O'HICKEY) legendary family of physicians to the O'Briens of Thomond 384 A/N
(OISIN) son of Finn MacCool, conversed with St. Patrick 200, 323 A/N
("O'Johnny, Lear") 599 see O'Leary, John
O'Keeffe student at U.C.D. P 229–32, 234–37
(O'KENNEDYS OF DUBLIN) former lords of Ormond, descended from Brian Boru 328 A/N
["Old Gummy Granny"] toothless personification of Ireland 595–600 A/N
(O'LEARY, CAOC) Caoch the piper—in ballad 624 A/N
*(O'LEARY, JOHN) Fenian editor 599 A/N
(O'LEE) heriditary family of physicians to the O'Flahertys of Connacht 384 A/N
*(Olhousen/OLHAUSEN, W.) pork butcher 434 N/T + *Thom's,* p. 1977
(Oliphant, Lancecorporal) one of the companions of the girl Edy Boardman is gossiping about 432
("Ollebo, Old, M. P.") 678 see Bloom, Leopold
(O'LOUGHLIN, J.) publican 47
(O'MALLEY, GRACE) 628 see Granuaille
(OMAR KHAYYAM) author of the *Rubaiyat* 433 A/N
(O'Mara) friend of Bags Comisky 618
(O'Molloy, J. J.) down-at-the-heels solicitor 124–44, 146–50, 225, 230–32, 319–45, S. Joseph (339), [463–74], [488]
(ONAN) biblical masturbator 729 A/N
O'Neill clerk in the Custom House S 105–9, 136–37, (159)
(O'Neill Russell) 192 see Russell, Thomas O'Neill
*(O'NEILL, HENRY J.) undertaker 71, 221, 302, 647 N/T + *Thom's,* p. 1978
(O'NEILL, HUGH) Earl of Tyrone, 16th/17th-century Irish rebel S 63
*(O'NEILL, J. J.) publican 233; D 88–89 N/T
(O'NEILL, OWEN ROE) 17th-century Irish military leader 296 A/N
(O'Neill, Sergeant) warned Mr. Casey of his impending arrest P 37
(O'NEILL, SHANE) 16th-century Earl of Tyrone, burned Armagh 296 A/N
("O'Nolan") 324 see Nolan, John Wyse

(OONA) nurse to Countess Cathleen in Yeats's play P 225 N

(OPHELIA) in Shakespeare's *Hamlet* 76, 194 A

(OPISSO, CATHERINE) dressmaker and milliner in Gibraltar 779 N

(O'REILLY, JOHN BOYLE) 19th-century patriotic poet S 157

(O'Reilly, "Maggot") an acquaintance of the Blooms, possibly Robert O'Reilly 449, 731

(O'REILLY, MYLES GEORGE) politician from Montenotte, Cork 316 N

*(O'REILLY, ALDERMAN ROBERT) merchant tailor and politician 155 N + *Thom's,* p. 1980

(O'REILLYS OF CAVAN) ancient Irish family 328 A/N

("Orelli") presumably an M. P. from Montenotte 316 see O'Reilly, Myles George

(O'Rourke, Father) friend of Father Flynn D 15–16, 17, 18

*O'ROURKE, LAWRENCE "LARRY" publican 57–58, 225, (281), [489], Larry Rhinoceros [538], [586], (750) N/T + *Thom's,* p. 1980

(O'ROURKE, TIERNAN) Prince of Breffni, whose wife deserted him in 1152 35, 132 A/N

(ORSINO) Duke of Illyria in Shakespeare's *Twelfth Night* S 29

O'Ryan, Terence curate at Barney Kiernan's pub 295–345 N

(OSCAR) son of Oisin, grandson of Finn MacCool 323 N

(O'Shaughnessy) student at U.C.D. P 210

(O'SHEA, KATHERINE "KITTY") mistress and later wife of Charles Stewart Parnell A woman 35, That bitch 650–52, they were fated to meet 654–55; P 36

(O'Shea, Kitty) someone Molly knew 751

(O'SHEA, CAPT. WILLIAM HENRY) first husband of Katherine O'Shea Her husband 650–51, the legitimate husband 655 A/N

(O'SHIEL) hereditary family of physicians to the O'Mahoneys of Oriel 384 A/N

(OSIRIS) ancient Egyptian god 142 A/N

(OSSIAN) 323 see Oisin

("Ostrolopsky") in Brini's genealogical list 495

(Osvalt, Esther) girl in Paris whose shoe Stephen tried on 49

(OTHELLO) Shakespeare's Moor 212, 443; S 29, 33 A/N

(OTTO) Duke of Bavaria 175 N

(OTTO, THOMAS) responsible for a harlequinade in *Sinbad the Sailor* 678 N
(OVID) Roman poet the elegant Latin poet 411; P 5, 179 A/N/N
(OWEN) 2nd- and 4th-century Irish kings 323 N
("Owen Caniculus") 339 see Garryowen

("P.") signature of satiric sketch in *United Irishman* 334 A/N see Griffith, Arthur; Parnell, Charles Stewart
("Paddyrisky, Pan Poleaxe") member of the F.O.T.E.I. 307 N
("Pagamimi, Avvocato") legal adviser to the president of the F.O.T.E.I. 308 N
Paget, the Hon. Mrs in second carriage of the viceregal procession 252–55 N
(PALESTRINA, GIOVANNI PIERLUIGI) 16th-century Italian composer 82 A/N
(PALGRAVE, MURPHY & CO.) Dublin steamship owners 639, 719 N
(PALISSE, JACQUES CHABANNES DE LA) French marshal killed in 1525 184 A/N
(PALLES, CHRISTOPHER) Lord Chief Baron of the Exchequer 131 A/N
(Palme*) ship that foundered off Irish coast 638 A/N
("Palme, Mrs Gloriana") participant in forest wedding 327
(PALMER, MRS BANDMAN) 76 see Bandman-Palmer, Mrs
("Panargyros") one of Bloom's silver children 494
(PANTHER) putative father of Jesus, according to Celsus 521 A/N
(PANZA, SANCHO) squire to Dox Quixote 192 A/N
(PAPARO, JOHN CARDINAL) first cardinal sent to Ireland, 12th century S 53
("Papli") 66 see Bloom, Leopold
(Pappin/PAPAN OF BALLYMUN, S.) 6th-century Irish abbott 339 N
(PARACELSUS/PHILLIPUS AUREOLUS PARACELSUS THEOPHRASTUS BOMBASTUS VON HOHENHEIM) 16th-century Swiss scientist and alchemist 297 A/N
("Parade, Sidney") not a person, but a place in southeast Dublin 297 N

(PARIS) Trojan prince who absconded with Helen and judged in Aphrodite's favor 191; D 192 A/N
Parker, Miss employee at Crosbie & Alleyne D 86, 90, (92)
(Parkes) voter canvassed by Henchy D 131
(Parkinson) presumably a remarkable tenor of the early 19th-century D 199–200 N
("PARLEY, PETER") P 53 see Goodrich, Samuel G.
PARNELL, CHARLES STEWART Irish Home Rule leader and "uncrowned king" (35), (95), (111), the chief's grave (112–13), (163), 165, (248), (298), P. (334), my famous brother (483), (492), [599], (640), (648–52), (654–55), coffin of stones (660-61), (681), (716) + mother (655); P. (7), (15), (16), (27), a public sinner (32), (34), (35–39), (70), (93), (184); this man D (122), (132–35) A/N/N/T
(PARNELL, EMILY MONROE) 165 see Dickinson, Emily Monroe
(PARNELL, FRANCES ISABEL "MAD FANNY") Charles Stewart Parnell's sister 165 N
*PARNELL, JOHN HOWARD Charles Stewart Parnell's brother and Dublin city marshal (165), (170), a long face 230, the marshal (247), 248, 253 [480], [483], [586] A/N
("Paronymous, S.") in religious procession 339 A/N
(PASCAL, BLAISE) 17th-century French philosopher + mother P 242 N
(PASIPHAË) wife of King Minos, mother of the Minotaur queens with prize bulls 207, 569 A/N
(PASTEUR, LOUIS) 19th-century French scientist 495 A/N
Pat bartender at O'Neill's D 88–89, (92)
Pat waiter at the Ormond (256), 263–91, [447] + "wife" (283)
(Pat and Bull) presumably characters in newspaper comics 119 N
("Pat, Father") proverbial priest S 55
*PATEY, T. M. in bicycle race 254
("Patrice, Saint") 645 see Patrick, S.
(PATRICK, S.) patron saint of Ireland 80, 169, 198, 200, 307, 323, 333, 338, 340, 482, 595, 645, 666 A/N
("Paul, oom") 749 see Kruger, Johannes Paulus
(PAUL, S.) early convert to Christianity 82, 102, apostle to the gentiles 333, 336; S 112 A/N
(Peake) in *Freeman's Journal* obituary 91

(Peake, "little") fired from Crosbie & Alleyne's 91, 272; D 92
(Pearcy, Mrs) presumably a cleaver murderess 593 N
(Peard, Harry) university crony of Mr. Dedalus P 90
(PEARS) manufacturer of soap 85 N
(PEARSON) London weekly penny magazine 354 N
("Pendennis") 156 Introduction see Penrose
(PENELOPE) wife of Odysseus 149, 201 A/N
("Penelope in Stratford") 202 see Shakespeare, Ann Hathaway
(Pennyfeather) apparently an old friend and/or rival of Mr. Dedalus P 250 N
Penrose boarder at the Citrons, then acquainted with the Blooms that priestylooking chap (155–56), (181), (519), [586], 731, 754
(PEPPER, JOHN) theatrical ghost performance 151 A/N
(PERDITA) daughter of Leontes in Shakespeare's *The Winter's Tale* 195 A/N
(PERICLES) title character of Shakespeare play 195 A/N
("Periplepomenos") 416 N see Fitzharris, James
(PETER NOLASCO, S.) 13th-century founder of the Mercedarians 339 A/N
("PETER THE HERMIT") Peter of Amiens, leader of the First Crusade 297 A/N
("PETER THE PACKER") 297 see O'Brien, Lord Peter
(PETER, S.) Christ's disciple and founder of the Church 82, 103, 109, 336, 390, 391, didst deny me 393, 401 A/N
("Peter, Uncle") 361 see Bloom, Leopold
("Petitépatant, Pierrepaul") member of the F.O.T.E.I. 307 N
(PHEDO) student of Socrates 215 A/N
(PHILIP II) 16th-century king of Spain 326 A/N
["Philip Drunk"] Philip of Macedonia 518–21 see Philip Sober
["Philip Sober"] 518–21 see Philip Drunk
(PHOCAS OF SINOPE, S.) gardener and martyr 339 A/N
(PHOEBE) girl addressed in song 774 A/N
(PHOTIUS) 9th-century Patriarch of Constantinople, twice excommunicated 21, 197 A/N
("Phyllis") typical girl's name in pastoral poetry 415 A/N
(PIAZZI, GIUSEPPI) 18th/19th-century Italian astronomer 700 A/N

("Pick and Pocket") typical law firm 289 see Collis & Ward
("Pickackafax, Peter") P 93 see Dedalus, Stephen
("Pidgeon, Jimmy") in Kitty's anecdote, probably intended as the Holy Dove 520
*(PIGOTT) piano and musical instruments dealer 253 N/T
(PILATE, PONTIUS) Roman governor of Judea, condemner of Christ 82, 131, 219 A/N
*(PILE, SIR THOMAS) High Sheriff of Dublin and Lord Mayor 679 N
*(PIM BROS.) Quaker merchant of linens and wool products D 51 N/T
("Pinbad") 737 see Sinbad the Sailor
(PINKER, J. B.) literary agent claimed by Beaufoy, actually James Joyce's 459 N
(Piper) apparently a minor Irish literateur 191, 214 N
(PIPER, PETER) in nursery rhyme 191
("Pippi, Dr") medical adviser to the F.O.T.E.I. 308
("Piscator, Peter") 391 see Peter, S.
(Pisimbo) Gibraltar name remembered by Molly 779
(PISISTRATUS) 6th-century B.C. usurper in Athens 415 A/N
(PITT, SIR WILLIAM) Prime Minister of England during Napoleonic Wars 17 A/N
(PIUS IX/GIOVANNI MARIA MASTAI-FERRETTI) Pope of Rome 1846–78 D 165, 167, 168–69 N
*(PLASTO, JOHN) hatmaker frequented by Bloom and Boylan 56, 92, 279 N/T + *Thom's,* p. 1987
(PLATO) 185–86; P 208 A/N/N
Playwood/HAYWOOD, CHARLES BURT) in marriage column of the *Irish Independent* 298 N
(PLUMTREE, GEORGE W.) manufacturer of potted meat 75, 154, 171, 675, 684 N/T
*(PLUNKETT, ELIZABETH MARY MARGARET, LADY FINGALL) patroness of Irish Industries Association 663 N
("Podmore") presumably a typical name 622 A/N
("Pokethankertscheff, Vladinmire") member of the F.O.T.E.I. 307 N
("Poll, Pretty") Lipoti Virag's epithet for alluring female 515
(POLONIUS) in Shakespeare's *Hamlet* G 10

(PONCHIELLI, AMILCARE) 19th-century Italian composer 69 A/N
*(PONSONBY, EDWARD) bookseller 253 N/T
(Ponto) Newfoundland dog, presumed violator of Mrs. Dandrade 536
(POOLE) traveling show 739 A/N
("Popinjay, Sir Fopling") man-about-town in Mulligan's discourse 402 A/N
("Poplar, Miss Grace") participant in forest wedding 327
("Poppens") D 39 see Hill, Eveline
(PORKORNY, JULIUS P.) professor of Celtic in Vienna and Berlin 249 A/N
(PORTER, SIR ANDREW MARSHALL) Master of the Rolls 175 N
(PORTINARI, BEATRICE) admired by Dante 637; G 11 A/N
(POTITUS) grandfather of St. Patrick 666 A/N
(Potter, Elsa) adolescent acquaintance of Milly Bloom 693
(POTTERTON) in lunacy case before the Lord Chancellor 236 N
(Pottlebelly) whom Mr. Dedalus knew at the university in Cork P 89
(Powell, Josie) 158 see Breen, Mrs. Josephine
Power, Jack employed by the Royal Irish Constabulary of Dublin Castle, friend of Martin Cunningham 87–101, 104–7, 112–13, (162), (238), 246–48, 336–45, [470], (647), (704), (773) + wife (93), (773) + father (162) + mistress (93), (773); D 152–55, 156–74 N
(POWER, JOHN, AND SONS) distillers 267, 272, 276 N
*(POWER, JOHN T.) whiskey merchant 306 N/T
Power, Miss guest at the Morkans' party D 182–84
*(POYNTZ, B.) clothing outfitter 405 T + *Thom's,* p. 1989
(PRAXITELES) 4th-century B.C. Greek sculptor P 205, 207 N
*(PRESCOTT, WILLIAM T. C.) cleaner and dyer 83, 180, 372, 775 N/T
*(Price, Henry/PRICE, GEORGE, & PRICE, HENRY) dealers in hardware and fancy goods 730 N/T + *Thom's,* p. 1990
*(PRICE, HENRY BLACKWOOD) cousin of Garrett Deasy, descendant of Sir John Blackwood, campaigner against hoof-and-mouth disease 33, 35 A/n

(PROBYN, GEN. SIR DEIGHTON MACNAGHTON) British cavalry commander 590 A/N
(PROSPERO) in Shakespeare's *Tempest* 212, 213 A/N
(PROTEUS) polymorphic Ancient of the Sea 50 N
(PSEUDO-AREOPAGITE) G 1 see Dionysius the Pseudo Areopagite
(PTOLEMY) 2nd-century Alexandrine astronomer and geographer 326 A/N
(PUE, RICHARD) edited first daily newspaper in Dublin in 1700 139 A/N
*PULBROOK, ROBERTSON & CO.) tea merchants employing Tom Kernan 239, 726, 729 N/T
(PULITZER, JOSEPH) American journalist of the "Bowery gutter sheet" 139 N
("PUNCH, MR") hero of Punch and Judy puppet play S 153
*(PURCELL, REV. F. T./THOMAS F.) of St. Saviour's Dominican Priory 318 N
Purdon, Father deliverer of businessman's sermon at St. Francis Xavier's D (164–65), 173–74 N see also Vaughan, Fr. Bernard
(Purefoy, "Bobsy") son of the Purefoys 421
(Purefoy, Charley) eldest son of the Purefoys 421
(Purefoy, Frederick Albert) deceased son of the Purefoys that died 397, 421
(Purefoy, Mamy) daughter of the Purefoys 421
(Purefoy, Mary Alice) daughter of the Purefoys 421
(Purefoy, Mortimer Edward) Mr. Purefoy's third cousin, employed in Dublin Castle 161, 421
(Purefoy, Mortimer Edward) Purefoy baby born 16 June 1904 boyaboy 383, born babe 384, of child (387), bullyboy 397, a bouncing boy 406, an heir had been born 410, baby 420, nurseling 423
Purefoy, Theodore husband of Mina Purefoy and accountant in Ulster Bank (161), Her hub (397), Glory Allelujerum (408), her dear Doady (420–21), (423–24), [491], [586], (742)
(Purefoy, Tom) son of the Purefoys 421
(Purefoy, Victoria Frances "Budgy") daughter of the Purefoys 421, budgers 742
(Purefoy, Violet Constance Louise) daughter of the Purefoys 421
Purefoy, Wilhelmina "Mina" wife of Theodore Purefoy, gives birth to her ninth child (158–59), (161), (163–64), (235),

"Putrápesthi, Countess Marha Virága Kisászony"
(280), (286), (373), Hope she's over (380), To her nothing (384), her thereto to lie in (385), the woman that lay (386), of child or woman (381), joy of her childing (388), (397), a lady, now an inmate (403), the lady who was *enceinte* (406), (408), the brave woman (420–21), In her (423), To her (424), (452), [586], [599], (729), (742) N

("Putrápesthi, Countess Marha Virága Kisászony") member of the F.O.T.E.I. 307

(Pyatt/PYAT, FÉLIX) 19th-century French revolutionary and journalist 137 N

(PYGMALION) whose sculpted Galatea came to life 176 A/N

(PYRRHUS) Greek king and general, 3rd century B.C. 24, 133–34 A/N

("Quaid, Brother") Stephen's mock name for typical Christian Brother P 166

("Quidnunc, Sir Milksop") typical busybody in Mulligan's anecdote 402

("Quiet, Doctor") personification of recommended prescription for mother and child 423

(Quigley, Mrs) neighbor of the Dignams 250

Quigley, Nurse at the Lying-In Hospital 392, [522]

*(QUILL, ALBERT WILLIAM) barrister and occasional poet 638 A/N

(Quinlan) in *Freeman's Journal* obituary 91

*(QUINNELL, GEORGE) printer 401 N/T

*(QUIRKE, THOMAS G.) solicitor, layman in religious procession 318 N

(QUIXOTE, DON) Cervantes' rueful knight 192 A/N

*RABAIOTTI, ANTONIO Italian ice cream vendor 225, 429, (434) N/T + *Thom's,* p. 1992

(RABELAIS, FRANÇOIS) 16th-century French monk and author 751 A/N

(RACHEL) sister of Leah in Old Testament 76 A/N

(RAFTERY, ANTHONY) 19th-century blind Irish poet 312 A/N

(RAHAB) harlot who aided in the destruction of Jericho 589 A/N

(RAKOCZY II, FRANCIS) Transylvanian whose army adopted the Hungarian march tune 343 A/N
(RALEIGH, SIR WALTER) Elizabethan courtier and poet 201, 478 A/N
(RALLI, BARON AMBRIGIO) resident of Trieste G 15
("Ramsbottom, Mrs") type of name deplored by Molly 761
(RAOUL) apparently the lover in *Sweets of Sin* 236, 258, 260, 263, 288, 382, 565
(RASCHID, HAROUN AL) Caliph of Bagdad in *Arabian Nights* 47, 540, 586 A/N
RATH, PATRICK "Paddy" pupil at Clongowes Wood P 13, 54
(RAVELLI) operatic tenor D 199
(RAWDON-HASTINGS, HENRY WEYSFORD) 19th-century English horse owner 32 N
("Raymonde"*) wax model in shoe shop 529
(RÉAUMUR, RENÉ-ANTOINE FERCHAULT DE) 18th-century French physicist 704
*(REDDY, RICHARD, AND DAUGHTER) antique dealers 243 N/T
(REDMAYNE, WILLIAM T.) in *Irish Independent* births column + wife and newborn son 298 N
*(REDMOND, JOHN) leader of the Home Rule party in early 20th century 599 A/N
("Reephen") S 165 see Daedalus, Stephen
(Reeves, Miss) student at U.C.D. S 131
("Reggy") lover in Bloom's amorous fantasy 169
(RENAN, ERNEST) 19th-century French critic 195, 205; S 175, 189–90 A/N
REPULSE horse owned by Lord Hastings (32), [573] N
(REUBEN) son of Jacob and Leah in Old Testament 93 A
(REYNARD) fox hero of medieval beast epic 553 A/N
(Reynolds, Bob) one of Stephen's creditors 31
["Rhinoceros, Larry"] 538 see O'Rourke, Lawrence
("Rhodes, Dusty") typical name for a tramp 427, 496 see M'Intosh
(RICCI, LORENZO) 18th-century General of the Jesuits P 56 N
(RICE, REV. EDMUND IGNATIUS) founded the Irish Christian Brothers 339 A/N
*(RICE, IGNATIUS S.) solicitor, for the Waterworks Committee 671 N + *Thom's,* p. 1996
(RICH, EDWARD) 8th Earl of Warwick P 115

(RICH, LADY PENELOPE) Sir Philip Sidney's "Stella" 149, 201 A/N
(RICHARD III) English king and Shakespeare villain 201, 209, 211 A/N
(RICHARD, S.) 13th-century English bishop and Chancellor of Oxford 339 A/N
Ricketts, Kitty whore in Bella Cohen's establishment 501–86, 587–600
(RIENZI, COLA DE) 14th-century tribune of Rome by usurpation 308 a/N
("Right, Miss") Bloom's personification of the ideal bride for Stephen 656
("Right, Mr") Bloom's conception of the ideal husband 369
(RIGHTAWAY) sire of Throwaway 648
(RIMBAUD, ARTHUR) 19th-century French poet S 32
("Rinbad") 727 see Sinbad the Sailor
("Rinderpest, Doctor") presumably a Russian cow-catcher but actually a bovine disease 399 N
Riordan, Mrs/"Dante" widow residing with the Dedaluses and then at the City Arms Hotel where she knew the Blooms (97), (174), an old one (305–6), [490], [586], (680–81), (738) + nephew (305); P 7–8, (10–11), (15), (16), (18), 27–39, (93) + brother P (35) N/N
(Riordan, Mr) husband of "Dante" Riordan 738
(RIPON, MARQUESS OF) 717 see Robinson, George Frederick Samuel
(Rippingham, Winny) acquaintance of Gerty MacDowell 357, 366
("Risabel") S 165 see Daedalus, Isabel
(RISTORI, ADELAIDE) Italian tragedienne 76 A/N
Rivière, André Canadian member of the car racing team D 42–48
(ROBARTES, MICHAEL) character in Yeats's poems P 251; S 178 N
(Roberto) subject in Italian dispute overheard by Bloom and Stephen 637
(Roberts) one of Bloom's clients, possibly George Roberts 69
(ROBERTS, LORD FREDERICK SLEIGH) British military hero of South Africa 421, 748 A/N
*(ROBERTS, GEORGE) literary businessman, managing editor of Maunsel and Co. 192 N

("Robinson") figure in Bloom's hypothetical advertisement 154
(ROBINSON, GEORGE FREDERICK SAMUEL, MARQUESS OF RIPON) English Liberal politician in favor of Home Rule for Ireland 717 a/N
ROCHE, GEORGE REDDINGTON "Nasty" pupil at Clongowes Wood P 8–9, 13, 52–53 + father (26) Sullivan, pp. 48–49
*ROCHFORD, TOM associate of Lenehen and Nosey Flynn 178–79, 232, (233), 253, (267), (299), [474], [598] N
(ROCHFORT, MARY) accused of adultery with her brother-in-law, recollected by Father Conmee 223 A/N
Rock bailiff employed at the subsheriff's office 170, (245) N
(ROCKEFELLER, JOHN D.) American multimillionaire 719 A/N
(RODOT) Parisian patisserie remembered by Stephen 42 N
(Rogers) an acquaintance of the Blooms 449
(ROGERS, PHILIP) sued by William Shakespeare 204
(ROMEO) 108, 333; D 186 see Montague, Romeo
(RÖNTGEN, WILHELM CONRAD) 19th-century discoverer of the X-ray 634 A/N
(ROONEY, ANDY) hero of Samuel Lover's *Handy Andy* 530 A/N
(ROONEY, MICKY) typical band in Irish songs 289 N
(Rory) 297 see Bloom, Rudolph
(RORY OF THE HILL) Irish rebel hero—in song 295 A/N
(ROSA, CARL) 19th-century opera company 618 A/N
(Rosales y O'Reilly) composite Spanish/Irish name remembered by Molly from Gibraltar 779
("Rosalie") whore in Mulligan's travesty 214, 217 A/N
(ROSE OF CASTILLE) heroine of Balfe opera 297 A/N see Elvira
(ROSE OF LIMA, S.) first canonized saint of Spanish America 339 A/N
(ROSE OF VITERBO, S.) 13th-century Italian saint 339 A/N
*[ROSENBERG, HARRIS] member of Dublin's Jewish community 544 Hyman, p. 328

(ROSSA, JEREMIAH O'DONOVAN) Fenian leader 297; D 31 A/N/N

(ROSSINI, GIOACCHINO ANTONIO) 19th-century Italian composer 82, 661 A/N

(Roth) Clongowes acquaintance of Stephen S 71 see Rath, Patrick

(Rotha Marion) 298 see Gillett, Rotha Marian

(ROTHSCHILD, BARON LEOPOLD) international banker and owner of 1904 Derby winner, St. Amant 174, 495, (or one of the other members of that family) 719, 728 A/N

(ROUND, JOHN) English manufacturer of cutlery 309 N

*(ROURKE, JAMES) baker 614 N/T

(ROUSSEAU, JEAN-JACQUES) 18th-century French philosopher 495; P 200; S 40 A/N/N

Routh English friend of the car drivers D 46–48

(ROWAN, ARCHIBALD HAMILTON) a leader of the United Irishmen E 45; P 10, 56 N

Rowan, Archie son of Bertha and Richard Rowan E (16–17), (19), (23–24), (25), 26–30, (43), 44–47, (51–52), (55), 56, (64), (66), 91–92, (100), (102), 109–10 Introduction

Rowan, Bertha Richard Rowan's common-law wife E (16–17), (19), (23–24), (25), (26), (27), 28–37, (39-40), (42–43), 45, (46), 47–56, (58), (59–72), 72–88, 89–98, 99–107, (107), (108–9), 110–12

Rowan, Richard Irish writer returned from self-exile in Italy E (15), (16), 17–25, (28), (33–34), 36–56, 58–75, (76–78), (80–88), (89), (90), (91–98), 98–100, 102–4, (105–6), 106–12 + father (15), (24–25) + mother (22–25), (52), (90), (103)

*(ROWE, ANDREW) publican 161 N/T

(ROYCE, EDWARD WILLIAM) 19th-century English actor 10 A/N

(Rubio, Captain) whose spyglass Molly remembers having borrowed in Gibraltar 762 Introduction

(Rubio, Mrs) Molly's servant in Gibraltar, possibly widow of the captain 759, 760, 779 N; Introduction

(Rublin, Mrs Gus) in testimonial for bust expander 545

(Ruby) heroine of book Molly has been reading 64, 454, 653, 751 A/N see also Cohen, Ruby

Rumbold, Harry barber/hangman whose soliciting letter Joe Hynes reads (303), (308–9), [471], [593–94] A/N

*(RUSH, FRANCIS "JOHNNY") rented carriages in Dublin D 17
(RUSKIN, JOHN) 19th-century English writer S 148
(Russell, Colonel) speaker at the debating society S 172–74
*RUSSELL, GEORGE/"A E" Dublin mystic/poet, editor of the *Irish Homestead* (31), (35), (140), (160), 165, 184–93, (195), (206), (372), (398) A/N
*RUSSELL, THOMAS lapidarian 241–42 N/T
(RUSSELL, THOMAS O'NEILL) Irish writer and language enthusaist 192 a/N
(RUTLAND, EARL OF/ROGER MANNERS) one of those credited with having written Shakespeare's plays 208, 214 A/N
("Rutlandbaconsouthamptonshakespeare") 208 see Bacon, Sir Francis; Rutland, Earl of; Shakespeare, William; Southampton, Earl of
(RUTTLEDGE) employed in the office of the *Freeman's Journal* 116, 282 N
(RYAN, FR FRANCIS/Mr) master at Belvedere College D 22 Sullivan p. 92
*(RYAN, FRED) writer and co-editor of *Dana* 31, 214 A/N
Ryan, Terry curate at Barney Kiernan's 295–345 see O'Ryan, Terence

(SABELLIUS) 3rd-century heretic 21, 208 A/N
(SACHER MASOCH, LEOPOLD VON) 19th-century Austrian novelist 235 A/N
(SADGROVE) a surveyor who sued for libel 321 A/N
(SAINT AMANT) horse that won the 1904 Derby 174 A/N
(SAINT FRUSQUIN) sire of Saint Amant 174
(SAINT LEGER OF DONEREILE) 178 see Aldworth, Elizabeth
(SALANCA, Peter/PATER) prior of Spanish Trappist monastery 243 N
(SALISBURY, LORD/ROBERT ARTHUR TALBOT GASCOYGNE-CECIL) Conservative British Prime Minister 133 A/N
(SALLUST/GAIUS SALLUSTIUS CRISPUS) 1st-century B.C. Roman historian 134 A/N

*SALMON, REV. DR GEORGE mathematician and provost of T. C. D. (164), (170), (253), [586], (690) N
(SALOME) mother of the Maccabees in Old Testament martyrdom 297 A/N
(SAMBO) black boy in children's story 443
(SAMUEL) Old Testament prophet 728 A/N
(SANDOW, EUGENE/EUGEN, pseudonym of FREDERIC) MULLER) performing strong man and author of book of exercises 61, 435, 681, 709, 721 A/N
(SANDOW-WHITELEY) 721 see Sandow, Eugene
("Saphiro") 322 see Wought, James
(SARA) Abraham's wife in Burns's poem 425 N
(Sarah, Nurse) in the Daedalus household S 101, 134
Sargent, Cyril pupil at Mr. Deasy's school 27–29 + mother (27)
(SARSFIELD, PATRICK) Earl of Lucan, Irish Jacobite general at Battle of the Boyne 296, 330; S 63 A/N
(SATAN) 83, 184, 203, 553; D 171; S 222 A see also Lucifer
(SAURIN, MICHAEL) pupil at Clongowes Wood P 13, (26) + father (26)
("Savorgnanovich") in Brini's genealogical list 496
(SAYERS, TOM) 19th-century English boxing champion 242, 318 A/N
*SCAIFE, C. in bicycle race 254
*(SCALLY, REV. MICHAEL D.) parish priest at St. Nicholas R. C. church 318 N + *Thom's,* p. 2006
(SCARLI) husband and wife in Italian play seen by the Blooms 769 A/N
SCEPTRE losing horse in Gold Cup backed by Boylan and Lenehen (128), (174), (265), (325), (415), Bass's mare (416), Mare (426), [573], (648) N
(SCHOLASTICA, S.) 6th-century nun, sister of St. Benedict 339 A/N
("Schwanzenbad-Hodenthaler, Leopold Rudolph von") member of the F.O.T.E.I. 307
("Schwarz") in Brini's genealogical list 495
(SCOTT, SIR WALTER) 19th-century English novelist P 228; D 25, 29 N
*(SCOTT, WILLIAM) tailor 240 N/T; Introduction
(SCOTUS, JOHN DUNS) 42; see Duns, John

(Sebastian, Father) a Passionist Father that Bloom suspects of having had an affair with Molly 731 N
(SEDDON, FREDERIC) executed for poison murder 593 A/N
Ségouin, Charles French racing car driver D 42–48
[Selene, Princess] prospective second Mrs. Bloom, named for Greek moon goddess 483 A/N
(SENAN, S.) 6th-century Irish monk 339 A/N
(Servasius/SERVATIUS, S.) 4th-century bishop of Tongres 339 A/N
*(SEWELL, JAMES WALTER) of Sewell, Son & Simpson, veterinarian 249 N/T
(Sexton) in *Freeman's Journal* obituary 91
*(SEXTON, WALTER) jeweler and watchmaker 165 N/T + *Thom's,* p. 2008
(Seymour) friend of Buck Mulligan 7, 22
*(SHACKLETON, GEORGE, & SONS) flour and corn merchants 239 N/T + *Thom's,* p. 2008
(SHAKEBAG) character in *Arden of Feversham* 209 see also Shakespeare, William
(SHAKESPEARE, ANN HATHAWAY) wife of William Shakespeare 189–91, 193, 196–97, 201–3, 206, 210, 211, 212, 215 + father's shepherd (203) A/N
(SHAKESPEARE, EDMUND) brother of William Shakespeare 209, 210, 211 A/N
(SHAKESPEARE, GILBERT) brother of William Shakespeare 209, 210 A/N
(SHAKESPEARE, HAMNET) son of William Shakespeare 188, 189, 208 A/N
(SHAKESPEARE, JOAN) sister of William Shakespeare 202–3 A/N
(SHAKESPEARE, JOHN) father of William Shakespeare a butcher's 187, 202, 206, 207 A/N
(SHAKESPEARE, JUDITH) daughter of William Shakespeare + husband 202–3 A/N
(SHAKESPEARE, MARY ARDEN) mother of William Shakespeare 202, 207, 208 A/N
("Shakespeare, Patrick W.") 297 see Patrick, S.; Shakespeare, William N
(SHAKESPEARE, RICHARD) brother of William Shakespeare 209, 210, 211, 213 A/N

(SHAKESPEARE, SUSAN) daughter of William Shakespeare + husband 202–3, 212 A/N
SHAKESPEARE, WILLIAM (18), (28), (30), (96), (152), (193–98), (201–15), (248), (280), the poet's (419), (432), (446), (505), [567–68], (570), (622), (634), our national poet (636), (661), (677), (690), (700), (708); D (157), (179); S (25), (29), (41), (79), (102–3), (172), (185); G 10 A/N/N
(SHAKTI) in Hindu religion the wife of male deity 510 A/N
("Shanganagh") pen name of Arthur Griffith 334 A/N
(Shannon) one of the boat club swells known by Miss Dunne 229
(Sharon, Larby) ? person or place remembered by Molly from Gibraltar 782
(SHAW, GEORGE BERNARD) Irish playwright 196 N
(SHEARES, HENRY and JOHN) brothers who belonged to the United Irishmen and were executed after the 1798 rebellion 305 A/N
(SHEBA, QUEEN OF) reputed mistress of King Solomon 201, 297 A/N
*(SHEEHY, DAVID) Irish Nationalist member of Parliament 165, 219 A/N/T
*SHEEHY, MRS DAVID wife of David Sheehy 219 + sons (219)
(Sheila) bride of fellow to be hanged 309–10
Shelley, Mr chief clerk at Crosbie and Alleyne D (87), 88, 89, 90, 92
(SHELLEY, PERCY BYSSHE) English Romantic poet 185, 194; P 96, 103, 213; S 129, 148 A/N/N
(SHELTON, R.) producer of *Sinbad the Sailor* at the Gaiety 678 N
(Sheridan) boarder at Mrs. Mooney's D 62, 65
(Sheridan) one of the reputed violators of Mrs. Dandrade 536
*SHERLOCK, LORCAN secretary of the Dublin Corporation (247), [479] N
("Shipahoy") 637 see Murphy, W. B.
(SHIPTON, MOTHER) 17th-century English prophetess 376 A/N
(SHIVA) Hindu deity, the Destroyer 510 A/N
("Shortall, Mary") poxy whore in Kitty Ricketts's anecdote + child 520 see Mary, B.V.

SHOTOVER Duke of Westminster's horse in picture on Deasy's wall (32), [573] A/N
Shuley pupil at Belvedere P 168–69
*[Shulomowitz, M./SHMULOWITZ, M] librarian at the Jewish Library in Dublin 544 N + Hyman, pp. 328–29
(SHYLOCK) moneylender in Shakespeare's *Merchant of Venice* 204, 313 A/N see also Bridgman
[SIBYL, VEILED] defender of Bloom 491–92
(SIDNEY, SIR PHILIP) Elizabethan courtier and sonneteer 205, 211 A/N
*(SIGERSON, GEORGE) Dublin doctor and man of letters 192 A/N
("Silberselber") one of Bloom's silver children 494
("Silversmile") one of Bloom's silver children 494
(SIMNEL, LAMBERT) 15th-century Yorkist pretender to the throne of England as Edward VI 45 A/N
(SIMON MAGUS) convert to Christianity who tried to buy the power of laying on of hands P 159; simony D 9 N
(SIMON STYLITES, S.) 5th-century anchorite 339 A/N
"Simonlionel" 289 see Dedalus, Simon; Lionel
(SIMPSON, GEORGE) founder of Dublin hospital 752
(Simpson, Georgina) friend of the Blooms from their courtship days 444, 742
(SINBAD THE SAILOR) character in *Arabian Nights* and pantomime subject 636, 678, 737 A/N
*(SINCLAIR, WILLIAM or HENRY MORRIS) grandsons of Morris Harris 166; Don't see him 170 Hyman, p. 148; Introduction
Sinico, Captain nautical husband of Emily Sinico D 110, (114–15) + great great grandfather (110)
Sinico, Emily Dublin housewife befriended by James Duffy (114), a lady who is dead? (333), (695), (711); D 109–12, (113–17) N
Sinico, Mary daughter of Capt. and Mrs. Sinico D 109, 110, (115)
"Siopold" 276 see Bloom, Leopold; Dedalus, Simon
(SIR HUGO) horse that won the 1892 Derby 647
(SIRR, MAJOR HENRY CHARLES) captured Lord Edward Fitzgerald 241; D 125 A/N/N
(SISYPHUS) condemned in Hades to constantly push a rock up a mountain 587 A/N
(SITTING BULL) Sioux Indian chief 552 A/N

(SKEAT, W. W.) English lexicographer S 26, 30
*(SKERRY, GEORGE EDWARD, & CO.) commercial college 766 N/T + *Thom's,* p. 1513
(SKINNER, JAMES) 19th-century British military adventurer in India 590 A/N
("Skin-the-Goat") 136 see Fitzharris, James
(SLATTERY) leader of a hard-drinking brigade in Percy French song 424 A/N
(Slattery, Rev. B. R.) in religious procession 318 possibly Rev. J. D. Slattery of St. Saviour's, Dublin
*(SLATTERY, WILLIAM) publican 335 N/T
[SLIGO, MAYOR OF] in procession for Bloom 480
("Slipperslapper, Mother") 475 see Cohen, Bella
(SLOPER, ALLY) English comic strip character 506 A/N
("Smerdoz") in Brini's genealogical list 495
("Smith") alias used by the boy relating the events D 26
*(SMITH, ELLEN) sailors' outfitter P 176 T
*(SMITH, PHILIP H. LAW) barrister 250 N/T
(Smith, Toad) presumably a hanged murderer 303 A/N
(Smythe-Smythe, Lieutenant) presumably a violator of Mrs. Dandrade 536
("So and So, Mr.") conversant with Mr. Fulham S 249
("So-and-So, Messrs") Bloom's designation for Parnell's successors 649
("Socks, Padney") 693 see Bloom, Milly
(SOCRATES) 190, 202, 213, 217, 432; S 117 A/N
Sohan, Jack Belvedere pupil, possibly son of John Sohan, pawnbroker 220 N
(SOLOMON) Hebrew king 285 N
(SOLOMON OF DROMA) 331 see O'Droma, Solomon
*(SOLOMONS, E. M./MAURICE E.) optician and Austro-Hungarian consul 254 N/T, p. 43 + *Thom's,* p. 2015
("Sometimes Godly, Mr") 396 see Madden, William
(SOUTHAMPTON, EARL OF/HENRY WRIOTHESLEY) Shakespeare's patron 208 A/N
(SPALLANZANI, LAZZARO) 18th-century Italian biologist 418 A/N
("Spark") 322 see Wought, James
*(SPARROW AND CO.) outfitters and linen merchants 360 N/T

("Speranza") 306 see Wilde, Lady Jane
(SPINOZA, BARUCH) 17th-century Jewish Dutch philosopher 284, 342, 687, 708, 769 A/N
("Spiro") 322 see Wought, James
(SPRAGUE, HORATIO JONES) U.S. consul in Gibraltar in late 19th century 757 A/N
(SPRAGUE, JOHN LEWIS) son of old Sprague and vice-consul in Gibraltar 757 A/N
*(SPRING AND SONS) coal factors 253 N
("Spurgeon") recent deceased overdue in heaven—in Bloom's joke 109
("Squaretoes, Thomas") S 145 see Cranly
(ST AUSTELL, IVAN/W. H. STEPHENS) sang with opera company in Dublin 664 A/N
(ST JUST, HILTON) sang with opera company in Dublin 664 A/N
(Stack, Miss) brought Bloom flowers when he sprained his ankle, remembered by Molly 738
(Stanhope, Hester) Molly's friend in Gibraltar 755–57, 782 A/N
(Stanhope, Mr/"Wogger") husband of Hester Stanhope 755–57, 782
(STANISLAUS KOSTKA, S.) 16th-century Jesuit novice and patron of youth 339; P 56 A/N/N
*(STARKEY, JAMES S./"SEAMUS O'SULLIVAN") Irish poet and editor 192–93 N
Starkie, Captain friend of Mr. Fulham S 242–44 + lady friend S (242–43)
("Staylewit") in mock Parliamentary debate 316
(STEAD, WILLIAM THOMAS) English editor of the *Review of Reviews* P 196; S 112 N
(STEEVENS, MADAME GRISSEL) 18th-century benefactress to the Dublin sick 411, 569 A/N
(STEPHEN PROTOMARTYR, S.) first Christian martyr 339, 481; P 159 A/N
("Stephaneforos") P 168–69 see Dedalus, Stephen
("Stephanoumenos") 210, 415; P 168 see Dedalus, Stephen
*STEPHENS, DAVY newspaper vendor and Dublin character 116, [469] N
(STEPHENS, JAMES) 19th-century Fenian Head Centre 43, 68, 163, 316, 484 A/N

*(STEPHENS, JAMES) poet and folklorist 192 N

(STERLING, ANTOINETTE) late 19th-century contralto 706 N

*STEVENSON, F. in bicycle race 254

("Stewart") 649 see Parnell, Charles Stewart

("Stink, Paddy") Mr. Dedalus's designation for typical student of the Christian Brothers P 71 see also Mud, Mickey

(STOCKMANN, DR) hero of Ibsen's *An Enemy of the People* S 86

(Stoer, Mr) neighbor of the Dignams 251, 351 + son (251) N

(Stoer, Mrs) neighbor of the Dignams 250 N

*(STOKER, SIR WILLIAM THORNLEY) surgeon 466 N/T + *Thom's,* p. 2018

("Stoom") 682 see Bloom, Leopold; Dedalus, Stephen

("STRATTON, EUGENE"/EUGENE AUGUSTUS RUHLMANN) American blackface comic 92, 222, 254, 443 A/N

("STRONGBOW"/RICHARD FITZGILBERT DE CLARE, EARL OF PEMBROKE) 12th-century invader of Ireland 44 A/N

*(STUBBS) insurers and debt recovery agents 320 N/T + *Thom's,* p. 45

*(STUBBS, HENRY G.) superintendent of Board of Public Works, Phoenix Park 160–61 N

(SUAREZ, FRANCISCO) Spanish Jesuit theologian, 16th/17th century P 242

(SULLIVAN, JOHN L.) 19th-century world heavyweight champion 297 A/N

Supple, Bertha friend of Gerty MacDowell and Edy Boardman (348), (352), (364), (365–66), 431–32

(SVENGALI) villain in du Maurier's *Trilby* 526 A/N

*(SWAN, REV. BROTHER WILLIAM A.) director of Institute for Destitute Children 219 N/T

(SWEDENBORG, EMANUEL) 18th-century Swedish mystic, nicknamed Daedalus Hyperboreus P 224; G 1 N

(SWEELINCK, JANS PIETER) 16th/17th-century Dutch composer 663; G 16 A/N

*SWENY, F. W. pharmacist 84–85, [440], (676) N/T

(SWIFT, JONATHAN) 18th-century satirist and Dean of St. Patrick's A hater of his kind 39, 588 A/N

("Swillale, Ape") 396 see Ape Swillale, Mr

(SWINBURNE, ALGERNON CHARLES "ALGY") 19th-century English poet 5, 37, 187, 249, 519 A/N

(SWITHIN, S.) 9th-century English bishop of Winchester 397 N

*(SWITZER AND CO.) drapers 767 N/T

*(SYNGE, JOHN MILLINGTON) Irish dramatist 193, 198, 200, 216 A/N

("Synonymous, S.") in religious procession 339 A/N

("Szombathely") in Brini's genealogical list 496

(TACITUS) 1st/2nd-century Roman historian 326; S 128 A/N

(TALAVERA, JUAN MARIANA DE) P 246 see Mariana de Talavera de la Reina, Juan de

Talbot pupil at Mr. Deasy's school 24–27

(TALBOT DE MALAHIDE, LADY MAUD) wife of Richard Talbot in 14th century maid, wife and widow 223 A/N

(TALBOT DE MALAHIDE, LORD RICHARD) 12th-century Lord Admiral of Malahide 223, 616 A/N

(TALBOT DE MALAHIDE, SIR RICHARD) 14th-century heir of the first Lord Admiral 223 A/N

(TALBOT DE MALAHIDE, RICHARD WOGAN) who sold Lambay Island in 19th century 402 N

Talbot, Florry prostitute at Bella Cohen's 501–86

(Talbot, Katherine) John Corley's grandmother 616

Talboys, Hanna/Mrs Merwyn aristocratic accuser of Bloom haughty creature (73), [467–74], [594] N

Tallon, Bertie pupil at Belvedere P 74, painted little boy (77)

*(TALLON, DANIEL) former Lord Mayor of Dublin 58, 679 A/N + *Thom's*, p. 2022

Tallon, Mrs Bertie Tallon's mother P 74

(TANDY, JAMES NAPPER) Irish revolutionary and secretary of the United Irishmen 44 A/N

*(TANDY, SHAPLAND MORRIE) taxing master, Supreme Court of Judicature 39 *Thom's*, p. 2022

(TANTALUS) condemned by the gods to a tantalizing torture in Hades 115 A/N

("Taptun, Master") typical medieval innkeeper who taps a tun of ale 336 see Kiernan, Bernard

("Tar, Jack") catchname for typical British sailor 329, 653 N
Tate, Mr English master at Belvedere P 79, 125; S (241–42)
Tatters dog belonging to cockle pickers on Sandymount Strand 46
("TAXIL, LÉO"/pseudonym of GABRIEL S. JOGAND-PAGES) mockingly anti-clerical 19th-century French author 41, 391 A/N
(TAYLOR, JOHN F.) 19th-century Irish barrister and orator 141–43, 464 A/N
(Taylor, Officer) paramour of adultress Belle Tupper in *Police Gazette* 324, 333
(TEARLE, GEORGE OSMOND) 19th-century English Shakespearean actor 690 A/N
(TEAZLE, SIR PETER) character in Sheridan's *School for Scandal* 8 A/N
("Teddy") D 198 see Malins, Freddy
(TELL, WILLIAM) legendary 14th-century Swiss hero 297, 626 A/N
Temple Stephen's acquaintance at U.C.D. and later his creditor (31), (39); P 196–201, 229–32, 234–37, (238), (242); S 105–9, 114–15, 173–74, 223–26 N
TENNYSON, ALFRED LORD Victorian poet (50), (202), [588]; P (80); S 148 A/N
(Terence, S.) either 1st-century bishop or 3rd-century martyr 339 a/N see also O'Ryan, Terence
(TERESA OF AVILA, S.) 16th-century Spanish reformer of the Carmelite order 339 A/N
(TERESA OF THE CHILD JESUS, BLESSED SISTER) 19th-century Carmelite nun 339 A/N
(THAISA) dead wife of Pericles, Prince of Tyre 195
("Thatbody, Dr") cited by Stephen as an authority on masturbation S 55
(THEODOTUS, S.) 4th-century martyr 339 A/N
("Theosophos") Stephen's mock prototype of a theosophist 416
("Theother, Miss") from Molly's mock list of patriotic sopranos 762
("This, Miss") from Molly's mock list of patriotic sopranos 762
("Thisbody, Dr") cited by Stephen as an authority on masturbation S 55

*(THOM, ALEXANDER) printer and publisher, Bloom's former employer 123, 155, 342, 377, 708, 772 N/T
("Thomas, John") personification of the penis 426 A/N see Leo XIII
(THOMAS, S.) 205 see Aquinas, S. Thomas
(THOMPSON, SIR HENRY) Parnell's London medical specialist 649 N
(THOR) Scandinavian god of thunder 394 A/N
*(THORNTON, JAMES J.) fruiterer and florist 227 N/T
*THORNTON, MRS midwife at the births of Milly and Rudy (66), (162), [494] N
(THOTH) Egyptian god of learning and magic 193; P 225 A/N
*THRIFT, H. in bicycle race 254
THROWAWAY horse that won the 1904 Gold Cup throw it away (85–86), (325), (335), (415), Hundred shillings to five (470), (534), A dark horse [573], (604), (648), (676), that outsider that won (750) N
THUNDER, CECIL schoolboy at Clongowes Wood P (9), 40–45, 52–53 Sullivan, p. 48
(TIBBLE, DR) brand of cocoa 635
(TICHBORNE, ROGER CHARLES) missing heir impersonated in 19th-century law case 650 A/N
(Tierney, Richard J.) Nationalist candidate for the Royal Exchange Ward D 119, Has he paid 121, 122, 123, that little shoeboy 127, he's not so bad 127, He's not a bad sort 128, 129, 131 + father 123
(TIETJENS/TITIENS, THERESE JOHANNA ALEXANDRA) 19th-century Hungarian-German soprano D 199
(Tighe) friend of John Corley 618
(Tilsit, Jessie) presumably a murder victim 303
Tim barman at the Scotch House D 94
"Tim" or "Tom" barman in Cork pub P 95
(Timothy) 424 see O'Brien, Sir Timothy
("Tinbad") 737 see Sinbad the Sailor
("Tittlemouse, Tommy") 500 see Bloom, Leopold
(Tivy, Dick) Cork acquaintance of Mr. Dedalus and Ned Lambert 102
*(TOBIAS, MATTHEW) solicitor 615 N + *Thom's*, p. 2028
(Tobin, Pat) responsible for Gumley's job as nightwatchman 639

(Toby, Uncle) presumably author of children's page in a newspaper 119
*(TODD, BURNS AND CO.) clothiers 102, 752 N/T
(TOFT) owner of a traveling amusement company 526, 578 N
("Toga Girilis") female poet in U.C.D. magazine S 182, 187
("Tom") Stephen's designation for a typical Irish peasant S 64
("Tom the Devil") Molly's contemptuous name of one of Bloom's clients 775
("Tom, Dick, and Harry") traditional names for typical man in the street 19, 650
("Tom, Peeping") tailor who ogled Lady Godiva in her nakedness 163, 368 A/N
("Tomkin") hypothetical replacement for the long-gone sailor 624
(TOMKINS, THOMAS) 16th-century English composer 662 A/N
(Tomlinson, lieutenantcolonel Tomkin-Maxwell ffrenchmullan) provost marshal at the epic hanging 310 + wife (310)
("TOMMASO MASTINO, SAN") 637 see Aquinas, S. Thomas
("Tommy") bookmaker at the racetrack; slang for money 573 N
(TONE, THEOBOLD WOLFE) Irish martyr of 1798 229, 297, 305, 593, 599; P 184 A/N/N/T, p. 72
(Torry/TORREY, REUBEN ARCHER) American revivalist in Dublin in 1904 151 A/N
("Tostoff, Toby") onanistic character in Mulligan's parody 217
*(TOWERS, FITZGERALD AND CO.) estate agents 61 T + *Thom's,* p. 2069
Towser pupil at Belvedere P 168–69
(TREBELLI, MME/ZELIA GILBERT) 19th-century French soprano D 199
(TREE, SIR HERBERT BEERBOHM) English actor 767 A/N
(TRILBY) title character of Du Maurier's novel 767 A/N
(TRISTAN) lover of Isolde 297 A/N
Troy, Inspector retired member of the Dublin Metropolitan Police and acquaintance of the Nameless One (292), [586]
(Truelock/TRULOCK, HARRIS & RICHARDSON) gun manufacturers 452 N/T + *Thom's,* p. 2028
("Trumps, Mynheer Trik van") member of the F.O.T.E.I. 307

("Tully") 394 see Cicero, Marcus Tullius
*(TUNNEY, WILLIAM JAMES) grocer 250, 251, 355, 568 N/T + *Thom's,* p. 2028
(Tupper, Belle) adultress in divorce scandal 324, 333
(Tupper, Norman W.) Chicago contractor with unfaithful wife, Belle 324
(TURGENIEFF/TURGÉNIEV, IVAN) 19th-century Russian novelist S 42
(TURKO THE TERRIBLE) king in pantomime 10, 57, 596 A/N
(Turnbull, Cecil) Bloom's acquaintance during adolescence 667 N
*[TURNBULL, DONALD] Bloom's friend from the High School, possibly same as Cecil Turnbull 548 N + *Thom's,* p. 2028
(TURPIN, DICK) 18th-century English highwayman 297; P 215 A/N
(TWANKEY, WIDOW) Aladdin's mother in pantomime 438 N
Tweedy, "Major" Brian Cooper Molly Bloom's father (56), (57), (72), (93), (269), (319) the old major (377), (409), (457), [596], [601], (652), (667), (710), (730), father was the same (738), the real father (741), father waiting (746), father being in the army (748), like father (752), your father (755), father talking (757), father was up (759), soldiers daughter am I (762), all father left me (763), he told father (765), father bought it (772), and father (782) N
*(TWEEDY, HENRY R.) Crown solicitor, County Waterford 93 N/T + *Thom's,* p. 2029
("Tweedy-Flower") grand opera company envisioned by Bloom 627
("Twelvetrees, Mrs Clyde") participant in forest wedding 327
*TWIGG, LIZZIE A E's protégée who answered Bloom's ad (160), 165–66, Rumpled stockings (372) N
(TYLER, WAT) 14th-century leader of English peasant revolt 495 A/N
(Tyson) student at Belvedere P 81

("Ueberallgemein, Kriegfried") member of the F.O.T.E.I. 307
[ULSTER KING OF ARMS] chief official of the College of Arms 480 N
(ULTAN, S.) 7th-century Irish missionary 389 A/N

(ULYSSES/ODYSSEUS) the wily Greek—in Shakespeare's *Troilus and Cressida* 195, 212 A/N
(Underdone's) apparently a Dublin restaurant P 97
(Urbright) in *Freeman's Journal* obituary 91
(Ursula) maid in the employ of Mulligan's aunt 6 A/N see also Ursula, S.
(URSULA, S.) martyred princess who led 11,000 virgins to be slaughtered by the Huns 339 A/N

(VALENTI, GIULIO) Italian embryologist 418 A/N
(VALENTINE) 2nd-century Gnostic heretic 21 A/N
(VALERA, JUAN) Spanish novelist 779 A/N
VANCE, EILEEN Stephen's (and Joyce's) childhood neighbor in Bray P 8, (35–36), (42–43), (69)
(VANCE, MR) Eileen Vance's father and presumably a teacher in the High School 72, 376; P 8 + wife P (8) N
(VANDERBILT, "COMMODORE" CORNELIUS) 19th-century American financier 478 N
(VANDERDECKEN) the legendary Flying Dutchman 478 A/N
(VAUGHAN, FR. BERNARD) English Jesuit whose sermon was heard by Bloom and Father Conmee 82, 219 N
(VAUGHAN, MABEL) heroine of 19th-century novel by Maria Cummins 363 A/N
("Velasquez, Patricio") composite figure in list of Irish heroes of antiquity 297 N
(VENUS) 176, 191, 206, 208, 371, 419, 466; P 205, 208, 209 A/N see also Aphrodite
(VENUS CALLIPYGE/KALLIPYGE) Roman statue of Venus 201, 490 A/N
("Venus Metempsychosis") 490 see Bloom, Molly
(VENUS PANDEMOS) Greek goddess of all the people 425, 490 A/N
(VERCELLIS, MME DE) Jean-Jacques Rousseau's mistress S 40
("Verity, Madame Vera") presumably beauty editor of a London weekly 349
(Verschoyle, Mr) superannuated lover of his wife 333 N + *Thom's,* p. 2030?
(Verschoyle, Mrs) superannuated beloved of her husband 333 N + *Thom's,* p. 2030?

(VEUILLOT, LOUIS) 19th-century French journalist 44; P 156 A/N/N
(Vial plana, Fr.) Gibraltar priest remembered by Molly 779 N
("VIATOR") pseudonymous author of travel book on Bloom's shelf 708 A/N
(VICTORIA, QUEEN) A crazy queen 20, 43, old hag 50, 85, 102, 161, old queen 170, 255, 300, 330, 334, *vieille ogresse* 592, 678–79, 757; his old mother D 132; P 28; S 60, 63 A/N
*(VICTORY, LOUIS H.) Irish poet and essayist 191–92 A/N
(VIDOCQ, EUGENE FRANÇOIS or FRANÇOIS EUGENE) 19th-century French criminal and police official D 29 N
("Vifargent") one of Bloom's silver children 494
(VILLIERS DE L'ISLE-ADAM, PHILIPPE AUGUSTE) 19th-century French symbolist 189 A/N
Villona Hungarian associate of the car drivers D 42–48
("Vinbad") 737 see Sinbad the Sailor
(VINCENT, THOMAS) in *Irish Independent* marriage announcements 298 N
(VINCENT DE PAUL, S.) 17th-century French cleric 339 A/N
("Vinegadding, Mrs Helen") participant in forest wedding 327
("Vingtetunieme") in Brini's genealogical list 496
(VINING, EDWARD PAYSON) author of an 1881 book on *Hamlet* 198 A/N
("Virag") antepenultimate figure in Brini's genealogical list 496
("Virag") friend claimed by Bloom in fictitious alibi 606
(Virag) Rudolph Bloom's 18th-century grandfather 724
Virag, Lipoti grandfather of Leopold Bloom poor papa's father (378), of Leopold (437), [511–23], [552], his grandfather's (708), (723), (766)
("Virag, Nagyaságos uram Lipóti") 342 see Bloom, Leopold
(Virag, Rudolf) 682, 723 see Bloom, Rudolph
(Virag, Stefan) second cousin of Rudolph Bloom 723
(VIRGIL) 390, the Latin poet 617; P 164 A/N
(VOISIN, LOUIS) London murderer 593 A/N
(VOLTA, ALESSANDRO) 18th/19th-century Italian physicist 297 A/N

(VOLUMNIA) mother of Coriolanus 208 A/N
(VULMAR, S.) 7th-century French abbot 339 A/N

(Wade, Francis) Bloom's friend during adolescence 716
(WAGNER, RICHARD) German composer 661; E 58 A/N
(Waldman, Professor) whose chest expander the Nymph recommends 545
(WALKER, JOHN) 18th-century English lexicographer 335 A/N
*(WALL, THOMAS J.) chief divisional magistrate of Dublin police district 162, 615 + son (162) N + *Thom's,* p. 2032
*(WALLACE BROS.) steamship owners 88 n/T
Wallis friend of Vincent Heron P 75, 82–83
*(WALPOLE BROS.) drapers and outfitters 780 N/T
*(WALSH, LOUIS J.) judge and amateur poet 364 A/N
*(WALSH, REV. DR WILLIAM J.) Catholic Archbishop of Dublin and Primate of Ireland 80, His grace 118, 121, 647, 648; Billy with the lip P 33; S 74 A/N
(WALSHE, JAMES "LYNCHEHAUN") Irish murderer who escaped to America 245 N
(WARBECK, PERKIN) 15th-century Yorkist claimant to the English throne 45 A/N
(Ward) canvassed by Mr. Henchy in the Royal Exchange Ward D 131
*WARD, GERALD aide-de-camp to the Lord Lieutenant of Ireland 252–55, fellow in the tall silk 257, Way he looked (270) N.
(WARWICK, EARL OF) P 115 see Rich, Edward
(WAT) a hare in Shakespeare's "Venus and Adonis" 191 A/N
*[WATCHMAN, MINNIE] presumably one of the circumcised 544 Hyman, p. 329; Appendix A
[WATERFORD, MAYOR OF] in procession honoring Bloom 480
*(WATERHOUSE AND CO.) gold- and silversmiths D 50 T
(Waters children) Eveline's childhood playmates D 36, 37
*(WATERS, REV. THOMAS) curate in charge of St. John the Baptist R. C. church 317 N + *Thom's,* p. 2035

Weathers English acrobat D 94–96, (97)
*(WEBB, GEORGE) bookseller D 188 T
("Weiss") in Brini's genealogical list 495
(WELCH, WIDOW) brand of medicine for women 348 N
(WELLESLEY, ARTHUR) 297 see Wellington, Duke of
(WELLINGTON, DUKE OF) 19th-century British military hero and prime minister 297, 332, 434; D 192 A/N/T
WELLS, CHARLES Stephen's tormentor at Clongowes, later a seminarian at Clonliffe P (10), 14, 21, (22), (24), 40–45; S 70–73, 74–75, 118, (127) + father S (70) Sullivan, pp. 48–49
(WELSH, ISABELLA HELEN) in *Irish Independent* obituary 298 N
*(WERNER, Lewis/LOUIS) ophthalmic surgeon 250 N/T + *Thom's,* p. 2036
(WERNER, LOUIS) musical conductor and accompanist to Mary Anderson 93 N
(WESTMINSTER, DUKE OF/HUGH LUPIS GROSVENOR) owner of Shotover 32, 573 A/N
*(WETHERUP, W.) employed by the Collector General of Rates 126, 660 N
(Wettstein, Pfotts) presumably Percy Bennett's second 319 N
(WEYGANDT, CORNELIUS) professor at University of Pennsylvania, the Yankee interviewer 140 A
(WHALEY, RICHARD CHAPELL "BURNCHAPEL") 18th-century Irish roisterer, father of "Buck" Whaley P 184
(WHEATLEY) manufacturer of non-alcoholic hop bitters 81 N
(WHEATLEY, HORACE) pantomime performer 296 A/N
Whelan College orator at U.C.D. S (39), 89–90, 101–5, 171–74, (179)
(Whelan) presumably a journalist for the *Express* 161
(Whelan) Florry Talbot's putative seducer 509
(WHELAN, MRS AND MISS) costumers for the *Sinbad the Sailor* pantomime 678 N
("Whinbad") 737 see Sinbad the Sailor
*(WHITBRED, JAMES W.) manager of the Queen's Theatre 167 N + *Thom's,* p. 2038
White billiards player S 217–18

*WHITE, DUDLEY barrister 252 N/T + *Thom's,* p. 2038
*(WHITE, MRS M. E.) pawnbroker 252 N/T + *Thom's,* p. 2039
("White, Miss"*) euphemism for a lavatory 353
(WHITESIDE, JAMES) 19th-century Irish Lord Chief Justice and M. P. 138–39 A/N
(WHITMAN, WALT) American poet 201 A/N
("WHITTIER, GREENLEAF") 678 see Withers, Greenleaf
*(WILDE, LADY JANE, "Speranza") Irish nationalistic poet and mother of Oscar Wilde 306 A/N
(WILDE, OSCAR) poet and playwright 6, 18, 39, 49, 198, 214 A/N
*(WILDE, WILLIAM) physician and father of Oscar Wilde 250 N/T
(Wilkins) Conservative candidate who withdrew in favor of Tierney D 131
*(WILKINS, W.) headmaster of the High School Bloom attended + wife 371 N + *Thom's,* p. 2040
Wilkinson, Mr befriender of Mr. Daedalus S 159–60, (161), 168, (231)
Wilkinson, Mrs wife of Mr. Wilkinson S (159), 160, (161) + 2 children (160)
(Wilkinson, William) presumably buried in Glasnevin 108
(WILL, "BLACK") character in *Arden of Feversham* 209 see also Shakespeare, William
(WILLIAM I—"THE CONQUEROR") 11th-century king of England 201, 211 N see also Shakespeare, William
(WILLIAM III) 17th-century king of England, victor over the Irish 253; D 208 A/N/T
(WILLIAM OF OCCAM) 14th-century English scholastic 40 A/N
*(WILLIAMS AND WOODS) confectioners 764 N/T
("Willie") prostitute's hypothetical name for Stephen P 100
("Wills, Hughie") 198 see Hughes, Willie
("Willy") whose hat figures in pornographic pictures 368
("Willy") subject of American nonsense song 373 A/N
*(WINE, BERNARD) jeweler and antique dealer 258 N/T + *Thom's,* p. 2042
(WINKLE, RIP VAN) somnolent hero of Washington Irving story 377, 495, 542, 624 A/N
("Winks, Billy") personification of sleep for children 363

(WITHERS, GREENLEAF) author of *Sinbad the Sailor* pantomime 678 N
(WOFFINGTON, MARGARET) 18th-century Dublin actress 296 A/N
("Wogger") 755 see Stanhope, Mr.
(WOLFRAM) in Wagner's *Tannhäuser* E 57
(WOLSELEY, SIR GARNET JOSEPH) 19th-century British general 757 A/N
(WOLSEY, THOMAS CARDINAL) counselor to King Henry VIII 219; P 10, 22 A/N/N
(WOLSTAN, S.) 11th-century Benedictine and bishop 339 A/N
(WOOD, MRS HENRY) 19th-century English novelist 756 A/N
*(WOODS, MR AND MRS R.) next-door neighbors to the Blooms 59 N/T +*Thom's,* p. 2043
(WORDSWORTH, WILLIAM) English Romantic poet 113, 206; D 107; S 124, 148 A/N
*(WORN, A.) stationer 182 T
(WORTHINGTON, ROBERT) Dublin railroad contractor 639 A/N
(WOUGHT, JAMES) convicted in Canadian swindle case 322 A/N
*(WREN, P. A.) auctioneer 99, 543, 710 N/T + *Thoms,* p. 2044
(WRIGHT) in *Irish Independent* marriage announcements 298 N
(Wylie, Reggy) adored by Gerty MacDowell the boy that has the bicycle 333, 349–50, 351–52, 358, 362, 363 + father (349), (351)
*WYLIE, W. E. bicyclist; brother of Reggy Wylie 237, (349), (351) N
(WYNDHAM, SIR CHARLES) English actor and manager 690 A/N
*(WYNN) hotel 735, 739 N/T + *Thom's,* p. 1408

("XX") algebraic unknown 658 see Murphy, W. B.
(XANTHIPPE) wife of Socrates 190, 202 A/N
(XENOPHON) 4th-century B.C. Greek historian 124 A/N
("Xinbad") 737 see Sinbad the Sailor

(YASODHARA) wife of Buddha 771; S 190
*(YEATES AND SON) optometrists 166 N/T
*(YEATS, ELIZABETH) sister of W. B. Yeats, one of the weird sisters of the Dun Emer Press 13, two designing females 424 A/N
*(YEATS, LILY) sister of W. B. Yeats, one of the weird sisters of the Dun Emer Press 13, two designing females 424 A/N
*(YEATS, WILLIAM BUTLER) Irish poet W.B. 184, 192, 216, 509 A/N
(YORK, DUKE AND DUCHESS) visited Dublin August 1897 679 N see George V
(YORKE, ELIZABETH) wife of Philipe Yorke, lord lieutenant when Emmet was hanged 240
*(YOUKSTETTER, WILLIAM) pork butcher 221 N/T + *Thom's,* p. 2045
(Young "Boasthard") 396 see Dedalus, Stephen
(Yvonne) Parisienne in Stephen's recollection 42

(ZACHARY) father of John the Baptist P 248 N
(ZARATHUSTRA) founder of Zoroastrianism, used as spokesman by Nietzsche 23, 393, 424 A/N
(ZARETSKY, BENJAMIN) Canadian swindle law suit plaintiff 322 A/N + Hyman, P. 175
(ZEPHYR) personification of the West Wind D 83
ZINFANDEL horse favored to win the Gold Cup (174), (178–79), (325), [573], (648) N
["Zoe-Fanny"] 509 see Higgins, Zoe
(ZOLA, ÉMILE) 19th-century French novelist S 92–93, French atheistic writer 172

Anonymous Listings

("adored one") in Bloom's suppositions on infidelity 642
(adulterer, onehandled) 148, 150 see Nelson, Admiral Lord Horatio
(adultress) 324 see Devorghil
(adultress) in *Wife of Scarli,* play seen by Molly 769
(agent) for candidate Tierney D 119
(agent, literary) suggested that Christ was a maniac S 189
(agents, land) 95 see Askin, Paul
(altar boy) who assisted Father Flynn D 17
altar boy in mortuary chapel at Isabel's funeral S 167
(American) talked stamps with Molly's father 741
(American "of the Bowery gutter sheet") 139 see Pulitzer, Joseph
[American, wealthy] collects money for Bloom 494
[anabaptist] in procession for Lord Mayor Bloom 480
(Andalusian) 750 see Manola
(angel, God's) 385 see Gabriel
[applewoman] voicing support for Bloom 484 see also applewoman, old
applewoman, old from whom Bloom buys Banbury cakes 153
(Arab) whose farewell to his steed the boy's uncle recites D 34
"arab, barefoot" street urchin outside Harrison's restaurant 157
(Arab, old) one-eyed musician in Gibraltar remembered by Molly 757
(archbishop) 121; S 74 see Walsh, Rev. Dr William J.
(archbishop) 231 see Creagh, Archbishop David
(artiste, operatic) for whom Duggan substituted D 142
assistant town clerk 246 see Henry, James J.
[assistants, two blackmasked] assisting hangman Rumbold 593
astroscopist, younger 700 see Dedalus, Stephen
attendant, noiseless 184 see Evans
aunt with whom the boy in "The Sisters" lives D 9–11, (12), 14–18

aunt   with whom the boy in "Araby" lives   D 31, 32, 33–34
aunt   Stephen Dedalus's, whom he visits   P 67
(aunt)   Buck Mulligan's   4, 5, 6, 88, 199, 425
aunt, maiden   of the Daniels   S 158
(author)   of *A Handbook of Astronomy* owned by Bloom   709   A
(author)   of a testimonial for Wonderworker   722
(author)   of *Sweets of Sin*   735, 765
(avuncular)   probably a pawnbroker   425

(babemaries)   mother and sister of Moses, conflated with the two Marys, Mary Magdalen and the mother of James and Joses   142   A/N
[babes and sucklings]   celebrating the crowned Bloom   486
(baby tuckoo)   P 7   see Dedalus, Stephen
(bailiff)   newly employed by the subsheriff   245
[baptist]   Church head at Bloom's coronation   480
bargeman   on the turf barge *Bugabu* newly arrived in Dublin   99, 221, (396)
baritone   at concert at the Antient Concert Rooms   D 143–44, 146, 147–48
barmaid   at the Greville Arms, Mullingar   S 250–51
(barmaid)   at Jury's or the Moira, mistress of Jack Power   93
barmaid, stout   at Adelphi Hotel   S 207–8, 217
bawd, elderly   pro-British, anti-Semitic, peddling "maidenhead"   431, 441–42, 593, 602
("Beast, Black")   man lynched in Georgia, as reported in *Police Gazette*   328
[Beatitudes]   goosestepping "medicals"   509   see Bannon, Alec; Costello, Francis; Crotthers, J.; Dixon; Lenehan, T.; Lynch, Vincent; Madden, William; Mulligan, Malachi Roland St John
(beauty, sleeping)   in Grimm's fairytale   211
(beggar)   to whom Stephen gave alms   P 104
[beggar]   to whom Bloom gives his coat   486
(beggar, absentminded)   Stephen's translation of "*le distrait*"   187   see Hamlet
(beggar, absentminded)   in testimonial for Wonderworker   722
(beggar, absentminded)   from Kipling's poem   748   A/N
beggar, lame   badgered by the children in Mullingar   S 244, (245)

("beggar, old") feared by Molly as an intruder 765
(beldam) woman who caused Pyrrhus's death 25
[bellhanger] expresses adulation for Bloom 482
(bellydancer) in Stephen's imagination as he sees jewels in a shop window 241
(betweenmaid) contemplated by Bloom for his dream house 713
[bidder] presumably at Dillon's auction rooms 539
("Big Brother") "Elijah" Dowie's God 508
(billiard sharp) in Gilbert and Sullivan song P 192
(biographer, English) of Jean-Jacques Rousseau S 40 see Morley, John
(bishop) who confirmed Kitty-Kate 508
("bishop") subject of Bloom's curiosity about Molly's sexual tastes 740
[Bishop of Down and Connor] at Bloom's coronation 480–82
(bishop, old) whom Molly remembers preaching about women's role 761
("bitch, dirty") in Bloom's pornographic photo 721, 753 see señorita, nude
("bitch, little") whom Molly suspects was with Bloom on 16 June 739, 773
[Black Rod] an official of the House of Lords 480 N
[blacksmith] admirer of Bloom 481
(Board ladies, two) of the Dublin by Lamplight laundry D 99
boarder in conversation with the prefect of the sodality at U.C.D. P 199
boatman at Sandycove discussing the drowning 21
(boatman) who rescued Reuben J. Dodd's son 94–95
(boatmen) at Bray who rented a boat to Bloom 764
(Bobby 14 A) 314, 333 see Constable 14A
(bondwoman) reputed mother of Antisthenes 149 see noble
(bookseller) at St. Patrick's Close S 166
bookseller at Merchants' Arch 235–37, [586] + wife (236)
(bootblack) at G.P.O., suspected by Bloom as one of Molly's lovers 731
bootlace vendor on O'Connell Street 93, [538] see O'Callaghan
(boots) employed at the Queen's Hotel in Ennis 97
boots employed at the Ormond Hotel in Dublin (256), 258, [564]

("bosthoon, Tipperary") assumed by Kernan to have left his horse unattended 240
boy narrator in "The Sisters" D 9–18
boy narrator in "An Encounter" D 19–28
boy narrator in "Araby" D 29–36
boy employed by Tierney at the Black Eagle D 128–29
(boy) at Clongowes chapel P 41
boy at Stephen's aunt's, carrying coal P 67
boy at Belvedere, bringing message P 83
(boy) at Belvedere, coming for the rector P 105
boy at Belvedere, on lookout for the rector's approach P 107
boy 101 see Dignam, Patrick Aloysius
boy, Belvedere brings gossip to Stephen S 35–36
("boy, christian") ritual sacrifice speculated about by Bloom 108 see Hughes, Harry
(boy, fat) in Dickens's *Pickwick Papers* 188 see Joe
("boy, nicelooking") contemplated by Molly 740
boy, ragged teases beggar S 244 + ragged friend S 244
boy, tall student at Belvedere P 105
boy, young in Clonliffe refectory S 184
(boy, little Italian) who mended statue for Molly 766
boys, two fighting for their caps D 32
("bride") in Madagascar, whose wedding rites are described in the hospital common room 392–93
("bride" and "bridegroom") nobility Conmee imagines marrying in days of yore 224
(Bride of Lammermoor) Scott heroine in list of Irish heroes and heroines 297 A/N
("bride, blushing") whom Bloom imagines as marrying chap of 70 373
("bridegrooms, two") whom Bloom imagines marrying sisters in typical newspaper photo 119
(brother and sister) Stephen's P 98 see Dedalus, Maurice
(brother, elder) of prodigal son in the biblical parable P 189 see prodigal
(brother, her husband's) with whom Mary Rochfort may have committed adultery 233
(brother, Kickham's) P 40 see Kickham, Alexander
("brother, little") whose family Bloom conjectures the husband accusing his wife of feeding 157 see Breen, Denis
(brothers and sisters) Stephen's P 18 see under Dedalus

[brutes, male] commenting as Bloom enters Bella Cohen's 501
[buckles*] commenting on Bloom's baby talk with Zoe 501
("bugger, noisy") 758 see coalman who tried to cheat Molly
(bully) on guard in Bride Street brothel 314
("burglar") whom Molly believed was in the kitchen 766
bursar at U.C.D. P (192); S (23–24), 24
businessman at Sandycove discussing drowning case 21
(butcher) 187 see Shakespeare, John
(butcher) on whom Molly practiced her prospective married name 761
butcher's boy whose basket Stephen exemplifies P 212
butcher's boy telling workmen about the drowned woman S 252
("butcher's boy") in Stephen's French-accented monologue 570
(butler) employed at Clongowes castle P 10

cabby in cabman's shelter, who looks like Henry Campbell 621–60 see also cabman; driver; jarvey
cabman who drove the Browne-Malins party from the Morkans' D 208-9
(canon) accused of preaching politics P 31
[cap*] Lynch's, scoffs at Stephen 504
(captain) of boat on which Mrs. Malins sailed D 190
"captain" dwarf in National Library P 227–29 + parents P (228)
(captain) of vessel from Bridgwater 647
(captain, American) friend of Mr. Dedalus's father P 92
(captain, Norwegian) humpbacked, remembered by Bloom 61 see *Finnegans Wake*
(captain, yeoman) trapped the Croppy Boy 285–86, 290
(Capuchin) with whom Stephen converses S 177
(cardinal) whose mausoleum is in Glasnevin 101 see MacCabe, Edward Cardinal
(cardinal, tardy) first one sent to Ireland S 53 see Paparo, John Cardinal
(caretaker) of the Morkan household, Lily's father D (175), 182
carman who brings Kernan home D 153–55

("carman") invented by Bloom as a ruse to draw Stephen away from Carr 589
(cashier) at shop where Chandler bought Annie's blouse D 82
cashier at Crosbie & Alleyne D (87), (90–91), 92
(cashier) at the *Freeman's Journal* 199
("cattleraider") constricted from planting by Lord Harry, according to Dixon 400
[cavaliers] dancing to Maginni's commands and the pianola music 576
chairman at the Literary and Historical Society S 103 see Keane, Mr
(chairman) of the debate between Fitzgibbon and Taylor 142
[chamberlain, lord great] high official at Bloom's coronation 480 N
("chap") employed at Jaffa dock, imagined by Bloom 60–61
(chap) in photo, seen floating in the Dead Sea 72
(chap) who sold Bloom a Swedish razor 290
(chap) who poked Bloom in the crowd around Parnell 654
(chap in dresscircle) who ogled Molly 284 see gentleman, unknown
(chap in the inland revenue office) engaged to Dan Dawson's daughter 126
(chap in the mortuary) 284 see Coffey, Fr M.
(chap in the paybox) of the turkish baths, whom Bloom believes helped Stephens escape 68 N see O'Brien, J. P.
("chap of seventy, old rich") bridegroom imagined by Bloom 373
("chap that wallops the big drum") imagined by Bloom as practicing for Micky Rooney's band 289
(chap that writes like Synge) in context Shakespeare; in origin Aeschylus 198 A/N
(chap with sandy hair, little) one of two gentlemen with Kernan at pub D 150, 159
chap you know 61 see whatdoyoucallhim
(chap, chalk-faced) S 116 see Butt, D., S. J.
(chap, football) S 126 see McCann, Philip
(chap, Italian) killed a man in Trieste, according to Murphy 628
("chap, old") the Holy Ghost 3
(chap, old) diner at the Burton 169
(chap, other) diner at the Burton, with his mouth full 170
(chap, decent young) D 160 see man, young, in cycling suit

(chap, other brass) in orchestra at concert remembered by Bloom 271
(chap, tall old) with earrings, remembered by Molly from Gibraltar 765
[Chapwith] one of Bloom's pursuers 586 see chap, other
("chargeant, first") in court case 322
(chef) in the kitchen of the Master of the Rolls, seen by Bloom 175
chemist 84–85 see Sweny, F. W.
("chemist, new") loved by nurse 333
(Chief Commissioner) of D.M.P. officiating at the hanging 306
(chieftain, negro) tenor singing in Gaiety pantomime D 198
(child) with woman in doorway at Clane P 18 see woman, standing at the halfdoor
(child) in coffin to be buried at Glasnevin 96, 101
("child") bit by bellows, in presumed news story 146
("child") whose enlarged head causes delayed birth, according to Bloom 161
(child) heard wailing in Nighttown 430
("child") imagined by Bloom to have been born to Murphy's wife 624
child, bandy in Nighttown doorway 430
child, little in lodge house at Mr. Fulham's S 239
("child, poor") to whom Molly feels she should have given dead Rudy's jacket 778
child, scrofulous whose hair is being combed in Nighttown 430
child, squatted playing marbles near Meade's timberyards 77
children teasing idiot in Nighttown 429
("chile, poo lil") subject of Bloom's self-deprecating song 463 A
(chimneysweep) whose gear endangered the eyes of the Nameless One 292
[choir] singing the prayer for the dying 579–80
Christian Brother buying creams at Graham Lemon's 151
citizen Gaelic enthusiast and chauvinist at Barney Kiernan's (293), 295–345, that bawler (380), that fireeater (436), [487], [498], [586], [593], [596], the offender (642–44), give him (metaphorically) one in the gizzard (657), blood and ouns champion (658), truculent troglodyte (729) + "sister-in-law" (380) N see Cusack, Michael

(citizen, very stout black-bearded) S 61 see Cusack, Michael
clergyman 230 see Love, Rev. Hugh C.
(clergyman) in testimonial for Wonderworker 722
("clergyman, protestant") whom Molly conjectures to be in the room next to hers in Belfast hotel 747
(clerk) in St. Catherine's church D 18
clerk dusting in a church S 146
clerk in Agriculture office, billiard-playing friend of Cranly S 207–8, 217 (224)
(clerk) in offices of the *Irish Times* where Bloom placed his ad 160
clerk in the Custom-House S 105 see Glynn
clerk in the Police Courts friend of Mr. Daedalus S 166
clerk, chief at Crosbie & Alleyne's D 88, 92
(clerk, chief) at Callan's D 93
clerk, elderly playing billiards at the Adelphi Hotel S 217–18
(clerk, government printer's) whom Bloom imagines falling from Howth hill 550 see Elijah
[clerk, managing] at Drimmie's, who pursues Bloom in Nighttown 586
(clown) in *Twelfth Night* S 28 see Feste
(clown) at Hengler's circus, who "claimed" Bloom was his father 696
(coachman) in stable behind Richmond Street D 30
(coachman) who put Queen Victoria to bed 330 see Brown, John
("coalman") subject of Bloom's curiosity about Molly's sexual tastes 740
(coalman) who tried to cheat Molly with wrong bill 758
(cobbler) from Tinahely, known to Cranly S 138 see also engine-driver
cocklepickers a man and a woman along Sandymount Strand 46–47
(colonel) regular customer at Bella Cohen's 539
colonel, retired S 172 see Russell, Colonel
(comedian) in music hall attended by Stephen and Cranley S 125
commercials, two brought to Nighttown by Corny Kelleher 606
(commission agent) employed by Jack Mooney D 62
(commissioner of police) forbids Irish games in Dublin park 315

competitor, French in car race in Dublin D 44
conductor of tram at Harold's Cross P 69–70, (222)
conductor of Conmee's tram 222–23
conductor of orchestra, remembered by Bloom 271
(confessor) Stephen's at Belvedere P 153
(confessor) Mrs. Daedalus's S 209–10
(confessor) Mary Rochford's 223
constable at Kernan's accident D 151–53, (160)
(constable) who arrested Comisky, according to Corley 618
constable off Eccles Street corner cuddler of Bloom's neighbor's servant (60), [586–87]
(Constable 14A) almost arrested Bob Doran; presumably in love with Mary Kelly 314, 333
Constable 57C salutes Conmee, chats with Kelleher 221, 225
(Constable 57E) gives evidence at Sinico inquest D 114
("Constable 65") bosthoon who catches his dinner cabbage D 161
[Constable 65C] in Nighttown 586 see watch, first
[Constable 66C] in Nighttown 586 see watch, second
(Constable 67) in Nighttown, whom the bawd considers a bitch 442
[constable, high] commander-in-chief of the army and navy at Bloom's coronation 480 N
(constabulary man in Santry) attacked by Garryowen 295
(constabulary men, two) in Malahide, who came upon Stephen worshipping P 232 see also laborer
("contractee, inconsiderate") who would pay Bloom at an increasing rate 718
contralto singing at the Antient Concert Rooms D 147
(contralto, leading) of opera company at Theatre Royal, praised by D'Arcy D 198
cook at Dublin by Lamplight laundry D (99), 100–101
("cook") advertised for in the *Irish Times* 160
("cook") for Bloom's dream house 713
(corn-factor) had employed Polly Mooney as typist D 63
(coroner) D 113 see Leverett, Mr
(coroner) 75; D 157 see Byrne, Louis A.
(coroner) at Rudolph Bloom's inquest in Ennis 97
(corpse) who tumbled into the road out of his coffin 98
councillor newly elected, sitting in the Gardiner Street church next to Fanning D 172–74 see Tierney, Richard J.
[couple, old] blessed by Bloom at his coronation 486

("courtesan") whom Bloom would like to fascinate 722
(creature, haughty) woman at polo match remembered by Bloom 73 see Talboys, Hanna
[crier] at Bloom's trial 460, 470
(criminal, hardened) murderer recalled by Molly 765
crone ragpicker accompanying the gnome in Nighttown 430
Croppy Boy subject of song, who confesses to false priest and is executed by the British (282–87), (290), [593–94]
[crowd] at horse race 573
crowd at Stephen-Carr fight 601
(Csar) P 194 see Nicholas II, Czar
curate in John Mulligan's D 95
curate one of several in pub who carries Kernan up D 150, brings him brandy D 151, and cleans up his blood D 153
curate at Larry O'Rourke's, mopping 58
curate at Davy Byrne's, serving Bloom 172
curate at Burke's, serving biscuits 427
(curates, two grudging) brought biscuits for Lenehan D 57 see curate at Burke's
cyclists, two in Nighttown, who almost run Bloom down 435

(dairyman) former lover of the slavey who now fancies Corley D 51
(dame, butcher's) meatfaced woman at horse race where Cranly took Stephen 32
(daughter, farmer's) whose bag Bloom rescued at Limerick railroad station 166
(daughter, Jew's) who lured Harry Hughes to his death—in ballad 691
("daughter, king of Spain's") from nursery rhyme and sea ballad, used symbolically by Old Gummy Granny and by Stephen 595, 652
(daughter, turnkey's) helped James Stephens escape, according to Bloom 163
[Daughters of Erin] pray for Bloom as the mob turns against him 498
(dean) S 23 see Butt, D., S. J.
(Dean of Clonliffe College) where Wells is a seminarian S 73
dean of studies at U.C.D. (205); P 184–90, (192), 199, (205), (240), (251) + "wife" P (199) see Butt, D., S. J.

("dean or bishop") sat in synagogue garden talking to Molly 740
(deputy coroner) at Sinico inquest D 133, 115
[Deputy Garter] executive officer for the Order of the Garter 480 N
(devil) claims dead policeman in Joe Hynes's quip 332
("devil, poor") rescued by Rochford from manhole 233
diner at the Burton 170
diner at the Ormond 263, 264 see Goulding, Richard
director of studies at Belvedere College, interviewing Stephen P 153–60, (162)
(disciple) P 189 see Matthew
("Disgusted One") author of letter about flogging in the British navy 328
(doctor) who treats Stephen at the infirmary in Clongowes P 23
(doctor) who treated Stephen's eyes P 51
(doctor) who treated Stephen's aunt Ellen P 68
(doctor) who treated Stephen's sister Isabel S 126, 151, 161, 163, 164
doctor who examines the drowned woman in Mullingar S 252
(doctor) who treats the demented woman at the Richmond Asylum 8 see also Norman, Connolly; Teazle, Sir Peter
(doctor of the Church, great) S 103, 205 see Aquinas, S. Thomas
door-porter at U.C.D. S 90
(doxy) inamorata shared by Beaumont and Fletcher 393
driver of cab taking D'Arcy-Conroy party from the Morkans' D 214–15 see also cabby; cabman; jarvey
driver of the tram at Harold's Cross P 69–70, (222)
driver of street sweeper outside cabman's shelter 662–65
(driver of the winning German car) D 42 see Jenatzy, Camille
driver, pugnosed of the tram that blocked Bloom's view of the woman's ankles noisy pugnose 74, (160), that tramdriver (368), fellow that balked me (436), [586]
drover of cattle down North Circular Road 97
(druggist) in Mullingar S 244
(drunkard) in priest's parable S 58–59
drunkard being ejected from Suffolk Street bar S 213
(drunks, two) at Glasnevin cemetery looking for Mulcahy, in O'Connell's story 107

(Dublin fusilier) soldier who reported Parnell alive in South Africa 649
(duchess, English) about whom Gallaher gossips to Chandler D 78
(duke) in *Twelfth Night* S 29 see Orsino
(duke, present) of Rutland, descendant of presumed author of Shakespeare's plays 214
dummy at Dublin by Lamplight laundry D (100), 101
[dummydummy] of Bloom falling from the Hill of Howth 550

"E" one of five sandwichboard men working for Wisdom Hely 154, 227, 229, 253 see also H; L; Y; 'S
[earl marshal] president of the College of Heralds at Bloom's coronation 480 N
[echo] mocking Bloom 548
(editor) of a nationalist weekly S 91 see Griffith, Arthur
(editor) of the *Review of Reviews* S 112 see Stead, William Thomas
[elector] hailing Bloom 478
(Emperor, German) about whom Bloom quizzes Molly as to her sexual tastes 740
End of the World* Scots octopus dancing in Bella Cohen's (165), [507] see Russell, George
(engine-driver) son of Tinahely cobbler, known to Cranly S 138
(engineer) who gave Kitty Ricketts sweets at a bazaar 526
(examiner, polyglot) who tested Father Artifoni S 215
(expert, phonetic) who analyzed Garryowen's verses 312

(farmer at the Royal Dublin Society's Horse Show) on Bloom's list of Molly's lovers 731 see below
(farmer in the ridingboots) whom Bloom remembers from horse show 374 see above
(farrier) whose shop Bloom and Stephen walk past 613 T see Kavanagh, J.
[fan*] carried by Bella, interrogates Bloom 527–29
(father) of Croppy Boy, died at siege of Ross 241, 285
(father) of "Lord Harry" 400 see Henry VII
(father Guardian) of Marsh's Library in Dublin S 177–78

(Father Minister) of Clongowes, who orders Stephen sent to the infirmary P 22, 40, 48
(Father Provincial) to whom Conmee mails his letter 220
(father, good) priest who frequented Bella Cohen's 520 see under priest
(father, old) dead drunk in Nighttown, his daughter being offered as maindenhead 441
(father, passionist) the source of Anne Kearne's Lourdes water 145
(faunman) drunk celebrating Good Friday 200
("favourite, newest stage") subject of typical adultery scandal in newspaper 654
(fellow) friend of Gallaher with whom he arranged to play cards D 79
(fellow) at Clongowes who threatened Cantwell P 9
(fellow) at Clongowes who had seen a rat in the ditch P 10, 14
(fellow) at Clongowes who asked Kickham to kick the ball P 11
fellow at Clongowes who reports about the smuggers having been caught P 40
(fellow) at Clongowes who reported who caught the smuggers P 40
fellow at Clongowes who encouraged Stephen to complain to the rector P 53, (54)
(fellow) at Clongowes who caused Stephen's glasses to be broken P 57
("fellow") with whom Stephen claims to have walked to Dolphin's Barn S 70
(fellow) told Mulligan in The Ship that Stephen was insane 6
(fellow) whom Kevin Egan knew in Barcelona 43
(fellow) from whom Crawford hoped to borrow money 147
fellow at the Burton sharpening knife and fork 169, knife and fork upright 170 see also diner
(fellow) whom Flynn knew was trying to join the Masons 177
(fellow) whom Miss Dunne hopes will be at the band 229
(fellow) to be hanged at Mountjoy 299
(fellow) with whom the Nameless One went to a Gaelic League musical evening 311
(fellow) one of the painters working in the Blooms' flat in Lombard Street 374
(fellow) 436 see driver, pugnosed
(fellow) playing music outside Bella Cohen's 505

(fellow) Murphy's shipmate who became a valet 630–31
(fellow) guitarist Molly remembers from Gibraltar boat 775
(fellow in the pit) who ogled Molly at the Gaiety 767 see gentleman, unknown
(fellow opposite) whom Molly remembers, watched her undress in Gibraltar 763
(fellow that died) when Bloom was working for Wisdom Hely 144 see Gilligan, Philip
(fellow that was something in the four courts) who jilted Atty Dillon 758
(fellow with a Ballyhooly blue ribbon badge) remembered by the Nameless One from a Gaelic League musical evening 311
(fellow, blackguardlooking) gypsy that Molly contemplates as potential seducer 777
(fellow, first) character in *Ruby, Pride of the Ring,* discussed by Molly 64
(fellow, old) employer of the slavey D 51
(fellow, old) Haines's father 7
fellow, old asleep in All Hallows Church 81
(fellow, old) 251 see Stoer, Mr
(fellow, old) bagpipe player at Gaelic musical evening 311
(fellow, other) at the bellows when Glynn played the organ 288
(fellowplayer) sued by Shakespeare 204 see Rogers, Philip
(fellows, two) seen by Corley in the company of his former mistress D53
[fellowthatslike] one of Bloom's pursuers 586 see cabby
(female) 638 see whore with black straw sailor hat
("female religious") "nun" in Bloom's pornographic photo 721, 738
(female, confiding) whom Lenehan speculates that Stephen seduced 392
female, elderly visiting the law courts and legal offices 232, 236, 252
(females, two designing) 424 see Yeats, Elizabeth; Yeats, Lily
[feminist] admiring Bloom 481
(figure) female in Stephen's erotic dream P 99
[figure, sinister] guarding the entrance to Nighttown 436 see Blanca, señorita
(fishwoman) hawking her wares outside the Rowan house E 107

flower girl who entreats Stephen to buy her wares P 183–84, (220)
[flybill*] against which Lipoti Virag butts his head 522–23
(fogey, old) pharmacist mocked by the Ormond barmaids 259–60 see Boyd, Samuel
[footballboots] one of Bloom's pursuers 586
(foreman) 118 see Nannetti, Joseph Patrick
(form) asleep against a dust bin in Nighttown 429, sprawled form 437
"Frauenzimmer" Stephen's designation for the two women on Sandymount Strand 37, Two old women 242, (579)
Freeman man D 144 see Hendrick, Mr
("French Celt") Deasy's source for the statement about the sun never setting on the British Empire 30 A/N
(Frenchman, solitary) Celtophile at Paris meeting S 62
(friend) of Mr. Dedalus and Mr. Casey, an outspoken Nationalist P 31
(friend) of Mr. Daedalus in the sheriff's office S 150
(friend) of a friend of Mr. Daedalus, in Dublin Castle S 166
friend of Mr. Daedalus, at Isabel's funeral S 167–68
(friend) of girl seen in Eustace Street adjusting her garter 74
(friend) presumably a publican hospitalized for acute alcoholism 293 see Kiernan, Bernard
(friend in court) prevented prosecution of Bloom, according to the Nameless One 293 see Falkiner, Sir Frederick Richard?
[friend of Lyons] in pursuit of Bloom 586 see M'Coy, C. P.?
friends, two of Lenehan, with whom he stops to chat D 58
friends, two of Mr. Fitzpatrick, in audience at Antient Concert Rooms D 140
(friends, two) medical students who had taken their exams P 216
(froeken) masseuse in Upsala who tried to massage Kevin Egan 43

(G. man) plainclothes policeman sought by litigious Breen 299
gaffer in Nighttown regaling loiterers with a salacious story 450
galoot, lankylooking 109 see M'Intosh

garçon bartender at Corless's D 74–82 see also François
gardener in Lord Iveagh's estate adjoining U.C.D. S 115
(gardener) at the cemetery in Ennis where Bloom's father is buried 113
(gardener, deaf) at Oxford, oblivious to the ragging party of undergraduates 7 his "resemblance" to Matthew Arnold is transposed to Philip Drunk and Philip Sober in Nighttown 518
(gentleman) pro-British hit by Dante with an umbrella P 37
gentleman giving directions to porter in Maynooth station S 238
(gentleman) who collects admission fees at Nelson's Pillar 145
("gentleman") subject of typical police inquiry 163
("gentleman") subject of typical feminine ploy in conversation 371
(gentleman friend) of Lydia Douce on moonlight walks during her holiday 282
(gentleman lodger) of the Supples who possessed erotic cuttings 365–66
("gentleman of fashion") Molly's designation for the writer of *Sweets of Sin* 765 see author
("gentleman of fashion") Molly's designation for the man that ogled her at the Gaiety 769 see gentleman, unknown
gentleman off Sandymount green 354 see nobleman, stroller
gentleman with the glasses on tram opposite Conmee 222
(gentleman, another) claimed by Bella Cohen as one of her customers 539
gentleman, elderly chivalrous to Maria in the tram D 102–3, (103)
("gentleman, fair") loved by M. B. 33 see Bannon, Alec; Boylan, Hugh
(gentleman, ruptured) whose testimonial for trusses appeared in *Photo Bits* 545
(gentleman, unknown) who ogled Molly in the Gaiety Theatre 284, 731, 767
gentleman, young overheard by Stephen on Eclles Street flirting with a young lady S 211
gentleman, young 279 see Boylan, Hugh
(gentleman, young) 18th-century figure on calendar in the MacDowell jakes 355
(gentlemen, two) D 150 see Harford; chap with sandy hair
gentlemen, two drinking stout in the Ormond bar 270–91

(gentlemen, two) remembered by Molly from railroad journey 748
gentlemen, two young flirting with salesgirl in the Araby bazaar D 35
(German lad) 330 see Albert, prince consort
(ghost) 202 see Hamlet, king
(gipsy, wildlooking) remembered by Molly from Rathfarnum 777
girl waitress in refreshment bar where Lenehan eats his peas D 57–58
(girl) shop assistant where Chandler buys a blouse for Annie D 82
girl waitress in restaurant where Duffy eats his dinner D 113
girl whose laughter Stephen hears with torment P 115
girl seen by Stephen wading on North Bull Island P 171, (172)
girl selling flowers P 183-84, (220) see flower girl
(girl) in Stephen's exemplary story who dies an accidental death + mother P 205
(girl) servant in Rowan household E 28
(girl) author of *The Female Fellow* S 187
("girl") in Bloom's fantasy, playing a dulcimer 57
(girl) apparent object of young Dodd's interest 94
girl selling plums at foot of Nelson's Pillar 95, (145)
girl with her mother in Glasnevin 101; S 167 see harpy; woman, hard
girl selling sweets at Graham Lemon's 151
(girl) remembered by Bloom as passing the Stewart Institution 182
(girl) remembered by Stephen as singing 220 see kitchengirl
(girl) remembered by Stephen as laughing at him 220
(girl) remembered by Stephen as taunting him 220
(girl) remembered by Bloom as playing the harp 271
(girl) presumably remembered by Bloom as blushing in the zoo 471
(girl) waitress at D.B.C. who directed Molly to the washroom 745
("girl") assumed by Molly to have married Mulvey 761
("girl") object of a man's pursuit, according to Molly's conjectures 777

(girl in Eustace Street) remembered by Bloom as settling her garter 74
(girl in Meath Street) whom Bloom encouraged to say obscenities 370
(girl in the office) informed Corley that no job was available 618 see Dunne, Miss
(girl in Tranquilla convent) whom Bloom claims liked to smell rock oil 368
girl, blonde shop assistant in Thornton's waiting on Boylan 227–28
("girl, lovely") imagined by Bloom as he hears Cowley sing 271 see Martha
girl, nextdoor servant at Bloom's neighbors 59, (59–60), The maid was in the garden (68), How did she walk (72), Crooked skirt swinging (280)
("girl, nice") Bloom's idealized masseuse 85
("girl, Resp") typical advertiser for position as shop assistant 160
girl, ringletted Stephen's cousin P 67
girl, smaller seen by Bloom holding her caskhoop near Brady's cottages 71
(girl, Yorkshire) subject of song, associated with Zoe Higgins who claims to be from Yorkshire (254), (575–78) A/N
(girl, young) attendant at Poole's traveling show 739
[girls, prison gate] sing obscene song in derision of Bloom 496–97
girls, two big neighbors of the Donnellys participating in Halloween festivities D 103–5
gnome rag-and-bone man in Mabbot Street 429–30
(god, Indian) shown by Bloom to Molly in National Museum 771 see Buddha, Gautama
(goddess, oxeyed) 322 see Juno
(godfather) Stephen Daedalus's S 48 see Fulham, Mr
[Gold Stick] officer of the English Royal Body Guard 480 N
("golfer, professional") typical subject of newspaper adultery scandal 654
(gospeller) Puritan preacher invited by Ann Shakespeare to New Place 206 A/N
(governor) of Gibraltar whose house sentry Molly remembers 782 see Napier, Lord Robert Cornelius

[gramophone*] accompanying Elijah's sermon on the end of the world 507–8
(grand Turk) presumed to have donated to Irish famine relief 329
(grandfather) either Leopold Bloom's or Rudolph Bloom's 724 see Virag, Lipoti
("grandmother") of Lord Harry 401
(grandoldgrossfather) 569 see Daedalus
(granduncle) Stephen's, who presented an address to Daniel O'Connell P 26
(grace, his) 118 see Walsh, Rev. Dr William J.
(graduate, young Oxford) offers to marry Sheila when her Irish lover is hanged 310
gravedigger, seventh at Glasnevin interment of Paddy Dignam 112
("greatgrandfather") whose recorded voice is heard after his death 114
[Green Lodges] greeting Sir John Blackwood 574
("groom") in Madagascar marriage rites 392–93
("guard") on Belfast train, that Molly thinks Boylan may bribe for privacy 748
guttersnipe, young newsboy mocking Bloom 129
(gypsy woman) who told Miss Daniel she would be an actress S 67 see also gipsy

"H" one of five sandwichboard men working for Wisdom Hely 154, 227, 229, 253 see also E; L; Y; 'S
hag vocally defends Stephen when he is hit by Carr 602 see hag, bent
hag, bent seen by Bloom carrying bottle, present at his coronation 61, (375), [538], 602
[handsomemarriedwomanrubbedagainstwidebehindinClonskeatram] one of Bloom's pursuers 586
("harlot, nasty") who sent Bloom used toilet tissue, according to Sins of the Past 537
harpist in Kildare Street playing "Silent, O Moyle" D 54, (56)
harpy, leanjawed woman with daughter in Glasnevin 101; P 167
hawker at Glasnevin, selling cakes and fruit 100
(He) with whom O'Molloy has influence on Lambert's behalf 320

(head centre) of the Fenians 43 see Stephens, James
hearer in the cabman's shelter 631 see cabby
"helmsman" 341 see jarvey who drives Bloom from Kiernan's
(her) singer Bloom remembers hitting high note 271
(her) mad wife of nobleman, presumably in song or play 364
(her) for whom a man gave up his life 767 see Manette, Lucie
(hero) who dies on the scaffold as an Irish martyr 309–10
(heroine of Jericho) 589 see Rahab
("hermit") on a diet of pulse 175
(High Sheriff of Dublin) addressed by Rumbold in quest of a hanging job 303
(highlander, Cameron) whom Molly remembers from Gibraltar exposing himself for her benefit 753
(highlander, married) with whom Edy Boardman accuses a friend of being involved 432
("highpriest, Egyptian") whom Taylor quotes regarding the superiority of Egyptian culture over Hebrew 142, 193
[hoof*] Bello's, as Bloom does up the bootlaces 529–30
"Hornblower" porter at the south gate of Trinity College 86, 254, [497], [586], (773)
[hours*] dancing to the pianola in Bella Cohen's 576–77
("housekeeper") whose information about the priest she works for interests Bloom 152
("housemaid") mentioned in typical advertisement for employment 160
(housesteward) who intends to collect the guts of the hanged martyr for his cats' and dogs' home 309
("housewife") at her chores early in the morning in Paris 34
("housewife") who bought trinkets from young Bloom 413
huckster bookseller whose wares Stephen peruses 242
[hue and cry*] in pursuit of Bloom 587
(huguenot) with whom Shakespeare presumably lived 188 see Mountjoy
(hurdygurdy boy) Italian organ grinder whom Bloom remembers having elicited Molly's interest 285 see organgrinder
(husband) of woman who lured Davin to come spend the night in her house P 183
("husband") who learns of his wife's escapade from rumors deriving from overheard confession 83

(husband) in *Sweets of Sin* whose wife spends his money on Raoul 236
(husband) who throttled Walter Bapty for seducing his wife 281
("husband") whose widow Bloom assumes is faring well 380
("husband") cuckolded by superior man, according to Bloom 624 see O'Shea, Capt. William Henry
("husband") cuckolded without recourse, according to Molly 777
("husband, goodman") whose wife died in childbirth 389
(husband, jealous old) Lillie Langtry's, whose chastity belt proved no obstacle for Prince Edward's oyster knife 751
("husbandman") convicted for planting 400 see cattleraider

I the boy or boys in the first three stories of *Dubliners* D 9–35
I narrator of the Cyclops chapter of *Ulysses* 292–345 see Nameless One
idiot deaf mute in Nighttown teased by the children 429
(idiot in the gallery) so dubbed by Molly for hissing the adultress in *The Wife of Scarli* 769, 780
(individual of sinister aspect) who once followed Milly down South Circular Road 693
[infant, female] accuses Bloom of misconduct 496
("inspector, ticket") on tramlines, who Conmee conjectures appears when one has discarded the ticket 222
("invalid") for whom Boylan buys his basket 227 see Bloom, Molly
Irishman putative founder of Socialism P 197 see O'Brien, James
(ironmonger) employer of Mr. Wilkinson S 159

(jarvey) to whom Bloom pointed out the stars, according to Lenehan 234–35
jarvey who drives Cunningham from Dublin Castle 246
jarvey who drives Cunningham, Power, and Bloom from Barney Kiernan's 341–45
jarvey who drives Kelleher and party to Nighttown 585–86, (606), 607–8 see Behan

jarvey in cabman's shelter, who looks like Henry Campbell 625, 632 see cabby
(Jesuit father) refuted by Father Butt S 25
(Jesuit, Belgian) author of *Le Nombre des Élus* 223 see Castelain, Father A.
(Jesuit, earnest) who recommended a clerkship in Guinness's for Stephen S 193 see Butt, D., S. J.
Jesuit, young visiting at Belvedere College P 84–85
Jesuit, plump freshfaced at Belvedere working on the theatrical P 84–85 see Doyle, Fr Charles
Jesuit, smiling welldressed P 84 see Jesuit, young
(Jew) father of girl who killed Harry Hughes—in ballad 690–91
Jew, little crossing on ferry D 23
("jewman") tailor who presumably made Ben Dollard's trousers 244
("josser, queer old") encountered by the truant boys D 24–28
Judge, County Court speaker at the Literary and Historical Society S 172
(junior partner) in James Duffy's bank D 112
(juror) at the Sinico inquest D 114
[jurors] convinced that Bloom won on Throwaway 470

(K C) barrister reputedly seen by Molly with prostitute 777–78
[keeper] of the National Museum, with lorry full of statues when Bloom is being lauded 490
(king of England) 589 see Edward VII
(king, silver) one of Bloom's desired reincarnations 728 see Denver
[kisses*] fluttering about Bloom 475
(kitchengirl) remembered by Stephen singing "By Killarney's Lakes and Fells" P 220

"L" one of five sandwichboard men working for Wisdom Hely 154, 227, 229, 253 see also H; E; Y; 'S
(labourer) in Malahide wood who discovers Stephen worshipping S 156 see also constabulary men, two
labourers, two crossing on the ferry D 23
lacquey at the Dillon auction rooms 226, 237–39, [539], (579)

(lad, young) British sailor to be flogged, in story told by the Citizen 329
ladies, two handsome friends of Farley D 46
(ladies, two plain middle-aged) friends of Robert Hand E 33
(ladies, two stylish dressed) noticed by Molly outside Switzer's being accosted by the unknown gentleman 767
("lady") who gave Anne Kearns the Lourdes water 145
(lady) in testimonial for Wonderworker 722
(lady) the queen in Molly's fortune cards 776
(lady who is dead) loved by the man in the macintosh 333
(lady, dark) subject of Shakespeare sonnets 196 see Fitton, Mary
(lady, old) who taunts Mr. Casey over Parnell P 36–37
lady, stout who gives coin to lame sailor 225 see M'Guinness, Ellen?
lady, young salesgirl at Araby bazaar flirting with the Englishmen D 35
(lady, young) at Eire Abu concert for whom Holohan brings lemonade D 140
lady, young who recites at the Eire Abu concert D 147–48
lady, young overheard by Stephen flirting with a young gentleman on Eccles St. S 211
(lady, young) who accompanied Captain Starkie S 242–43
[lady, rich protestant] pursuing Bloom in Nighttown 586
lady, stylish young shop attendant at Downes' cake shop D 102
(ladylove) figure on Gerty's calendar 355
(lamplighter) in Sandymount, anticipated by Gerty 363
(landlady) of James Duffy D 109
(landlady) in Stamer Street, whose hats drunken Richie Goulding wore 88
("landlady") who, Bloom worries, would cheat Stephen 656
("landboro lordboro") landlord of the Dedaluses, as dubbed by Stephen's young siblings P 163
("Lantern Jaws") a Jesuit priest 39; P 161 see Campbell, Foxy
lapidary 241 see Russell, Thomas
"Lardyface, Old" 333 see Bloom, Leopold
(lass that loves a sailor) D 39 see Hill, Eveline
("Last of the Mohicans") in parade of Irish heroes of antiquity 297; also p. 660* A/N

lay-brother ushers the gentlemen to their seats in the Gardiner Street church D 172
lay-brother collects contributions in the Gardiner Street church S 119
lechers, two silent brought by Kelleher to Nighttown 585–86
(legal luminary) who saved Fitzharris from execution 642 see Adams, Richard
(librarian) at the National Library S 122, 179
(librarian) at Marsh's Library S 176
(librarian, Quaker) 184 see Lyster, Thomas William
loafer lounging on Dawson Street 180
loafer number two one of the denizens of the cabman's shelter 632 see cabby
loafer with a patch outside Barney Kiernan's mocking Bloom 342
(lodgers, two buck) resident with Mrs. Egan in Paris 43
lodge-woman at Clonliffe, opening gate for Stephen S 75
loiterers guffawing over scurrilous story in Nighttown 450
(Londoner, little blond) artiste who incurred Jack Mooney's wrath D 68
"longshoreman number one" one of the denizens of the cabman's shelter 632 see cabby
(lord) for whom Mary Fitton presumably spurned Shakespeare 202 see Herbert, William
(Lord Mayor) rumored to have sent out for a pound of chops D 128
("lord mayor") imagined by Bloom in a gingerbread coach 170
("lord mayor") in Cissy's game with baby Boardman 353
"lord of his creation" 662 see driver, of streetsweeper
[lord, my] judge presiding at Bloom's trial 459
(lord, noble) presumably Bloom's "patron" 409 see Kearney, Mr
("lover") of Spanish girl in window in Ronda, as imagined by Molly 782
(lyricist, modern) alluded to regarding Garryowen's poetic performance 312 see Yeats, William Butler?

maid domestic in Cork watering plants P 91
("maiden all forlorn") once married to the man in the macintosh 427 A/N

("maidenhead") advertised virgin being hawked by bawd in Nighttown 431, 441–42
male form customer at Bella Cohen's whose hat and waterproof are on the rack (502), 525, male cough and tread (526)
("male religious") in Bloom's pornographic photo 721
(malefactor) prisoner being tried by the high sinhedrim 323
man serving dinner on Farley's yacht D47
(man) bookseller accused of peddling pornography S 166
(man) rescued by Mulligan from drowning 45, 621
("man") who leads Stephen in his dream 47
man with woman boarding outsider at Grosvenor Hotel 73
man on barge 99 see bargeman
(man) sidewalk artist observed by Gerty 357
man customer in the cabman's shelter reading newspaper 629 see also cabby; jarvey
man customer in the cabman's shelter reading postcard 629 see also cabby; jarvey
man customer in the cabman's shelter reading Murphy's discharge papers 629 see also cabby; jarvey
("man") yearned for by Molly 740
(man) who sacrifices his life for woman he loves 767 see Carton, Sydney
man all tattered and torn 427 A/N see M'Intosh
(man at the corner) who Molly noticed has a false arm 371–72
(Man for Galway) in parade of Irish heroes of antiquity 297 A/N
(man from Belfast) who built houses on Eveline's playing field D 36
man in buffsuit "partial" mourner seen by Bloom from his carriage 91–92
(Man in the Gap) in parade of Irish heroes of antiquity 297 A/N
("man in the gap") supposed by Bannon to be the actual father of Mina Purefoy's child 408
man in the macintosh seen at Dignam's funeral 109 see M'Intosh
(man in the hotel) who cooked the fish for Mrs. Malins in Scotland D 191
[man in the street] one of Bloom's pursuers 586
[man in the street, other] one of Bloom's pursuers 586

(man killed in Trieste) knife victim in Murphy's story 628, 636
(man making bottles) glassblower remembered by Gabriel Conroy D 213
(man of seventy) bit off a piece of his tongue, in Kernan's story D 158
man out of the last house observed by Eveline coming home D 36
man spitting diner spitting back his food 169, chap in the Burton (271), (370)
(Man that Broke the Bank at Monte Carlo) in parade of Irish heroes 297 A/N
(man that was drowned) whose body is expected to wash up on 16 June 1904 21, 45–46, Found drowned (50), drowning case (75), found drowned (659)
"man that was so like himself" 354 see nobleman, stroller
man with an infant's saucestained napkin eating soup at the Burton 169
(man with the curly hair) remembered by Molly as an admirer in the Lucan dairy 745
("man with the hat") farmhand remembered by Stephen for his oddities P 162
man, awkward observed by Father Conmee on the tram 222
(man, city) in testimonial for Wonderworker 722
man, consumptive seen by Stephen in the street P 177
(man, dark) who handed Bloom the throwaway 676 see man, sombre Y.M.C.A. young
[man, darkvisaged] bids for Bloom 540
man, elderly assisting at the Belvedere College theatricals P 84–85
man, elderly priest swimming at the Forty Foot in Sandycove 22–23
man, fat friend of Farley in charge of the two handsome women D 46
("man, first") contemplated by Molly as the first she will meet in the morning 780
("man, hardworking") reprieved by Falkiner from debt conviction 322
("man, live") advertised for in the *Irish Times* 160
man, old porter in the Gresham Hotel seeing the Conroys to their room D 125–26

(man, old) peasant in Mulrennan's story of the west of Ireland P 251–52 see also peasant, old
(man, old) seen by Stephen dozing in church S 146
(man, poor) mender of pots and pans remembered by Molly 758
(man, tall) in Stephen's dream in the infirmary P 27 see Michael, Brother
man, weary-looking door attendant at Araby bazaar D 34
man, young in checked suit with two women at John Mulligan's D 95
man, young in cycling suit who assisted Kernan when he fell D 151–53, (160)
man, young at the Daniels' party S 43
man, young at the Daniels' party S 46
man, young friend of Mulligan whom he meets at Sandycove beach area 21–22
("man, young") imagined by Stephen in an autumnal scene in a mountain hotel 684
(man, awkward old) who took communion from Father Conmee, an incident remembered by Conmee when he sees an awkward man on the tram 222
man, dullgarbed old 93 see bootlace vendor
man, effervescent young billiards player S 217–18 see White
man, flushed young 224 see Lynch
man, lean young club swinger at the Belvedere theatricals P 73
man, squat young P 234 see Glynn
man, thickset young clerk playing billiards at the Adelphi S 217–18
man, pallid suetfaced young polishing his eating utensils at the Burton 169
(man, plump smiling young) French delegate at Wolfe Tone memorial P 184
man, sombre Y.M.C.A. young hands Bloom the throwaway on Dowie 151, (676)
(manager) Joe Donnelly's superior to whom he made his wise remark D 104
manager of the bar where Kernan had his accident D 150–53
(marinedealer) whose shop on Burgh Quay Stephen passes P 176 T see Smith, Ellen
marker at the Adelphi Hotel billiards tables S 218

(marquess, noble) 133 see Salisbury, Lord
(marshal) whose ghost haunts Clongowes P 19 see Browne, Count Maximilian Ulysses von
massboy assisting at mass at All Hallows, observed by Bloom 82–83
(master) at the boy's school, annoyed by failing interest in schoolwork D 32
master of mathematics at Belvedere P 105
master of English history at Belvedere P 126
(master) of Harry Hughes's school—in ballad 691
(master at arms) flogging British sailor, in Citizen's account 329
[master of horse] officer of the Royal Court at Bloom's coronation 480 N
(Master of the Rolls) in whose kitchen area Bloom remembers the chef preparing a feast 175 see Porter, Sir Andrew Marshall
("master, young") suspect about whom the policeman quizzes the housemaid 163
(matron) at Dublin by Lamplight laundry D 99, 100
(matron, Ephesian) type of widow whose excessive mourning quickly evaporates when she is wooed by another man 408 A/N
mechanic at the refreshment bar where Lenehan has his meal D 57
(medical) at Holles Street hospital, remembered by Molly for his obliviousness to her blandishments 757
medical student, big attacks clerk over political difference, invites Temple to the brothels, offering to pay for Cranly S 207–8, 223–26
medicals, two on spree with Temple after their examinations S 223–26 see medical student, big
("member for Shillelagh") referred to in mock parliamentary debate 315
men, two counting the proceeds at Araby bazaar D 35
men, stupid young two of them at the Gaelic League class, the younger embarrassed by the Irish word for lover S 60–61
men, two unlabouring lounging outside pub, greet Conmee 221
("merchant of jalaps") to whom Stephen in his mock biblical speech feels he has been betrayed 393

(mermaid) on poster advertising cigarettes in the Ormond and at Daly's 263, 289 N
messenger Belvedere boy announcing time for confession P 126
(messengerboy) from Thornton's who delivered Boylan's basket to Molly 747
[methodist] head of the Church at Bloom's coronation 480
milkman with whom Stephen goes riding P 63–64
(milkman) with whom Archie goes riding E 16, 46, 91–92, 110
milkwoman at Sandycove delivering to the tower (12), 13–15, (16)
[millionairess] admiring Bloom 481
(minister) at Clongowes 40, 48 see Father Minister
(miser) dead landlord whose building Wilkinson occupies with the Daedaluses S 159
("missus") to whom the maid threatens to report the advances of the young master 163
(mistress) of Jean-Jacques Rousseau S 40 see Vercellis, Mme de
[mob] threatening to lynch Bloom 492
(monarch, "German") D 121 see Edward VII
[Moravian] head of Church at Bloom's coronation 480
("mortal, lucky") the lover in Bloom's imagined eternal triangle 642
(mother) of St. Columbanus 27
("mother") in doorway in Bloom's fantasy of the Near East 57
(mother) of Socrates 190, 202
(mother) of William Davenant 202
(mother) of the Croppy Boy 284, 594
(mother) of five children in testimonial for Wonderworker 722
("mother") of hardened criminal seen by Molly in newspaper 765
(Mother of the Maccabees) martyred mother in Old Testament, here in parade of Irish heroes and heroines of antiquity 297 see Salome
(mother, old) D 132 see Victoria, Queen
(mother's sister) of "Kitty-Kate"—who married a Montmorency 508
motorman who almost runs Bloom down in Nighttown 435, Insolent driver (436), mangongwheeltracktrolleyglarejuggernaut (452)

(murderer) reported ghost in Clongowes P 19
("murderer") in Molly's fantasy of being attacked 777
("mute, hired") professional wailer at funeral, according to Mulligan 8
mystery man on the beach subject of Bloom's novelistic intentions (376), [587] see nobleman, stroller

Nameless One collector of bad debts who narrates the Cyclops chapter 292–345, [470], [586]
navvy, drunken lurching through Nighttown 430, 433, 447, 450–52, 596
neighbour one of the denizens of the cabman's shelter 638 see cabby; jarvey
(neighbours, nextdoor) two girls Bloom remembers practicing the piano 278
(nephew) of Mrs. Riordan whom Bloom got drunk 305–6
newsboy hawking the Racing Special and mocking Bloom 146
newsboy, another hawking the Racing Special 144
newsboy, first hawking the Racing Special 144
(noble) reputed father of Antisthenes 149 see bondwoman
"nobleman" stroller along Sandymount Strand seen by Gerty and Bloom 354, 375–76, [587] see gentleman off Sandymount green; man that was so like himself; mystery man on the beach
(nobleman) who has his wife committed, from some work of literature known to Gerty 364
("nobleman"—with a cock-eye) whom Henchy and O'Connor consider a traitor to Ireland D 125
(nobleman, spendthrift) 221 see Aldborough, Lord
[noblewoman] admiring Bloom 481
(Number One) presumably the leader of the Invincibles 138
("nun") whom Bloom assumes invented barbed wire 155, 369, 553
("nun") debauched by vampire in Paris performance described by Stephen 570
("nun") in Bloom's pornographic photo 738 see female religious
nun, mad whom Stephen hears screeching P 175
(nun, nice) whom Bloom remembers from Tranquilla Convent 155, 368 see Agatha, Sister

nurse followed by Lynch and Stephen P 248
nurse ogled by Moynihan and Stephen S 150
(nurse) at Lying-In Hospital who reported to Josie Breen on Mina Purefoy's condition 159 see Callan, Nurse; Quigley, Nurse
("nurse") who loves the new chemist 333
("nurse") in household from whom young girls learn things, according to Bloom 372
(nurse) in testimonial for Wonderworker 722
(nurse) to whom Bloom would play up to if hospitalized, according to Molly 738
(nurse) whom Molly remembers pursued the medical in Holles Street 757 see Callan, Nurse
nymph from *Titbits* on the Blooms' bedroom wall (65), [544–54], (753)
("nymph, immortal") anticipated bride of Bloom in his role as Noman 727
"nymphs" crowd around Bloom's fleeing cab 341

officer who reports his conversation with the old peasant S 242–44 see Starkie, Captain
(officer, British naval) in testimonial for Wonderworker 722
(old one) Liffey Street bookseller 233
(old one) at City Arms Hotel 305–6 see Riordan, Mrs
(old salt) retired seaman remembered by Bloom at Dollymount 630
(one) who stayed at New Place with Ann Shakespeare 206 see gospeller
(one) 750 see shop girl, at Lewer's
(one in the cream muslin) whose clothes could be seen through, remembered by Molly 746
(one of them) girl whom Corley boasts of having taken advantage of D 53
[Orange Lodges] jeering at Deasy's stumbling race horse 573
(orator, College) S 39 see Whelan, College orator
(organgrinder, Italian) whom Bloom assumes to have been one of Molly's lovers 285, 731 see boy, hurdygurdy
(organ-player) Italian whom Mr. Hill contemptuously sent away D 40
[orphans, Artane] taunting Bloom 497

("other, absent") whose ignorance Bloom ridicules before Molly as a ploy 687

(paramour) of adultress Devorghil 324 see MacMurrough, Dermot
("parent, aged bedridden") claimed by Bloom in his defense 462
(parson) who witnesses the flogging of the young sailor 329
("particular party") known to Kelleher and Constable 57 C 225
("pater") invoked by Stephen 210 see Daedalus
[pavior and flagger] lauds Bloom 481
(peasant, old) in anecdote about rural ignorance S 242–43 see also man, old, peasant
(pedagogue) Stephen's role in Belvedere theatrical P 73
[peers] genuflecting in homage to Bloom 482–83
penitent who emerged from confession box in Church Street chapel P 142
penitent who entered confession box in Church Street chapel P 142
penitents, two P 141–42 see penitent who emerged; penitent who entered
(person) who directed Murphy to a urinal 638
(person, another) credited with Bloom for bringing the potato from America 478 see Hawkins, Sir John
(personage, sympathetic) 659 see cabby
(philosophaster, Scotch) 205 see James I
(philosopher, rabbinical) Aristotle's mentor, according to Bloom 687 A/N
[pianola*] in Bella Cohen's playing "My Girl's a Yorkshire Girl" 575–78
(playwright) forced to change an unhappy ending, according to Dillon S 98
("plumber, working") credited with responsibility for Kitty-Kate's downfall 508
(poet) who conflated genius and madness D 168 see Dryden, John
("poet chap") imagined by Bloom as his less fortunate rival 369
(poet, Latin) author of the *Metamorphoses* 411 see Ovid
pointsman of tram, observed by Bloom 91

policeman stationed at St. Stephen's Green S 140, (141)
policeman approaching drunken students near Noblett's corner S 225
("policeman") incapable of poetry, according to Bloom 166
policeman saluting Cunningham at Castleyard Gate 246
policeman, burly at theatre riot over *The Countess Cathleen* P 226
("policeman, dead") claimed by the devil, according to Hynes's quip 332
[policeman, fat] tripped by Bloom who is currying favor with the crowd 486
(policeman, horse) who cracked his head during T.C.D. riots over Chamberlain 162–63
policeman, illdressed bearded seen by Stephen on the docks P 66
(pontiff, sovereign) P 147 see Leo XIII
(pope) who declared infallibility a dogma of the Church D 168–69 see Pius IX
(pope) who banned women from church choirs D 194 see Leo XIII
(pope) who sent the first cardinal to Ireland S 53 see Innocent II
(pope, late) D 165 see Pius IX
porter at the Grosvenor Hotel 73
porter at Trinity College south gate 86 see Hornblower
porter at the *Freeman's Journal* saluting Braydon 117
porter, doddering at U.C.D. pinning up a notice P 204
porter, garrulous at Queen's College, Cork, interviewed by Mr. Dedalus P 89
("porter, railway") blamed for the "bad" language of the Holy Ghost by Mr. Dedalus P 32
porter, railway at Maynooth station attending to a case of machines S 238
Portuguese, little pupil at Clongowes Wood P 13, 54
postmistress at Westland Row station where Bloom collects his letter 72, [586]
(preacher) horrified to hear Jesus called a maniac S 189
prefect at Clongowes, on the playing field P 8
prefect at Clongowes, having his sleeves knotted P 14 see McGlade
prefect of the chapel at Clongowes P 17–18

prefect at Clongowes, bidding the boys in the dormitory goodnight P 19
prefect at Clongowes, waking up the boys in the dormitory P 21 see McGlade
prefect at Belvedere, officiating at the theatricals 74, (77)
prefect of studies at Clongowes P 44 see Dolan, Father
prefect of the sodality at U.C.D., considered by Stephen to be grave and serious P (192), 199
(prelate) gives the last rites to the Irish martyr before the hanging 308
[presbyterian moderator] at Bloom's coronation 480
president of U.C.D. P (192), 200; S 29 see Dillon, Rev. Dr W., S. J.
("President, Mr") "Elijah" Dowie's God 508 see also Big Brother
(president, venerable) of Sluagh na h-Eireann 316 see Citizen
(priest) former occupant of the boy's house, now deceased D 29, 31 + sister (29)
(priest) friend of Mr. Hill, now emigrated to Australia D 37
(priest) who granted Mrs. Mooney a separation from her husband D 61
(priest) who had heard Bob Doran's confession D 65
(priest) who had come to visit old Ellen P 68
priest viewed by Stephen outside Belvedere before the theatricals P 73
priest viewed by Stephen in church P 147
priest overheard by Stephen discussing the sanctity of Lord Macaulay P 156
priest in National Library disturbed by Stephen and Cranly P 227 see priest, red-faced
(priest) warned Maurice against single companions S 57
(priest) whose story of the dying drunkard Maurice retells S 58–59
(priest) whose list of the world's three greatest men a seminarian recounts S 74
priest who hears Isabel's dying confession S 164
priest who officiates at Isabel's funeral at Glasnevin S 167 see Coffey, Fr M.
priest emerging from a swim at the Forty Foot 22–23, garland of grey hair (40)

priest officiating at All Hallows 80–83, Like that priest (154), Priest with the communion corpus (284)
priest seen by Bloom on Westmoreland Street 154
(priest) sought for confession by the Croppy Boy 283
(priest) customer at Bella Cohen's 519–20, 526
(priest) remembered by Molly in Gibraltar 759
("priest") for whom Molly assumes dying atheists go howling 782
(priest in the Fermanagh will case) whose composure in the witness box Bloom admires 83
(priest, American) scheduled to lecture at the Mansion House D 144
(priest, another) with Father O'Rourke when Father Flynn was found in the confessional D 18
(priest, false) disguised British officer who tricked the Croppy Boy 285
(priest, little) teacher at U.C.D. who writes devout verses P 192
("priest, odd") whom Molly imagines occasionally disturbs a nun's sleep 781
priest, old Capuchin to whom Stephen confesses P 142–45
(priest, Portuguese) whose book on Latin verse Stephen learns from P 179 see Alvarez, Manoel
priest, red-faced disturbed trying to read at the National Library S 183; P 227
(priest, suave) Emma's uncle P 222 see Healy, Father, brother of Mrs. Daniel
(priest, burly black-vested) typical of those Stephen encounters in the Liberties S 146
priesteen seen conversing with Lyster in the National Library 215 see Dineen
(Prince of Wales, first) in parade of Irish heroes 297 a/N see Edward II
(prince, gracious) presumably granted civil rights to Catholics 409 see George IV
("prisoner, Spanish") donor of valuables that would compound as a fortune, in Bloom's scheme 718
(prodigal) in the biblical parable P 189 see brother, elder
professor lecturing on physics at U.C.D. P 190–94
(professor) of English composition at U.C.D. S 27 see Keane, Mr
(professor) at U.C.D. who heard good reports of Ibsen S 41

(professor) at the Medical School, rumored to be an owner of brothels S 65
(professor of economics) at U.C.D. P 192
(professor of Italian, plump roundheaded) at U.C.D. P 192 see Ghezzi, Fr Charles
(professor of mental sciences, young) at U.C.D. P 192
professor, young at U.C.D. seen talking to the dean of studies P 194
proprietor of pub at Chapelizod Bridge serving a drink to Duffy D 116
(proprietor) of the Adelphi Hotel S 208
(proprietor, rustic) neighbor of Mr. Fulham S 241
(prostitute) seen by Molly with a K. C. 778
("prostitute, reformed") presumed by Bloom to be a typical Salvation Army confessional speaker 83
(provost) of Trinity College 170, 253 see Salmon, Rev. Dr George

("queen") loved by king 333
(Queen of England) S 60, 63 see Victoria, Queen

[rabbi, chief] at Bloom's coronation 480
[ragman, sackshouldered] blocks Bloom's path in Nighttown 436
("railway bloke") 426 see Lenehan, T.
(rancher, indignant) who had quarreled with Bloom when he worked at Cuffe's 409
Rector at Belvedere College P (75–76), 105, 106, 107–8, (179); S (35–36) see MacNally
redcoats, two 450 see Carr, Pvt Harry; Compton, Pvt
(referee) of the Keogh-Bennett fight 319
(reporter) who records the death of Mrs. Sinico D 115
("reporter") who calls the hansom cab death tragic, in Stephen's story P 205
reporter who discusses Maeterlinck with Stephen S 39–40
[resident, old] praises Bloom 484
(robber, public) P 119 see Barabbas
rough in Nighttown melee between Stephen and Carr 593
[rough, burly] pursues Bridie Kelly in Nighttown 441

("Royal Dublins, two") for whom Stephen imagines the gypsy buying drinks 47

"'S" one of the five sandwichboard men working for Wisdom Hely 154, 155, 227, 229, 253 see also E; H; L; Y
sacristan at Church Street chapel P 141
sailor on Dublin docks where the boy searches for green-eyed sailors D 23
("sailor") whom Molly contemplates picking up 777
sailor, onelegged en route through the Dublin streets begging for alms 219, 225–26, 248, lame crutch and leg sailor [579], (747)
("sailorman") watching belly dancer in Stephen's imagined vignette 241 see bellydancer
(saint, holy) presumably a Jesuit who was vouchsafed a glimpse of hell P 132
("sandman") personification of sleep invoked for baby Boardman 363
(Savourneen Deelish) song title ("My Precious Darling"); among Irish heroes and heroines of antiquity 297 A/N
[Sawhimbefore] one of Bloom's pursuers 586 see nobleman, stroller
(scholar, eminent) credited with translating Garryowen's verse 312
[schoolboy, bluecoat] cheers Bloom 484
scullion, clumsy serving in Clongowes refectory P 12–13
secretary of the Literary and Historical society S 100–105
"secretary of state for domestic affairs" one of the carousers in the hospital commons room when baby Purefoy is born 410
[secretary of the society of friends, honorary] at Bloom's coronation 480
(secretary, papal) who puts atheistic writers on the Index S 41
(señorita, nude) in Bloom's pornographic photo 467, 721
("sentry") at city gates in Bloom's fantasy of the Near East 57
(sentry) from Molly's recollections of Gibraltar 762
(sentry) from Molly's recollections of the governor's house in Gibraltar 782
(sergeant) in Cunningham's anecdote of mealtimes in the police barracks D 161
(sergeant) remembered by Bloom looking up at Molly in the window 89

sergeantmajor, plump bald in Belvedere gymnastic event P 73
("servant") one of those buying milk, observed by Stephen from the cart P 64
servant heard by Stephen and Cranly singing "Rosie O'Grady" P 244
servant, old in Clongowes, guides Stephen to rector's office P 56, 58
("servant, proper") yearned for by Molly 768
(servant, false priest's) in song about the Croppy Boy 283
(servant-girl) whom Rousseau allowed to be accused of theft S 40
"server" altarboy assisting Father Coffey at the funeral service 103–4
server, illgirt waiter at the Burton 170
(Shah of Persia) 284, 290 see Nasr-ed-Din
("shawls," two) prostitutes seen with Bob Doran in Bride Street 314
("she") example of mindless dying woman Mulligan sees in the hospitals 8
(she) waitress Stephen remembers from Paris 42–43
(she) whose ankles Bloom tried to see 73–74, 160 see woman, horsey
("she") whom Bloom imagines in flirtatious conversation 371 see MacDowell, Gerty
("she") 392–93 see bride, in Madagascar
("she") prostitute Molly supposes Bloom had been with 772
shebeenkeeper haggling with British soldiers in Nighttown 450–51
(shepherd, woful) mourning for Lycidas in Milton's poem 25
(sheriff) in whose office doorway Cowley is seen by Bloom 265 see Fanning, "Long" John
(shop girl) at Lewer's, where Molly bought stockings that immediately laddered 750
(shop girl) in Grafton Street, whom Molly considered insolent 752
shopman bookseller at Merchants' Arch who rents Bloom *Sweets of Sin* 235–37
(Siamese, delicate) whom Stephen remembers from Paris library 25
[sightseers] died saluting Bloom 485
[sins of the past] accusing Bloom 537

(sister) of the husband of the woman who tried to lure Davin into her house P 183
(sister) remembered by William Shakespeare in his will 203 see Shakespeare, Joan
(sisters, weird) 13 see Yeats, Elizabeth; Yeats, Lily
("sixfooter") imagined by Bloom with a diminutive wife 373
slavey Corley's paramour, employed in house in Baggot Street D (50–54), 54–56, (57), 59–60
[sleepy hollow*] calling Rip Van Winkle 542 A/N
"sloppy eyes, old" 336 see Bloom, Leopold
slut shouting at Bloom outside Barney Kiernan's 342
slut on Mabbot Street combing her child's hair 430
[sluts and ragamuffins] jeering Bloom 466
sluts, two in the Coombe, whom Bloom remembers singing (78–79), [552–53]
(Soldier Boy, Bold) in parade of Irish heroes of antiquity 297 A/N
("solicitor") for the husband in Bloom's imagined love triangle 654
(solicitor, Nationalist) father of Gaelic League language teacher, Mr. Hughes S 60
(solicitor, well-known) whose death is reported in the *Evening Telegraph* S 221–22
somebody one of the denizens of the cabman's shelter 629 see cabby; jarvey
("somebody") who always comes to the door at the most inconvenient time, much to Molly's annoyance 747
("somebody") object of Molly's sensual desires 754
("someone") to whom Hughes reveals his dislike of Stephen S 115 see Clery, Emma
("someone") involved in flirtatious female conversation imagined by Bloom 371
("someone else") whom Bloom assumes Gerty was thinking about 371
(someone of the poor class) whose funeral coincides with Isabel's S 167
(son) of Queen Victoria 102 see Edward VII
(son) of Bella Cohen, presumably in Oxford, according to Zoe 475, 585
("son, cook's") one of several sons alluded to in Kipling's "Absentminded Beggar" 589 A/N see also Cook, Thomas, & Son

(soothsayer) who warned Julius Caesar about the Ides of March 193 A/N
Spaniard P 13, 54 see Arana y Lupardo, José
("Speaker of the House") Mr. Daniel's role in parliamentary charade S 45
(specialist) whom Parnell refused to call in 649 see Thompson, Sir Henry
"specimen in the corner, old" one of the denizens of the cabman's shelter 659 see cabby; jarvey
("sponger") owner of bawdyhouse where Bloom imagines Murphy will go 658
(sprinter) who broke Stephen's glasses on the cinder path P 41
("squarepusher") with whom Edy claims she saw her friend 432
("squire, sham") 241 see Higgins, Francis
(stationer) 182 see Worn, A.
(statue, little gimcrack) 543, 766, 775–76 see Narcissus
steward one of those attending at the Eire Abu concert D 142, 145
(stonecutter) near Glasnevin cemetery 99 see Dennany, Thomas H.
["Strangeface"] one of Bloom's pursuers 586
streetwalker 632 see whore with black straw sailor hat
stripling, blind piano tuner helped across the street by Bloom 180–81, 250, 254, The tuner (263), (264), Tap 281, 283–91, [486], [538]
(strumpet, nocturnal) with whom Sins of the Past accuse Bloom of cloacal acts 537
student at Clonliffe, overheard by Stephen praising the Archbishop S 74
("student, broadshouldered") whom Stephen imagines carving "Foetus" P 90
student, heavybuilt stares with wonder at MacAlister's antics in the physics theatre P 193
student, lean P 196 see Temple
student, medical quarrels with clerk, suggests going to the brothels to Temple S 207–8, 223–26 see also medicals, two
student, Scotch 404 see Crotthers, J.
student, stout P 230 see Goggins

("student, young") whom Bloom imagines tampering with the household maid 163
student, big countrified asks Stephen about longhaired artists S 34 + father S (34)
(student, nice young) who dressed Bloom's bee sting 97 see Dixon
student, stout ruddy listening to the exchange between Stephen and MacCann P 197–99
student, tall consumptive listening to Temple prattle on library steps P 230–32, 234–37
(subsheriff) who had employed M'Coy D 158 see also Fanning, "Long" John
(sub-matron) of the Dublin by Lamplight laundry D 99
(Sunamite) woman who kept King David warm 528 see Abishag
superintendent of Prospect Cemetery, Glasnevin S 167 see O'Connell, John K.
(swashbuckler) in Costello's bawdy song 392

(tart) with whom MacNally was seen S 36
(tart) reported to have hit Mac for insulting her S 224
("tart, bloody") whom Corley believes Stephen brought into his lodgings 617
(teacher, Irish) employed to teach Irish to Kathleen Kearney D 137
telegram boy reading Father Flynn's death notice D 12
telegram boy delivering telegram to the *Freeman's Journal* 118
(telegramboy) involved in illegal scheme on horse race 426 see Hand, Stephen
teller in Bank of Ireland where Stephen claims his prize money P 96
[tenants, evicted Irish] threaten Bloom 496
tenor, first at Eire Abu concert D (138), 143–44, 146, 147–48
(tenor, Italian) praised by Mr. Browne D 199
("thing in the gallery") hissing the adultress in *The Wife of Scarli* 780 see idiot in the gallery
(third, a) one of the denizens of the cabman's shelter 632 see cabby; jarvey
ticket-collector at Kingstown station, as the boy goes to Araby D 47
timekeeper of trams at Nelson's Pillar 116

("toff, Kildare Street club") whom Kernan supposes was the original owner of his coat 240
("toff, Kildare Street club") who, according to eyewitness Bloom, fired a shot in Truelock's gun shop 452
[torchbearers] cheer Bloom 479
(torero, muscular) in Bloom's pornographic photo, described by Mrs. Talboys 467 see also torero, nude
(torero, nude) in pornographic photo in Bloom's drawer 721 see also torero, muscular
(tramdriver) at Harold's Cross, whom Bloom tried to prevent from mistreating his horse 454 see also driver; motorman
tramp, old emptying his boots on the curbstone near Glasnevin 99
(trombone) musician Bloom remembers from a concert 271
(Tsar of Russia) 589; P 194, 196, 198; S 112–15 see Nicholas II
[twins] wheeled in pram by Bloom as he attempts to please the crowd 486
typesetter at the *Freeman's Journal* 121, 122, [484]
[typesetters, chapel of *Freeman*] cheering Bloom 484
(typist) remembered by Bloom on stairs showing off her underclothes 372

uncle of the boy who was being taught by Father Flynn D 10–11, (13) see Jack, the boy's uncle
uncle of the boy who wanted to go to the Araby bazaar D (30), 32, 33–34
("uncle") Jesus Christ's 342 see Joseph, S.
urchin, cringing newsboy at the *Telegraph* office 128
[urchins] warn Bloom of approaching cyclists 435
urchins, two barefoot pick up coin for one-legged sailor 225–26
(usher) in Paris post office closing door on Stephen 41–42

("vampire man") in Stephen's narration of a Paris club skit 570
(vampire, pale) in Stephen's quatrain 48, 132
(vet) tipster who presumably gave Bella Cohen advice on Throwaway 475

[veteran, palsied] whose bedsores Bloom kisses while campaigning 486
(vicechancellor) with whom Robert Hand arranges for Richard Rowan to dine E 38, 42, 44, 51, 58–59, 105, 107
(vice-chancellor) who, Bloom tells the watch, is Stephen's uncle 585
(vicereine) 160 see Dudley, Lady
(VILLAGE BLACKSMITH) in parade of Irish heroes of antiquity 296 A/N
virago in Nighttown, insulting the British soldiers 430, 593
("virgin") whom Stephen ogled in front of Hodges Figgis's shop 48–49
("virgin, budding") potential customer for young Bloom's trinkets 413
(visitor) at the Mulligan household when Stephen was present 8
(visitor, English) who attempted to photograph Milly 693
(voice) at Araby bazaar calling for lights out D 35
(voice) in pub calling for air for Kernan D 150–51
(voice) on Clongowes playing field calling the students in P 11
(voice) in newspaper office calling Monks 121
[voice] denouncing Bloom as a traitor 457
[voice] challenging Bloom's authenticity as a messiah 495
[voice] mocking Ben Dollard's garb 522
[voice] sneering at Reuben J. Dodd 539
[voice] demanding that Bloom swear 543
[voice from the gallery] deriding Bloom 459
[voice of all the blessed] at the Last Judgment celebrating God 600
[voice of all the damned] at the Last Judgment celebrating God backward 599
(voice, shrill) heard by Bloom at Sandymount hawking the stop press edition 379
[voices] commenting on the bidding 540
[voices] sighing after Bloom has been sacrificed 544
[voices] commenting on the Stephen-Carr-Cissy altercation 587–88
[voices] calling for the police after Stephen has been knocked down 598
[voices, distant] shouting that Dublin is burning 598

waggoner driving cart with granite block to Glasnevin 101
(waiter) in hotel grounds in Bray, observed by Stephen and Eileen P 43
waiter in Victoria Hotel, Cork, interviewed by Mr. Dedalus P 89
(waiter) in the Star and Garter, at whom Mrs. Deasy threw the soup 132
(waiter) on train to Marlborough, to whom Bloom refused to surrender his soup 748
(waitress) in Paris serving Stephen and Kevin Egan 42
waitress at the D.B.C. serving Mulligan and Haines 248–49
[waitress, blushing] with whom Bloom flirts while campaigning 486
("Wandering Jew") 217 see Ahasuerus; Bloom, Leopold
(wanton, court) 202 see Fitton, Mary
(warden) remembered by Molly locking gates in Gibraltar 757
(warder, head) at Kilmainham who reported on Joe Brady's erection after hanging 304
watch, first in Nighttown 430, [453–74], [586], 602–5, (608) see Constable 65 C
watch, second in Nighttown 430, [453–74], [586], 602–5, (608) see Constable 66 C
(watchman) *sereno* in Algeciras remembered by Molly 782–83
(watercarrier) 553, 671 see Aquarius
[waterfall*] at Poulaphouca, where young Bloom went on a high school excursion 547–53
(wench) pregnant in Costello's bawdy song 392
"whatdoyoucallhim" hunchback known to Bloom who pursues him in Nighttown 61, [586] see also captain, Norwegian
("wheelwright, cunning") whose spokes are like a ray of nymphs, in carriage conceit, as Bloom is sped away from Barney Kiernan's 341
whore who calls attention to Stephen's torn coat as he flees from Bella Cohen's 584
whore with black straw sailor hat, frowsy seen by Bloom at various places, once tried to solicit Stephen 290–91, 632, wretched creature (633), in the shape of a female (638); S 189, (190), (192), (203) Introduction
(whore, high class) remembered by Bloom in Jammet's 371
whores luring Bloom in Nighttown; pointing out the direction in which Stephen fled 450, 583

widow   seen by Bloom outside All Hallows   83–84
(widow)   remembered by Bloom outside Cramer's   380–81
[widow]   consoled by Bloom as he campaigns   486
("widow, fast")   according to Molly, easy prey to men   777
(widow, fubsy)   ogled by Stephen on Serpentine Avenue   40, 571
("widow, young")   whom Bloom contemplates meeting in Glasnevin   108
("widower")   whom Bloom feels sympathy toward   381
wife   of workman seen by Stephen leaving Gardiner Street church   S 121
(wife)   of Jack Power   93
("wife")   of would-be polygamist   151
(wife)   of Pericles   195   see Thaisa
(wife)   of Socrates   202   see Xanthippe
wife   of gentleman with glasses, seen by Conmee on the tram   222
("wife")   of Pat, the waiter at the Ormond   283
("wife")   of chap that wallops the big drum   289
("wife")   of poor hardworking man who comes before Falkiner as a debtor   322
("wife")   of the proverbial sailor who has one in every port   378
(wife)   of Buddha   771   see Yasodhara
(wife)   in *Fair Tyrants*   777
(wife)   of the K. C. seen by Molly with a prostitute   778
(wife of a barrister, divorced)   whom Robert Hand seduced in a cab   E 107–8
(wife of a compatriot)   dismembered by Voisin, according to Rumbold   593
(wife of a stockbroker)   mistress of Robert Hand   E 65–66
(wife, burgher's)   whose affair with Burbage was interrupted by Shakespeare   201
("wife, poor")   of hardened criminal seen by Molly in newspaper   765
(wife, lord lieutenant's)   who drove down the street after Emmet was hanged   240   see Yorke, Elizabeth
("wife, other chap's")   from whom Bloom is glad to escape   370
(wife, wife's lover's)   of Belluomo in Paris, as imagined by Stephen   42
("wifey")   diminutive spouse of "sixfooter"   373

(wine-merchant, Catholic) Bob Doran's employer D 65
see Leonard, Mr
(witch, laughing) in Beaufoy's "Matcham's Masterstroke" 69
woman penitent at Church Street chapel P 142
(woman) found drowned in Mullingar S 252
("woman") typical communicant eager for confession, as Bloom imagines 83
("woman") whom Bloom assumes laid flowers before the statue of Smith O'Brien 93
woman who stares at Josie Breen 158
(woman) who became a Mason 177–78 see Aldworth, Elizabeth
(woman) wife of Merchants' Arch bookseller 236
(woman) who had died in childbirth at the Lying-In Hospital 388–89
(woman) whose screams are heard in Nighttown 430
(woman at midnight mass) whom Bloom remembers attracting him in church 80
(woman he keeps) Jack Power's mistress 93 see barmaid, at Jury's
(woman in the big hat) who attracts Farrington at John Mulligan's D 95, (97) see also women with big hats, two
woman in the black straw hat S 190 see whore with black straw sailor hat
("woman in the next lane") whom the "idiot in the gallery" had, Molly assumes 769
woman in white stockings observed critically by Bloom on Grafton Street 168, (372)
["woman of the house"] addressed by Bloom as Irish peasant 499
(woman we had in) who washed the dead body of Father Flynn D 15
(Woman Who Didn't) in parade of Irish heroes and heroines of antiquity 297 A/N
(woman . . . with the watercress) from whom Molly intends buying Stephen's presumed breakfast 779
(woman standing at the halfdoor) reported by a pupil at Clongowes to Stephen P 18, 183 + child
(woman, beautiful) Raoul's married mistress in *Sweets of Sin* 236
woman, hard with her daughter at Glasnevin 101; S 167
see harpy, leanjawed

woman, horsey whose ankles Bloom tried to see on Westland Row 73–74, (160), (436) + "husband" or "brother" (73)
("woman, married") whom Molly views as an easy prey for men 777
("woman, night") assumed by Molly to have spent the evening with Bloom 738–39
woman, old Stephen's aunt P 68
woman, old who directs Stephen to the Church Street chapel P 141
(woman, old) whose cakes King Alfred allowed to burn S 104
(woman, old) praying in chapel, observed by Stephen S 146
woman, old selling her Sandycove milk to the tower residents 13–15
woman, old peeping out at the Dignam funeral procession 87
woman, old who left the tram Conmee was riding on 222
(woman, old) who was murdered by the hardened criminal 765–66
(woman, other) author of *Henry Dunbar* 756 see Braddon, Mary Elizabeth
("woman, other") whom Molly considers inviting to a picnic for Bloom 764
"woman, pigmy" child swinging on rope between rails in Nighttown 429
("woman, robber of a") who, Molly assumes, found her lost gloves 745
("Woman, Scarlet") whom Dowie accuses Bloom of worshipping 492
("woman, some") subject for a poet's writings, according to Molly 775
("woman, some") typically vicious, according to Molly 778
woman, standing urinating in Mabbot Street 449–50
woman, young Stephen's first whore P 100–101
(woman, young) who tried to lure Davin into her house 182–83, 238
woman, young 224 see Kitty
("woman, young") in a mountain hotel, in Stephen's imagined vignette 684
("woman, good matronly") whom Bloom projects for widower O'Connor 381
woman, small old taking communion at All Hallows 80
[women] adoring Bloom 486
women with big hats, two in John Mulligan's pub D 95

women, two overheard by Stephen praising a sermon at Gardiner Street church S 121
women, two old trudging through Irishtown with cockles 242 see Frauenzimmer
women, two poor reading Father Flynn's death notice D 12
work-girls, two in refreshment bar where Lenehan eats his meagre meal D 57
(workman, common) whom Molly remembers for allowing her privacy in a train to Howth with Bloom 748
workman, young overheard by Stephen praising a sermon at Gardiner Street church S 121
worshippers, two seen by Bloom at the holy water font at All Hallows 83
(wretch with the red hair) whom Molly remembers had exposed himself to her 753
(Writer, Holy) author of Genesis 408
(writer, French atheistic) S 172 see Zola, Émile

"Y" one of five sandwichboard men working for Wisdom Hely 154, 227, 229, 253 see also H; E; L; 'S
(yankee interviewer) whom AE presumably told of Stephen's visit 140, 185 see Weygandt, Cornelius
[yews*] commenting on young Bloom in the woods 545–53
(yokel, dullbrained) who won Gertrude's favors 202 see Claudius

Appendix A
The Joycean Method of Cataloguing

There are at least a dozen catalogues of named characters in *Ulysses*, primarily in Cyclops and Circe—counting those lists that include at least a dozen. That the epic convention of including such catalogues is being parodied in *Ulysses* seems apparent to any reader, but the schemes by which Joyce chose his components remain mysterious and deserve careful scrutiny. With comic juxtaposition often the main reason for selection, logical analysis may well be frustrated by a factor of sheer whimsy, but even extravagant absurdity is not necessarily without design, and few would suppose that Joyce's artistry would allow for totally random inclusion. *Notes for Joyce*, among other works, makes various attempts to explain individual identities within several of the catalogues, and certainly diagnosing pun possibilities within specific names and isolating the contributing factors in them are important approaches to the problem. Equally important is determining whether a pattern exists in each confabulation and whether an overall scheme can account for the complete accumulation.

Where a particular function is predetermined, the design is immediately apparent, as in the gathering of a minyan of Dublin Jews at Bella Cohen's. Actually, there are only nine listed (ten are required for a service) and we can assume that Bloom, although he is playing the part of a crybaby Christ, is the significant tenth (544). Corroborative evidence from *Thom's Directory* and Louis Hyman's *The Jews of Ireland* demonstrates that all nine were actual Jewish residents of Dublin (Bloom, after all, is probably the only fictional Dublin Jew in *Ulysses*), although in some cases their names have been somewhat tampered with. In several instances these names have appeared before and are already known to the reader, mostly as past friends of Leopold Bloom. The intrusive element in the minyan is Minnie Watchman, presumably a female in a group that by religious law must be totally male. It is tempting to conjecture that the Joycean joke is that Minnie's name merely looks feminine, and that *he* could actually be a man, but Louis Hyman not only locates *her* in Dublin but acknowledges that Minnie Watchman was his great-aunt. The joke, then, is in her "impossible" presence among the "circumcised," and it may be intended to parallel

Nosey Flynn's (accurate) story about the woman who became a Mason, Elizabeth Aldworth.

In another series a basic motive provides the punning factor which accounts for the complete pattern: the marriage of the trees (327), occasioned by John Wyse Nolan's innocent plea for the reforestation of Ireland. Lenehan's comment ("Europe has its eyes on you") transforms Nolan's Irish name into its French approximation, Jean Wyse de Neaulan, but his bride is a tree, Miss Fir Conifer, and all the members of the weddings are botanical as well. There are twenty-nine female participants, a number that should cause a flutter in the hearts of enthusiasts of *Finnegans Wake,* and the method of punning involves floral/arboreal factors with the possibilities of very real feminine given names and equally plausible surnames, the composite often providing the balance of person and plant. Some provide echoes of other aspects of naming in *Ulysses:* Mrs. Barbara Lovebirch suggests the sadistic pornographer, James; Mrs. Arabella Blackwood, the ancestor of Garrett Deasy, Sir John; and Mrs. Gloriana Palme, a reminder that Antisthenes "took away the palm of beauty from Argive Helen and handed it to poor Penelope" (149)—Mrs. Helen Vinegadding is also present at the ceremony. That the bride's sisters are named Spruce and Larch derives from their also being in the Conifer family, while their father, the M'Conifer of the Glands, anticipates The O'Donoghue of the Glens in a later cluster of antagonistic Irishmen. The disguised presence of Bloom (Henry Flower) as the Portuguese organist Senhor Enrique Flor returns the forest fantasy to local reality, and the combined marital name of the wedded couple as "Mr and Mrs Wyse Conifer Neaulan" recalls Bloom's own fictional coupling of "Mr and Mrs L. M. Bloom" (69).

Whereas a single punning principle is operative in the forest festivities, multilingual punning informs the naming of the delegation of the Friends of the Emerald Isle (307). Each of the seventeen delegates, including its Italian doyen, has the burden of the particular pun dependent upon his own language, although occasionally the pattern includes English puns as well (Pokethankertscheff/Pockethandkerchief; Hokopoko/Hocus Pocus; Kobberkeddelsen/Copper Kettle). The particular nationalities involved include most of the major European countries, plus some dominant ones of Asia, excluding of course England and its colonies. The nationalities at first glance seem to be those of the Great War, particularly the first ones listed, which is perhaps corroborated by the name of the German at the end (Kriegfried). They are: Italian, French, Russian, Austrian, Hungarian, American, Greek, Arabic, Spanish, Japanese, Chinese, Danish, Dutch, Polish, Slavic,

Swiss, German. At least two reveal real people, Hi Hung Chang (based, as Hugh Staples found, on Li Hung Chang) and Paddyrisky (as Don Gifford notes, an Irished Paderewski). The Austro-Hungarian components reveal names very close to home in Leopold, Rudolph, and feminine Virag, while an aura of the obscene, the scatalogical, and the putrid hangs over the delegation.

Although the Anglo-Saxons are understandably missing from the F. O. T. E. I., they are well represented in the catalogue provided by that scourge of the Sassenachs, the Citizen, as he reads from the notices in the *Irish Independent* of 16 June 1904 (298). As Gifford indicates, the Irish chauvinist is *actually* reading from the newspaper and all the names ticked off appeared in that issue, but his method of reading is highly selective. Never indicating that he is eliminating the large inclusion of Irish, he concentrates exclusively on the English, his half-truth concocted for the sake of political truth and his maliciousness compounded by purposeful mispronunciation of Cockburn. A couple of the names are altered somewhat: Playwood for Haywood seems playful, while Carr for Cann adumbrates a particularly unpleasant English representative. And if the decade of Dublin Jews seems somewhat exclusive, it is balanced in Cyclops with an ecclesiastical parade of two dozen Christian clergymen and two laymen (317–18). For this one Joyce seems to have emptied the churches of Dublin (by way of *Thom's*), starting with the president of Stephen's university and followed by its rector, Roman Catholics all.

Such literalness is rarely the rule, however, although the twelve good men and true who compose the "high sinhedrim" (323) seem significantly Irish, despite their positions in an Israelite court with Protestant Sir Frederick Falkiner apparently presiding. Although somewhat casual in composition, this distinguished dozen (Patrick, Hugh, Owen, Conn, Oscar, Fergus, Finn, Dermot, Cormac, Kevin, Caolte, Ossian) are certainly Irish, ancient and heroic, and essentially cut from the same cloth. Not so that major catalogue of Cyclopian giganticism, the "Irish heroes and heroines of antiquity" (296–97). This outpouring contains some ninety-nine separate individuals, although the placement of one comma may be random and the persons listed as Michaelangelo and Hayes may actually be one Michaelangelo Hayes, a nineteenth-century Dublin artist. With even the exact number in doubt (Michaelangelo can stand alone, but can Hayes?), the enormity of the problem of identification becomes apparent, especially since certain compounded names seem to cry out for separation (is Saint Patrick present in Patrick W. Shakespeare? and, if so, what about Patricio Velasquez?).

The catalogue begins legitimately enough with actual Irish heroes of antiquity, and it's hard to decide where it first goes wrong. Does Shane O'Neill's compact with Elizabeth disqualify him, or was he sufficiently devious in acting against the English monarchy? Father John Murphy, a priest, looks out of place among these warriors, but that is deceptive since he was a leader and martyr in the 1798 rebellion. The first eight heroes are in chronological order, but the next three go back to the centuries before Murphy. Nonetheless, even considering the end of the eighteenth century to be "antiquity," the spirit of the definition seems secure until the twelfth name, Red Jim MacDermott, the real Judas. Following after *Red* Hugh O'Donnell he looks as if he could sneak by, and if he hadn't betrayed the Fenians he might have deserved inclusion. Two other legitimate heroes follow him before the next traitor appears, the sham squire Francy O'Higgins, and by now the obvious absurdity of the list can hardly be overlooked. Two rotten apples have been discovered in the barrel, and M'Cracken essentially ends the pattern of listing Irish activists.

The inclusion of Goliath completely destroys the accuracy of the list's description. He may be ancient but he's hardly Irish, and he certainly isn't *our* idea of a hero. The brand of absurdity his name introduces is complemented by that of Horace Wheatley, a music hall entertainer, so that perhaps all three conditions for inclusion may be missing. That Thomas Conneff as yet defies identification provides another (if unintentional) failing in the list, but at least he has a name—more than can be said for the Village Blacksmith. The new pattern now emerging appears to be how many different ways the proper list of announced personages can be perverted; yet the next addition provides something totally new, albeit hardly unexpected. Peg Woffington is the first "heroine" and as an actress parallels Wheatley, and her surname echoes the double *f* in Conneff.

We next have a pair of captains, both involved in Irish land reform agitation, but on opposite sides. Pairing becomes the next principle, in fact: two Italians, two Irish saints, two military leaders, the first of whom was at least of Irish extraction although he provided his heroics for the French, and the second, the great king of the Franks. Wolfe Tone's appearance disturbs this pattern but does return the listing to its nominal function; however, it acts as a transition, into a new design with which it has no apparent relationship. Like Wolfe Tone, the Mother of the Maccabees was martyred, but this heroine is followed by the Last *of* the Mohicans and the Rose *of* Castille. The format now depends totally on the arrangement of the words—the first trio maintains an exact inner scheme while the next trio finds unique variations: The Man that

Broke the Bank at Monte Carlo, The Man in the Gap, The Woman Who Didn't.

The return to named persons does little to establish the credibility of the catalogue process, and the next dozen or so seem as random as any in the entire list. Representing various countries, professions, centuries, and marks of distinction, they bear little resemblance to ancient Irish heroes, the disputable Hayes being the only real Irishman among them. Women continue to be included at every third or fourth juncture, but in no particular positions numerically. The two Peters are a revival of the pattern of pairing, but they could hardly be less similar, especially since the Packer returns to another figure hostile to Irish nationalism. There is one more female, the Dark Rosaleen—a personification of Ireland that stands in contradistinction to Peter the Packer—and a new scheme develops: unlikely compounds of names. The surnames are immediately identifiable—Shakespeare, Confucius, Gutenberg, Velasquez—with nothing much in common except that they have nothing much in common. The first three given names are distinctively Irish (Patrick, Brian, and Murtagh) and seem to belong at the beginning of the list, while the fourth at least is of the same language group as its surname, although we may be suspicious that Patricio has its Irish origins as well.

With the next dozen names or so a random order occurs again. In their own way, however, such casual groupings in themselves form a pattern, a sequence of non-sequiturs that follows the earlier techniques of sudden disruptions, ironic juxtapositions, and meaningless couplings. Minor figures go unnoticed: associated persons linked together (Tristan and Isolde, Thomas Cook and Son), although hardly of the same relationship; designations in lieu of names (the first Prince of Wales, the Bold Soldier Boy, the Colleen Bawn); and the women in particular go unnamed, in a pattern that has been developing, from the Woman Who Didn't through the Rose of Castile, Savoureen Deelish, the Bride of Lammermoor, and the Colleen Bawn. Women are, after all, absent from the Cyclops chapter to as great an extent as in any in *Ulysses,* but a distinctly Gaelic coloring distinguishes these as Irish heroines (Dark Rosaleen, Arrah na Pogue, *et al.*). Since anonymity is important in Cyclops, the various uses of titles and tangential designations form an on-going design in the progression of characters, and particularly noteworthy then is Captain Nemo, a surrogate for the Odyssean Noman. In at least one other way the essentials of the chapter itself are reasserted in the catalogue: the subtitle of Boucicault's *Colleen Bawn* reveals the presence of Garryowen.

Even nicknames can act as disguises: if Waddler Healy is actually the

Bishop of Tuam, then at least he is nicely paired with Angus the Culdee as an Irish religious leader, but Weldon Thornton tentatively suggests that this is Tim Healy, whose presence would reintroduce the theme of Irish political betrayers. The next trio introduce a new comic vein since they are not people at all but punned versions of Dublin place-names: Dollymount, Sidney Parade, the Hill of Howth. The next dozen or so once again suggest complete formlessness, with certain familiar elements: the heroines (Lady Godiva, the Lily of Killarney, the Queen of Sheba); men of Irish birth or ancestry, a motif begun with Marshall MacMahon and John L. Sullivan and now added to with Arthur Wellesley and Boss Croker; the wildest of juxtapositions (Jack the Giantkiller between Herodotus and Buddha); and finally a patterned construction that sandwiches Balor *of* the Evil Eye between Lily *of* Killarney and the Queen *of* Sheba.

The vast parade winds down with the inclusion of a pair of publicans, Dublin brothers who localize and delimit the "tribal images of many Irish heroes and heroines," especially when they are defined by their nicknames. Volta, the Italian physicist who comes next, however, may not be as remote as first appears: Joyce was involved in setting up the Volta picture house on Henry Street, while the Nagles had their pub on its extension, Earl Street, on the other side of Sackville. To complete the procession, there are two grandiose Irish names, Jeremiah O'Donovan Rossa and Don Philip O'Sullivan Beare, the former a latter-day Irish hero and the latter an older Spanish historian—but of Irish birth. They conclude the most ambitious and most complex catalogue in *Ulysses,* in which an introductory rubric acts as a partial format more often violated and distorted and patterns within are developed for various kinds of comic effects.

How much simpler, then, are those two other stately processions, the flow of saints in Cyclops (339–40) and the march of dignitaries in Circe (480). The first contains both a vast horde of unnamed and unnumbered ecclesiasts of varying types and a definite parade of specific individuals. Well might Gertrude Stein ask, "How many saints are there in it?" Several, like Benedict and Francis and Clara and Dominic, are represented by their followers, while designated leaders of the parade are Saints Albert and Teresa of Avila, along with Edmund Ignatius Rice, a layman who became a Christian Brother but hardly expected to be canonized (as a Christian Brother he is distinguished by a middle name more suitable to a Jesuit, the first note of incongruous humor introduced into the catalogue). The "saints and martyrs, virgins and confessors" that flood by seem to number eighty-one, not counting the eleven thousand virgins that trail after Ursula. Except for the obvious perversions, the saints have a legitimate claim to their right to participate in the procession, although they range from the well known to the most obscure. As Michael Groden shows in *Ulysses in Progress,* Joyce usually added to his lists in the various stages of his manuscript, but with this one he seems to have thrown in whole handfuls at a time, eventually quadrupling the original collection.

Joyce's method of wholesale insertions indicates the significance of clusters of names in the cataloguing. Like items are linked: two saints of the same name, three saints who were patrons of youth (echoes of *A Portrait*). Irish saints form a large compact segment and female saints are also banded together in an important pocket. The elements of humor are varied, but the more obvious sort makes itself known when the process breaks down and such non-saints as Anonymous, Eponymous, and their ilk creep in, only to be once again succeeded by real saints. A later intrusion occurs when a quite proper Brother Aloysius Pacificus is complemented by an aggressive imposter, Brother Louis Bellicosus. The best cluster is that of the actual saints who have their named counterparts among the characters of *Ulysses.* The first hint comes with the pairing of Saint Simon Stylites and Saint Stephen Protomartyr; then the denizens of Kiernan's pub are gathered together under their saintly guises, Martin Cunningham, Alfred Bergan, J. J. (Joseph) O'Molloy, Denis Breen (passing outside the pub), Cornelius Kelleher (originally scheduled to be there, but dropped in the final version and only mentioned), Leopold Bloom, Bernard Kiernan (not present but of course implied), Terence O'Ryan, Edward Lambert, and Owen Caniculus (Garryowen). The cluster is not complete, nor (as indicated) completely exact, and given the presence of two highly important anonymous characters, the Citizen and the Nameless One (Saint Anonymous follows immediately after the dog-saint), it is clear that anonymity is intrinsic to the chapter.

Bloom's coronation parade differs somewhat by the far greater emphasis on titles than on proper names. Only four names are included: John Howard Parnell, city marshal; Joseph Hutchinson, Lord Mayor of Dublin; and the two primates of Ireland, Cardinal Logue and Dr. Alexander, Roman Catholic and Church of Ireland respectively. The range of dignitaries is broad and wide, from maharajahs to Italian grocers, the mayors of major Irish cities and the tradesmen of Dublin, but with special attention to the various religious denominations and to the representatives of British court pomp. Church and state offer up their factotums, and as comic as such items as Black Rod, Deputy Garter, and Gold Stick may seem to the uninitiated, they are specific heralds of courtly ceremony and appropriately real.

Of a very different order from those who march in honor of Bloom are those who pursue him through the streets of Nighttown (586–87). They form the collective Hue and Cry and are to be numbered among Bloom's detractors, although many of them would not know him at all and others one would assume might ordinarily be sympathetic to him. Including the ringleader, the Hornblower who is the porter at Trinity College south gate, they number some eighty, plus a dog and Mrs. Dandrade's lovers. (The lovers may well be the group listed by Bello—seven named males, plus a team of eight rowers, a dog, and a duchess—536.) There is no single common denominator for the group of antagonists, and we can even suppose that Hornblower's role is merely traditional, his tally-ho cap identifying him as leader of the fox hunt. That the two night watchmen in Nighttown should be in the front ranks follows logically from their interrogation of Bloom earlier, so that if the pursuers constitute Bloom's imagined "enemies," their part in that pattern is established. Although it should be safe to say that every one of these characters is in some way known to Bloom, it proves impossible, but we can discern some overall patterns. In most cases the people are also known to us, having "appeared" previously in *Ulysses.*

Linear progression may not adequately reveal the pattern of the pursuers: unlike a stately and continuous parade—down the street or across a page—a pack of pursuers tends to bunch together. Initially threatened by representatives of the law (the watch), Bloom may easily associate them with Menton, a lawyer and known enemy. Menton, Hely, and Val Dillon all date back for Bloom some sixteen or seventeen years, establishing a time frame for the association: Bloom worked for Hely then, Menton danced with Molly then (at Dillon's brother's house), and John Henry Raleigh speculates that Bloom may have worked for Val Dillon at about the same time. Bloom's employers of the past and his present work associates band together here (Hely, Nannetti, Keyes, Cuffe) with Larry O'Rourke an intrusive element (Nannetti's name may be responsible for O'Rourke's presence since Bloom was thinking about the *Freeman* when he encountered Larry that morning—57). Cuffe's name triggers recollections of Bloom's residence at the City Arms Hotel, which accounts for Mrs. O'Dowd, Pisser Burke, the Nameless One, and Mrs. Riordan, while mention of the Nameless One recalls the afternoon scene at Barney Kiernan's and invokes the Citizen and Garryowen.

With anonymity once again the informing principle, the Citizen and the Nameless One recall a quintet of "names" formed from phrases regarding people with forgotten names, but each of these probably has an actual antecedent: "Whatdoyoucallhim" is the hunchback Bloom had earlier seen and attempted to identify (61); "Sawhimbefore" is probably the man Bloom notices taking his constitutional along Sandymount Strand (375–76); "Chapwith" suggests one of the two diners in the Burton, designated there as "Other chap" (170). "Fellowthatslike" presents an interesting possibility of a projection into the next chapter, where one of the cabbies is constantly referred to as looking like the town clerk; this is a concept that violates psychological possibility but supports the contention that Circe is a chapter of phantasmagoria in which reality cannot fully explain all of the phenomena. Even "Chapwith" offers the same possibility when Corley asks about Bloom. "Who's that with you? I saw him . . . with Boylan" (618)—which would make Bloom one of his own pursuers.

There may be some clue in the cluster of unnamed persons to suggest what follows, but what binds it together is obvious: Callinan, Cameron (one is tempted to opt merely for alliteration until the full scheme is apparent), Dollard, Lenehan, d'Arcy—all were present with the Blooms at the Glencree dinner. Lenehan is the link with the next grouping, the noon scene at the newspaper office (present: Lenehan, Hynes, Murray, Brayden; mentioned: Healy, Fitzgibbon). Healy would of course suggest Parnell, but in this case it's the living brother, and Bloom saw him as he strolled through central Dublin after leaving the newspaper office. That stroll occasions the next series of pursuers: Bloom thinks about Joly and Salmon (even to the extent of "permanently" altering his first name), meets Josie Breen, and hears from her about Denis and the Purefoys. The next cluster of street-scene encounters reverts back several hours (could the image of Theodore Purefoy behind the grille of his bank conjure up the postmistress behind the grille at the Westland Row office?), and the dramatis personae are directly out of that experience, where two things are happening simultaneously. While M'Coy is blabbing about Lyons and Holohan and Doran (is he the friend of Lyons mentioned?), Bloom is attempting to concentrate on the "rich protestant lady" and her ankles. He conjectures whether the man with her is her brother or husband (resulting in *two* "men in the street," and possibly even "Footballboots," since Bloom shifts from thinking about *her* boots to thinking of the man as a "fallback"—73–74), but the pugnosed driver interferes with Bloom's line of vision.

If this cluster looks dense, what follows looks chaotic: the hunters seem to come pouring pell-mell from various points, and locating their aspects of similarity becomes progressively more difficult. Only a half dozen of them actually had contact with Bloom during the course of the day (Davy Byrne, Lidwell, Cowley, Crofton, Nolan, and the *Sweets of Sin* bookseller), and of those several were only seen by him. Another handful he either thought of or heard about: Dawson, Miss Dubedat, Figatner, Mrs. Dandrade, the Eccles Street constable, the man on Sandymount Strand, and the trio of known acquaintances, Mastiansky, Citron, and Penrose. We can also assume that he is familiar with Bob Doran's wife, Mrs. Gallaher and Mrs. Galbraith (since Molly indicates that she knows them both), and the clerk at Drimmie's. The same should be true for Jimmy Henry and Bloom the dentist, since both appear earlier in Circe hallucinations involving Bloom, and we have been informed that Bloom knows Mrs. Nolan through her dairy shop. Several new names appear on this list for the first time in *Ulysses* (Laracy, Mrs. Kennefick, the handsome woman, the Mesdames Moran, Hayes, Mrs. Galbraith, and Dr. Brady). The last will turn up again on the list of Molly's "lovers" and in Molly's thoughts, while the handsome woman seems derivable from Bloom's past experiences. Laracy and Hayes are authority figures in the Dublin community and have a logical status in the context of the chase; but there are several people with whom Bloom has no connection that we can be aware of. Mrs. M'Guinness in no way crosses paths with him nor crosses his mind: she exists in *Ulysses* in relation to the Dedalus girls, to Father Conmee who sees her on the street just after he encounters the son of Mrs. Gallaher, and to the lame sailor—if she is the stout woman who, like Molly, gives him money. And the Herzog-Geraghty-Troy trio are out of the Nameless One's experiences, with no Bloom connection that the reader is ever privy to.

How coherent and even clinical by comparison is the list of Molly's presumed lovers presented in Ithaca (731). Almost every one of them has his firm roots in past events of the novel, while the few remaining will be accounted for in Molly's soliloquy. The way in which each one had at some time come into contact with Molly, and the way in which Bloom could be made aware of each, can be logically deduced, even down to the most casual of the unnamed characters. However, the fox hunt in Circe which appears to have recalled almost everyone has its early origins, at least, in Bloom's immediate contacts, and it is also significant because of those absent from it. For various reasons, of either potential friendship or special relationship, the following are not among the pursuers: Stephen and Simon Dedalus, Cunningham, Power, Richie Goulding, Kernan, Nosey Flynn, Boylan, Bannon, Mulligan, Dixon, and Gerty MacDowell. This negative evidence in itself is rather eloquent.

The single most intriguing catalogue, however, is the genealogical chart presented by Papal Nuncio Brini, which is prompted by a performance in which Bloom assumes the resemblances of some fourteen historical personages (495). This mini-catalogue of Bloom's is interesting because it reveals some of his inner identifications. Some are with Jews (converted and unconverted) like Disraeli and the three Moseses; others indicate his interest in wealth (Rothschild), good looks (Byron), science (Pasteur), investigation (Sherlock Holmes), and even revolutionary zeal (Kossuth and Wat Tyler)—and only the last seems somewhat out of Bloom's logical field of knowledge.

The Brini list (495–96), on the other hand, displays no such cohesiveness and seems to be the most arbitrary and even capricious exercise in cataloguing, especially since most of the persons included are not really persons at all. The initial distortion actually pre-exists the catalogue itself: Brini seems to be an Italianate corruption of Breen, apparently based on the Nameless One's nasty comment that Denis Breen's father's cousin was a "pew opener to the pope," from which he constructs "signor Brini from Summerhill, the eyetallyano, papal zouave to the Holy Father" (321). From such doubtful origins it is understandable that unreliability and distortion will readily occur. The format is a parody of biblical begats, so starting with Moses and proceeding to Noah makes a kind of sense. At the other end is the ultimate product of the progression, Emmanuel, and thus the movement is from Old to New Testament. That Emmanuel's father is Bloom and grandfather is Virag moves that magnificent birth very close to home, identifying Christ with dead Rudy, although there is little need to assume that by the Bloom in the list we must necessarily mean Leopold Bloom. The positing of "real" people seems less germane to the parody than the creation of a series of names. After all, by a linguistic accident a biblical Enoch has been altered into Eunuch, from whom we can expect no actual issue, making the genealogical list merely academic on that level.

Both Thornton and Gifford have made heroic efforts to track down the participants or, that failing, to dissect the names into component elements. It is soon apparent that none of this works. The essence of the catalogue is in what it mocks: the genealogy of a self-professed messiah. Bloom is both the mother of the messiah and the messiah himself, and from his collection of facial impersonations he derives one component element of the genealogy, that of wealthy Jewish financiers. From Baron Leopold Rothschild the generation of "Leopoldi" includes Le Hirsch and Guggenheim (and Lewy Lawson suggests Leonard Lewisohn), rendering Bloom the son of Mammon (the actual answer to whether he is the Messiah ben Joseph or ben David may be in "Ben Maimun"). Le Hirsch and Guggenheim may well be the only real people in the list between the opening Moses/Noah and the closing Virag/Bloom—from biblical to fictional, with the frame reversed from Leopoldi to Emmanuel. However, a basic tone of Hebraicism pervades because of the context, with a secondary level of Hibernicism (O'Halloran, O'Donnell) since Ireland suggests the lost tribes of Israel. A single factor, the familiar Agendath Netaim, splits into two successive elements; opposing qualities of white and black become generational as German Jewish family names, Weiss and Schwarz; the modern Judaic split between Sephardic and Ashkenazic can be found in Aranjuez and Ostropolsky; the crucifixion is prefigured in the nativity (Christbaum). The Wandering Jew, an archetypal tramp, is also the thirteenth at the funeral, the man in the macintosh (Dusty Rhodes). And even a strain of place names (Adrianopoli, Aranjuez) filters through, especially since it leads to Szombathely, the Bethlehem of the Virag-Blooms.

The essence of the catalogue is not in its components but in its construction, which is somewhat akin to the HERE COMES EVERYBODY catalogue in *Finnegans Wake* (FW 88), where attempts to pinpoint the eighteen "people" whose initials form the acronym have proven disappointing. Joyce took his structure from an entry in Debrett's *Peerage*, noting that the Dysart family christened an heir with fourteen names that spelled out the acronymic LYONEL THE SECOND. Retaining many of the same names that would fit his own acronym, tampering with a couple of them for particular puns, adding the others to fill out his pattern (even including other names in the Dysart entry in Debrett's to fit his needs), Joyce composed his democratic emblem upon the aristocratic one compounded by the noble family of Dysart. His method of selection allowed for a certain degree of accident, plus a dollop of the whimsical, and even a direct transfer from the original. As each experiment in mock epic cataloguing takes place in *Ulysses* (as well as in the *Wake*) new characteristics enter the design. The overall pattern perseveres, but internal changes develop from the particular context, inner wheels rotating within the outer wheels, determined by a rhythm and logic perversely their own.

Appendix B
Molly's Masculine Pronouns

The special quality of difficulty arranged by Molly's shifts in thought accounts for the blur of masculine pronouns in the chapter, although we may assume that she is clear in her own mind about their individual identities. The following page-by-page tabulation (with line numbers) attempts to isolate the men concerned, citing references to the various indications of "he, "his," and "him," as well as some plurals involving males.

Page	lines	
738	1–5:	Bloom
	17:	Mr. Riordan
	19–43:	Bloom
739	1–3:	Bloom
	4–9:	Menton
	10–40:	Bloom
740	2–8:	Bloom
	11:	Boylan
	12:	Bloom
	13:	("him") Boylan; ("hes," "he") Bloom
	14:	Bloom
	15:	Boylan
	18–20	hypothetical "nicelooking boy"
	24–28:	Bloom
	30:	man Molly is supposed to be thinking about
	31:	the German Emperor
	32–35:	Bloom
	40:	hypothetical
	42:	("hes") Bloom; ("his") hypothetical
741	2–3:	subject of Molly's confession
	6–14:	Father Corrigan
	14–18	"theyre" hypothetical priest
	20–31:	Boylan
	42–43:	Bloom
742	1:	Bloom
	2–32	Boylan
	33–42:	Bloom
743	1–40:	Bloom
	41:	Lord Byron
744	10–16:	Denis Breen
	17–19:	Bloom
	20–24:	Denis Breen
	25–34:	Bloom
	35:	Mr. Maybrick
	36:	Bloom
	42:	Boylan
745	1:	("we") Molly and Bloom
	2:	Boylan
	5–9:	Bloom
	11–17:	Boylan
	19–25:	Bloom
	26–28:	There seem to be three possibilities regarding the Katty Lanner compliment: (1) that it came from foot-fetishist Bloom and he was the one she tried to question about it; (2) that it came from Boylan, who has been seen to admire Molly's feet, and that it was the

Page	lines	
		stop press on Throwaway that interrupted Molly's question; and (3) that Bloom initially made the allusion but it was to Boylan that Molly's subsequent question was addressed. The odds seem to be on Boylan since he is the punter who thinks in terms of odds.
	29–30:	the man in the dairy
	31:	Bloom
	32–37:	Bartell d'Arcy
	39–43:	Bloom
746	1–41:	Bloom
	42:	"his" Tweedy
	42–43:	Bloom
747	1–5:	Bloom
	5:	"he was" Henny Doyle
	6–17:	Bloom
	17:	"hell" Boylan
	18:	Boylan
	24–25:	Goodwin
	28–30:	Boylan
	33–41:	Bloom
	42:	Boylan
748	1–3:	Boylan
	4–15:	Bloom
	17–19:	Boylan
	21:	"us" Molly and Bloom
	22:	workman
	25:	Boylan
	31–39:	Bloom
	40:	Arthur Griffith
	41:	("him") Griffith; ("he") Bloom
749	1–11:	Gardner
	18–35:	Boylan
	37–38:	Mastiansky
	39–43:	Boylan
750	1–2:	Boylan
	3–4:	Lenehan
	6–7:	Val Dillon
	19–20:	Boylan
	26–27:	Boylan
	29:	Bloom
	34–38:	Larry O'Rourke
	41–42:	Bloom
751	1–3:	Bloom
	13:	"you" Bloom
	29–30:	Prince of Wales
	33:	Mr. Langtry (or some other jealous husband)
	34:	Prince of Wales
	35:	Bloom
	40:	Rabelais
	41–42:	Bloom
	43:	character in *Ruby*
752	2–3:	character in book
	8–11:	Prince of Wales
	12–21:	Bloom
	22–23:	Joseph Cuffe
	26–37:	Bloom
	40–43:	Cuffe
753	1–3:	Cuffe
	4:	Bloom
	5–6:	Cuffe
	7–11:	Boylan
	16–17:	men in general
	19–25:	Bloom
	28–29:	wretch with the red hair
754	1–4:	Bloom
	5–6:	Bloom
	8–9:	Bloom
	12:	Penrose
	13–17:	Bloom
	20–31:	Boylan
	32:	Bloom
	33–37:	Boylan
755	1–5:	Bloom
	19–31:	Mr. Stanhope
	41:	Bloom
	43:	"them" Mr. and Mrs. Stanhope
756	9–12:	Mr. Stanhope
	21–22:	Bloom
	25:	Bloom
	29:	Bloom
	35:	"they" Mr. and Mrs. Stanhope
	39–40:	Mr. Stanhope
757	4:	"they" Mr. and Mrs. Stanhope

Page	lines	
	6–7:	hypothetical lover
	10:	President Grant
	13:	Sprague
	19:	warden
	21–29:	Capt. Grove
	33:	old Arab
	41–43:	that medical
758	5:	noisy bugger
	8:	Bloom
	9:	"him" Bloom; "his" Boylan
	10:	Bloom
	15–18:	Mat Dillon
	23:	Bloom
	26–37:	Boylan
	41:	fellow in the Four Courts
759	21–35:	Mulvey
	36:	Miguel de la Flora
	37–43:	Mulvey
760	4–25:	Mulvey
	31–34:	"they" men in general
	35–43:	Mulvey
761	2–12:	Mulvey
	13:	"they" men in general
	15–25:	Mulvey
	27–29:	that old bishop
	30–37:	Bloom
	39:	"we" Molly and Mulvey
762	2–3:	Mulvey
	4–6:	"they" sailors in general
	8:	Mulvey
	13–19:	Mulvey
	20–24:	Gardner
	43:	Gardner
763	1–2:	Tweedy
	3–4:	Gardner
	6–7:	Boylan
	9:	Bloom
	12:	d'Arcy
	16:	Boylan
	17:	Bloom
	20:	Bloom
	29:	Bloom
764	1–12:	Bloom
	27:	1st "him" Boylan: 2nd "him" Bloom

Page	lines	
	29–30:	Bloom
	33:	Boylan
	35–43:	Bloom
765	1–4:	Bloom
	5:	Nosey Flynn
	7–9:	Pisser Burke
	10:	Bloom
	12:	Paul de Kock
	25–35:	Bloom
	37–38:	hypothetical tramp
	39–42:	that hardened criminal
766	1–2:	"they" criminals in general
	4–16:	Bloom
	22–32:	Bloom
	38:	Bloom
767	16–19:	man in the theatre
	28:	Martin-Harvey
	31:	Sydney Carton
	36:	Bloom
	37–38:	Rudolf Virag
768	11:	Bloom
	14:	Bloom
	17:	Boylan
	23–24:	Bloom
	26:	1st "his" Stephen Dedalus; 2nd "his" Simon Dedalus
	27–28:	Simon Dedalus
	29:	Stephen Dedalus
	30–31:	Bloom
	33:	"him" Stephen; "he"/"his" Bloom
	36:	Bloom
	37:	Stephen
	42:	Mr. Fleming
769	5–7:	Boylan
	10:	"we" Molly and Bloom
	11–12:	Bloom
	14:	"his" gentleman of fashion; "him" Bloom
	15:	Spinoza
	20–23:	that idiot in the gallery
	25–43:	Boylan
770	1–8:	Boylan
	18:	Bloom

Page	lines	
	20–43:	Dr. Collins
771	1:	Dr. Collins
	2–35:	Bloom
	36:	Buddha
	37:	"his" Buddha; "he" Bloom
	39:	"him" Buddha; "hes" Bloom; "he" Buddha
	40–41:	Buddha
	43:	Bloom
772	1–2:	Bloom
	6:	old Cohen
	7–8:	Bloom
	9–10:	"we" Molly and Bloom
	11–24:	Bloom
	25:	"himself" Arthur Griffith
	26:	Bloom
	27–28:	Griffith
	30–38:	Bloom
	39:	Aristotle
773	1–14:	Bloom
	15:	Denis Breen
	16:	"him" Breen; "hes" Bloom
	17:	Bloom
	19:	"his" Hornblower; "he" Bloom
	20–21:	Bloom
	27:	Tom Kernan
	36–38:	Jack Power
	41–43:	Bloom
774	2–7:	Paddy Dignam
	8–13:	Ben Dollard
	14:	"him" Dollard; "he" Simon Dedalus
	15–25:	Dedalus
	26:	"hes"/"his" Dedalus; "he" Bloom
	27:	Stephen
	28:	Bloom
	29:	Stephen
	31:	"he" Bloom; "him" Stephen
	32–33:	Stephen
	34–35:	Rudy
	36:	Bloom
	37–42:	Stephen
	43:	Boylan
775	1:	Boylan
	7–8:	Stephen
	11–12:	Bloom
	13–17:	Stephen
	18:	Bloom
	19:	"he" Bloom; "him" Stephen
	20:	Stephen
	21:	"hes" Stephen; "he" Goodwin
	23, 29:	Stephen
	33:	Bloom
	35–36:	Stephen
	41:	Bloom
	42:	statue of Narcissus
776	1–3:	statue of Narcissus
	4–18:	Stephen
	19–30:	Boylan
	31–32:	a lion
	33:	Boylan
	42–43:	uncle John
777	8–11:	cuckolded husband (as in *Fair Tyrants*)
	12–13:	the seducer
	16–24:	Bloom
	41–42:	Boylan
	43:	that K.C.
778	2–3:	that K.C.
	4–12:	Bloom
	24–26:	Stephen
	28:	Bloom
	29:	"we" Molly and Bloom
	31:	Rudy
	33–34:	"our"/"we" Molly and Bloom
	36:	Stephen
	37:	Bloom
	38–39:	Stephen
	42:	Stephen
779	3–6:	Stephen
	22:	"wed" Molly and her father
	23–29:	Stephen
	34:	Bloom
	35–39:	Stephen
	40:	1st "he" Bloom; 2nd "he" Stephen
	41–43:	Bloom
780	6:	Bloom

Page	lines	
	15–23:	Bloom
	24:	Boylan
	26–43:	Bloom
781	1–15:	Bloom
	20:	the priest
	24:	Bloom
	28:	"he" Bloom; "him" Stephen
	30:	"we" Molly and Stephen
	31:	Stephen
782	4:	Bloom
	12–25:	Bloom
	29:	the sentry
783	1:	the watchman
	8:	Mulvey
	9–14:	Bloom

Explanations of Controversial Decisions

Page	line	
740	42:	Molly is tempted by the idea that Bloom would be present as an observer while she is being seduced by another man.
741	14:	Although it is tempting to assume that Molly saw Bloom cry at the death of his father, that death was the year before he met Molly.
743	41:	Some readers have assumed that Molly thought Bloom too beautiful for a man, but the reference is a familiar one for Byron and the immediate afterthought supports this identification.
747	17:	Molly is relieved that Bloom will not be in Belfast sharing her hotel room while Boylan is in the next room overhearing their lovemaking.
750	27:	For Molly to accidentally encounter her husband in the city might be disconcerting, but to meet her prospective lover would be a greater annoyance since it would spoil the anticipation of the afternoon tryst.
751	40:	Molly may be remembering Rabelais's face from the book cover.
755	22:	If this is a continuous recollection, Mr. Stanhope is the donor, but Molly may be intruding a later recollection of Bloom buying her musical exercises.
755	41:	It seems reasonable that the bell lane is Bell's Lane in Dublin.
769	39:	Molly may be maliciously contemplating shocking Bloom by shaving her pubic hair, but it seems more likely that it is her lover for whom this audacious intimacy is intended.
778	42:	Since it is Stephen who is roaming the streets at night, it may well be Stephen who Molly supposes wants "what he wont get."

Appendix C
Table of Corresponding Pages

The following table relates the pagination of the New Random House edition of *Ulysses* (1961) to that of three other editions: Old Random House (1934), New Bodley Head (1960), Penguin (1968). The figures show the pages on which fall the last lines of the relevant pages in the New Random House edition.

New RH	Old RH	New BH	Penguin	New RH	Old RH	New BH	Penguin	New RH	Old RH	New BH	Penguin	New RH	Old RH	New BH	Penguin
5	7	4	12	**200**	198	257	201	**395**	389	517	393	**590**	575	689	522
10	12	11	17	**205**	203	264	206	**400**	394	524	398	**595**	580	693	524
15	17	18	22	**210**	208	270	210	**405**	399	530	403	**600**	585	696	527
20	22	24	27	**215**	213	277	215	**410**	404	537	408	**605**	589	699	530
25	26	30	31	**220**	217	283	220	**415**	408	544	412	**609**	593	703	532
30	31	37	36	**225**	222	289	225	**420**	413	551	417	**615**	599	708	536
35	36	44	41	**230**	227	296	230	**425**	418	558	422	**620**	605	714	541
40	41	50	46	**235**	232	302	235	**430**	423	563	426	**625**	610	721	546
45	46	57	51	**240**	237	309	240	**435**	428	567	429	**630**	615	728	551
50	51	64	56	**245**	242	316	245	**440**	433	571	432	**635**	620	735	556
55	55	66	58	**250**	247	323	250	**445**	438	575	435	**640**	625	742	561
60	60	73	63	**255**	251	328	254	**450**	443	579	438	**645**	630	749	566
65	65	79	68	**260**	256	335	259	**455**	447	582	441	**650**	635	756	571
70	69	85	72	**265**	261	342	264	**460**	452	586	444	**655**	640	763	576
75	74	92	77	**270**	266	348	269	**465**	457	591	448	**660**	645	769	581
80	79	99	82	**275**	271	355	274	**470**	462	596	451	**665**	649	776	586
85	84	106	87	**280**	276	362	279	**475**	467	599	454	**670**	654	782	591
90	89	113	92	**285**	281	369	284	**480**	471	603	457	**675**	659	789	596
95	94	119	97	**290**	286	375	289	**485**	476	607	460	**680**	665	796	601
100	99	126	102	**295**	290	381	294	**490**	481	611	463	**685**	670	802	606
105	104	133	107	**300**	295	388	299	**495**	485	615	466	**690**	674	808	611
110	109	140	112	**305**	300	395	304	**500**	490	619	469	**695**	680	815	616
115	114	147	117	**310**	305	402	309	**505**	495	623	472	**700**	685	822	622
120	119	153	122	**315**	310	409	314	**510**	500	627	475	**705**	690	829	626
125	124	160	127	**320**	315	416	319	**515**	504	632	478	**710**	695	835	631
130	129	166	132	**325**	320	422	324	**520**	509	636	482	**715**	700	842	637
135	134	172	137	**330**	325	429	329	**525**	514	640	485	**720**	705	849	642
140	139	178	141	**335**	329	436	334	**530**	519	644	488	**725**	710	855	646
145	144	184	146	**340**	334	442	339	**535**	524	648	490	**730**	715	862	652
150	148	189	150	**345**	339	449	343	**540**	528	652	494	**735**	720	869	657
155	153	196	155	**350**	344	456	348	**545**	533	656	497	**740**	725	875	662
160	158	203	160	**355**	349	462	353	**550**	537	660	499	**745**	730	882	667
165	163	210	165	**360**	354	469	358	**555**	542	663	502	**750**	735	889	672
170	168	217	170	**365**	359	476	363	**560**	547	667	505	**755**	740	895	677
175	173	224	175	**370**	364	483	368	**565**	551	670	507	**760**	744	902	682
180	178	230	180	**375**	369	490	373	**570**	556	673	510	**765**	751	909	687
185	184	237	186	**380**	374	496	378	**575**	561	677	513	**770**	756	916	692
190	188	244	191	**385**	379	503	383	**580**	565	681	516	**775**	761	923	697
195	193	251	196	**390**	384	510	388	**585**	570	685	519	**780**	766	930	702

SOURCE: Clive Hart and Leo Knuth, *A Topographical Guide to James Joyce's* Ulysses (Colchester, England: A Wake Newlitter Press, 1975).

Legend

Editions employed:
D *Dubliners* [Viking Press "definitive" edition]
P *A Portrait of the Artist as a Young Man* [Viking Press "definitive" edition]
E *Exiles* [Viking Press]
S *Stephen Hero* [New Directions]
G *Giacomo Joyce* [Viking Press]—named characters only
Ulysses [Random House 1961]

Name in Regular Type: character created by Joyce
Name in FULL CAPITALS: character pre-existing Joyce's fictional use; fictional, historical, legendary, or contemporary
*Name preceded by asterisk : actual resident in Dublin
Name* succeeded by asterisk : not actually a person in this case
"Name" in quotation marks : pseudonym, nickname, alias, nom de plume, conjectured name, misnomer, stage name, mock title, punned name
Name unadorned by either parentheses or brackets : actually present
(Name) in parentheses : mentioned, referred to, alluded to, thought about
[Name] in brackets : appears in hallucination in Circe chapter
! : exclamation mark indicates expletive or ejaculation rather than a person
? : question mark indicates that identity or appearance in doubt

Discrepancies between ACTUAL NAME and Joyce's variant are indicated by inclusion of both, differentiated by appropriate type.

Designation or description of character listed : Well-known historical or fictional persons whose names are obviously unique to indicate themselves alone receive no identification (e.g., Jehovah, Jesus Christ, Moses, Shakespeare, Molière); others are given brief identifications. Joyce's own creations are identified by the roles they play in the works.

Page and book indicators: *Ulysses* items are offered first, without any preceding letter to specify book; others follow with letters indicating the work as above. If the character never actually appears in the work, his name is in parentheses, and all page numbers therefore are understood to indicate references to him; names without parentheses are characters who appear in person on those pages without parentheses, are referred to on those pages in parentheses, and appear as a hallucination in those pages bracketed.

Animals and inanimate objects: Although this directory is limited to "human" characters, the unusual nature of *Ulysses* dictates that (1) all dogs (like Garryowen) and horses (like Throwaway) must necessarily be included, provided that they have names, (2) that those inanimate objects that have speaking roles in Circe be included—as hallucinations.

Further references: For fuller information on most of the persons alluded to and on many of the Joycean characters, the following are noted after the entries. Capital letters refer to the specific volume when we feel that the information is essentially accurate; lowercase letters indicate a serious instance of misinformation.

A Weldon Thornton, *Allusions in Ulysses: An Annotated List* (Chapel Hill: University of North Carolina Press, 1968).

N Don Gifford with Robert J. Seidman, *Notes for Joyce: An Annotation of James Joyce's Ulysses* (New York: E. P. Dutton, 1974).

N Don Gifford with the assistance of Robert Seidman, *Notes for Joyce: Dubliners and A Portrait of the Artist as a Young Man* (New York: E. P. Dutton, 1967).

T Clive Hart and Leo Knuth, *A Topographical Guide to James Joyce's Ulysses* (Colchester, England: A Wake Newslitter Press, 1975).

A plus sign (+) also indicates references from the following where especially pertinent; in many other cases the reader can also find additional information in them.

+ Robert M. Adams, *Surface and Symbol: The Consistency of James Joyce's Ulysses* (New York: Oxford University Press, 1962).
+ Zack Bowen, *Musical Allusions in the Works of James Joyce: Early Poetry through Ulysses* (Albany: State University of New York Press, 1974).
+ Louis Hyman, *The Jews of Ireland: From Earliest Times to the Year 1910* (Shannon: Irish University Press, 1972).
+ Richard M. Kain, *Fabulous Voyager: James Joyce's Ulysses* (Chicago: University of Chicago Press, 1947).
+ Kevin Sullivan, *Joyce among the Jesuits* (New York: Columbia University Press, 1958).
+ *Thom's*. 1904 *Thom's Official Directory of Dublin*